Science for mechanical engineering technicians:
a Part 1 course (T1, T2)

Consulting editor
C. T. Butler
*Head of Department of Mechanical and Production Engineering
Trent Polytechnic*

Other books in the Technical Education Series
BROWN: Mechanical Engineering Craft Studies (C & G 503)
FIRTH and VANDER WILLIGEN: Engineering Drawing Technology
  (C & G 293 Part 2)
KNIGHT and MELLOR: Mathematics for Mechanical Engineering
  Technicians: a Part 2 Course (T3, T4)
MORRIS: Control Engineering (C & G 57, C & G 293)
SCHOFIELD: Physics for ONC Engineers (ONC/D)
STOTT and BIRCHALL: Electrical Engineering Principles
  (C & G 57, 49, 434, 451, Part 1)
TITHERINGTON and RIMMER: Mechanical Engineering Science (ONC/D)
TITHERINGTON and RIMMER: Applied Mechanics (ONC/D)
WARD: Electrical Engineering Science (ONC/D)

Science for mechanical engineering technicians:
a Part 1 course (T1, T2)

G. L. Houpt, C.Eng., M.I.Mech.E.
Barnet College of Further Education

McGRAW-HILL
London · New York · Sydney · Toronto · Mexico
Johannesburg · Panama · Dusseldorf · Singapore
Rio de Janeiro

Published by
McGRAW-HILL Publishing Company Limited
MAIDENHEAD · BERKSHIRE · ENGLAND

07 094262 5

Copyright © 1970 McGraw-Hill Publishing Company Limited. All rights reserved. No part of this publication may be reproduced, stored in a retrieval system, or transmitted, in any form or by any means, electronic, mechanical, photocopying, recording, or otherwise, without the prior permission of McGraw-Hill Publishing Company Limited.

MADE AND PRINTED IN GREAT BRITAIN

Preface

At the time of writing this introduction, many engineering students in Great Britain are taking part in a year's study which, for the first time, is exclusively in SI units (Système International d'Unités). Since the change from Imperial to SI units is bound to take place gradually, exact co-ordination is difficult because students working in SI units at college may at the same time be called upon to use equipment calibrated in Imperial units. If the change to SI units is to have any point, however, it should be complete, and courses of study in these units should make no reference at all to Imperial units.

The object of this book is to provide a text in SI units to cover the engineering science syllabus for Part I of the Mechanical Engineering Technicians' course (MT1 and MT2). Emphasis has been given to worked examples, and in view of this the explanatory text, though effectual, has been kept to a minimum.

The author would like to thank Mr W. Cooper for his help and advice in connection with the chapter dealing with electricity, and the Consulting Editor for his helpful comments and suggestions.

Some of the problems and examples are taken from past City and Guilds of London Institute examination papers. Where necessary, the units have been modified from Imperial to SI, and the acknowledgements (GGLI) and (CGLI modified) are made at the appropriate places. The author thanks the City and Guilds of London Institute for their kind permission to use these questions, the answers to which are solely the responsibility of the author.

G. L. HOUPT

SI Units

Quantity	Unit	Abbreviation or symbol
Mass	kilogramme	kg
Length	metre	m
Time	second	s
Force	newton	N
Energy and work	joule	J
Power	watt	W
Moment	newton metre	N m
Pressure and stress	newton per square metre	N/m^2
Temperature	kelvin	K
Quantity of heat	joule	J
Electric current	ampere	A
Resistance	ohm	Ω
Potential difference; and electromotive force	volt	V
Luminous intensity	candela	cd

Multiples and sub-multiples

Multiplying factor	Prefix	Abbreviation or symbol
$1\,000\,000\,000 = 10^9$	giga	G
$1\,000\,000 = 10^6$	mega	M
$1000 = 10^3$	kilo	k
$0.001 = 10^{-3}$	milli	m
$0.000\,001 = 10^{-6}$	micro	μ

It is strongly recommended that multiples and sub-multiples of SI units should be taken only at intervals of 10^3 as shown above.

Contents

		Page
Preface		v
Chapter 1	Basic chemistry	1
	1.1 Atoms and molecules	1
	1.2 Elements, compounds, mixtures, and alloys	2
	1.3 The composition of air	4
	1.4 Oxidation and reduction	4
	1.5 Corrosion	5
	1.6 Combustion	6
	Problems	8
Chapter 2	Electricity	11
	2.1 The effects of an electric current	11
	2.2 Conductors and insulators	12
	2.3 Electric current, voltage, and resistance	13
	2.4 Ohm's law	16
	2.5 Resistances in series and parallel	19
	2.6 Electrical power	29
	2.7 Magnetism and magnetic materials	34
	2.8 Permanent magnets and magnetic fields	34
	2.9 Electromagnets	36
	2.10 Magnetic devices in the workshop	38
	Problems	39
Chapter 3	Effects of heat	44
	3.1 Common changes due to heat application	44
	3.2 Thermometers and temperature measurement	45
	3.3 Coefficient of linear expansion; expansion and contraction fits	45
	Problems	51

CONTENTS

			Page
Chapter 4		Quantity of heat	56
	4.1	Changes of state	56
	4.2	Sensible heat	56
	4.3	Specific heat	56
	4.4	Measurement of heat quantity	57
	4.5	Latent heats of fusion and vaporization; dryness fraction	59
	4.6	Heat transfer in workshop problems	63
	4.7	Calorific value and combustion	68
	4.8	Consideration of heat losses in workshop problems. Thermal efficiency	68
		Problems	71
Chapter 5		Forces in equilibrium	78
	5.1	Vector representation of forces	78
	5.2	Triangle and parallelogram of forces	79
	5.3	Resolution of forces into vertical and horizontal components	88
	5.4	The principle of moments	92
	5.5	Simply supported beams	95
	5.6	Simple and cranked levers	99
	5.7	Couples and torque	104
	5.8	Centre of gravity	106
	5.9	Centre of area	109
		Problems	118
Chapter 6		Elementary strength of materials	132
	6.1	Stresses and strains, and their classification	132
	6.2	Hooke's law and the elastic limit	141
	6.3	Tensile and compressive tests, yield point and tensile strength	142
	6.4	Factor of safety and working stresses	143
	6.5	Percentage elongation and reduction of area. Ductility	143
	6.6	Proof stress	147
		Problems	149
Chapter 7		Friction	158
	7.1	The laws of dry friction	158
	7.2	Coefficient of friction	159

CONTENTS

7.3	Useful and wasteful friction in the workshop	164
7.4	Methods of reducing friction	171
	Problems	172

Chapter 8 Work and power transmission — 177

8.1	Work done by a constant force	177
8.2	Work done in overcoming friction	181
8.3	Work diagrams and work done by a variable force	183
8.4	Speed and velocity	186
8.5	Power consumption in machining operations	189
8.6	Output to input efficiency calculations in work and power	192
8.7	Loss of power due to friction	197
8.8	Work done and power transmitted by a constant and variable torque	198
8.9	Frictional torque and journal friction	208
	Problems	211

Chapter 9 Simple machines — 220

9.1	Mechanical advantage, velocity ratio, and efficiency	220
9.2	The law of a machine	234
9.3	Limiting efficiency and overhauling	235
9.4	Pulley drives and gear wheel ratios	238
9.5	Simple and compound gear trains for screw-cutting and other workshop applications	248
	Problems	256

Chapter 10 Conversion of energy — 267

10.1	Heat produced by friction and machining	267
10.2	Conversion of electrical power to mechanical and heat energy	270
10.3	Conversion of heat energy to mechanical work and electrical energy. Thermal efficiency	276
	Problems	278

Index — 283

1. Basic chemistry

1.1 Atoms and molecules

All material substances are composed of a vast number of tiny particles called atoms. This is true whether the substances are in a solid, liquid, or gaseous form. Each atom is so small that it cannot be seen, even under a microscope providing a high magnification. In fact, an atom is the smallest part of a substance which can take part in a chemical change. In view of this definition it is important at this stage to distinguish between chemical and physical changes.

A chemical change involves the production of a new substance with different properties, such as the rust produced in the corrosion of iron or the exhaust gas from a motor car produced by the combustion of the petrol.

In a physical change no new substance is produced and generally it is only a change of state that is involved, such as melting or evaporation. The three possible states of existence are solid, liquid, and gaseous, and these may be defined as follows:

(a) a solid resists an attempt to change its shape or size, and will remain at the same volume while its temperature is constant,

(b) a liquid resists an attempt to change its volume, but not an attempt to change its shape, and will also remain at the same volume while its temperature is constant,

(c) a gas takes up the shape of its containing vessel and will always fill this vessel, therefore the volume of a gas will only remain constant while it is in a vessel of unchanging volume.

The structure of an atom consists of a nucleus with a positive electrical charge surrounded by electrons each with a negative electrical charge. The nucleus contains protons, each of which bears a positive electrical charge, and neutrons which have no electrical charge, that is, they are neutral. The number of protons in the nucleus is characteristic of the element concerned and is known as the atomic number, for example, a hydrogen atom has one proton, the helium atom has two protons, hence the atomic numbers of hydrogen and helium are 1 and 2 respectively. With the exception of hydrogen, each proton in the nucleus is accompanied by at least one uncharged particle called a neutron.

A molecule is the smallest part of a substance that can exist in a free state (independently) and retain the properties of the substance. A molecule can consist of one or more atoms.

All substances have an atomic weight and/or a molecular weight depending on whether they are elements or compounds. Stating the atomic weight of a substance is a means of expressing relative magnitudes of the weights of atoms, for example, the atomic weight of aluminium is 27 and that of silver is 108, that is, the atomic weight of silver is four times that of aluminium. In general, the atomic weight of any element is based on one unit of atomic weight being equal to one twelfth of the atomic weight of carbon (12).

1.2 Elements, compounds, mixtures, and alloys

An element is a pure substance which cannot be decomposed into simpler substances. Elements are frequently represented by a symbol together with a numerical subscript indicating the number of atoms per molecule, for example, hydrogen may be represented by H_2, the subscript '2' indicating that there are two atoms in one molecule of hydrogen. The following table gives a few common elements together with their symbols and atomic weights (correct to the nearest whole number).

Element	Symbol	Atomic weight	Element	Symbol	Atomic weight
Aluminium	Al	27	Mercury	Hg	201
Antimony	Sb	122	Nitrogen	N	14
Carbon	C	12	Oxygen	O	16
Chromium	Cr	52	Phosphorus	P	31
Copper	Cu	64	Silicon	Si	28
Gold	Au	197	Silver	Ag	108
Hydrogen	H	1	Sulphur	S	32
Iron	Fe	56	Tin	Sn	119
Lead	Pb	207	Tungsten	W	184
Magnesium	Mg	24	Uranium	U	238
Manganese	Mn	55	Zinc	Zn	65

Compounds are formed by the chemical combination of two or more elements in fixed proportions by weight, so that the composition of a compound is always the same however it is prepared. A molecule of an element consists of one or more atoms. A molecule of a compound contains one or more atoms of each element present in the compound.

Typical simple compounds are: carbon dioxide CO_2 (one atom of carbon + two atoms of oxygen forming one molecule of carbon dioxide), and copper sulphate $CuSO_4$ (one atom of copper + one atom of sulphur + four atoms of oxygen forming one molecule of copper sulphate). A compound can only be reduced into its constituent elements by means of a chemical change.

Both elements and compounds have molecular weights. The molecular weight of an element is equal to the number of atoms per molecule multiplied by the atomic weight. The molecular weight of a compound is the sum of the weights of all the atoms present in the compound. The following table gives a few elements and compounds together with their molecular weights and chemical symbols.

Acetylene	C_2H_2	26	Hydrogen	H_2	2
Benzene	C_6H_6	78	Nitrogen	N_2	28
Carbon	C	12	Oxygen	O_2	32
Carbon dioxide	CO_2	44	Sulphur	S	32
Carbon monoxide	CO	28	Sulphur dioxide	SO_2	64
Copper sulphate	$CuSO_4$	160	Water	H_2O	18

A mixture is obtained by intermingling the particles of two or more substances in random proportions by weight and without chemical reaction. Examples of mixtures are: sand and salt, water and sand, iron and brass filings, milk and water, oxygen, nitrogen, and argon as in dry air, carbon dioxide in water, sugar in water. If the mixture of sugar and water is stirred vigorously, the sugar becomes invisible and a perfect mixture (or solution) is obtained, the sugar (the solute) has been dissolved by the water (the solvent). A cutting fluid often used as a coolant for machining operations consists of a mixture of 'soluble' oil and water producing a liquid with a milky appearance. The word soluble here is an unfortunate misnomer because this mixture is not a true solution, but is a suspension of very small globules of oil in water. Such a mixture is called an emulsion.

If some pieces of tin are added to a quantity of molten copper the tin will be dissolved and a solution obtained. If this mixture is cooled and allowed to solidify we have what is known as an alloy, this particular alloy is known as bronze. Generally speaking, if two or more metals are fused together and allowed to solidify an alloy is obtained; however, the degree to which one metal is soluble in another in a solid state varies from those where it is so small as to be negligible such as zinc and tin, to those which have complete solubility for all proportions in the solid state, such as copper and nickel. An alloy of great importance to engineers is steel, where the two basic constituents are iron and carbon, amounts of carbon being small compared with iron. Some of the iron combines with the small amount of carbon to form iron-carbide (cementite), so that steel is, strictly speaking, an alloy of iron and iron-carbide.

1.3 The composition of air

Although the composition of dry air free from carbon dioxide is very nearly constant it cannot be called a compound because a compound always has a definite exact composition. Air is, therefore, a mixture (it is really a solution of gases). Dry air free from carbon dioxide contains roughly 78% nitrogen, 21% oxygen, and 1% argon by volume. The air surrounding us in the atmosphere contains varying degrees of moisture and traces of the inert gases helium, neon, krypton, and xenon. In addition, in an industrial area, the atmosphere will contain minute quantities of such impurities as: carbon monoxide, hydrocarbons, hydrogen peroxide vapour, sulphur compounds, inorganic and organic dust particles. Such impurities may occur due to motor-car exhaust gases, chimney-flue gas emission, mining, and quarrying. In the workshop, dust particles may be present because of such operations as: grinding, metal-polishing, paint-spraying, sand-blasting, and the machining of wood or plastic materials. In some of these cases the provision of dust extractors is obligatory. Moist air has a severely corrosive effect on many metals, and the dust in the atmosphere, in addition to being a health hazard, is most undesirable where very accurate measurements are being made such as those required for inspection purposes.

1.4 Oxidation and reduction

These are both processes in which a chemical reaction takes place. The full explanation of the meaning of these two terms is beyond the scope of the course covered by this book, however, at this stage oxidation may be considered as a chemical process in which oxygen is added to an element or compound. Reduction is the reverse of oxidation and may be considered as a chemical process in which oxygen is removed from a compound. Most metals combine with oxygen to form oxides and is part of the phenomena known as corrosion. Another example of oxidation occurs in the heat treatment of metals (particularly steel) when oxygen is present in the furnace atmosphere, in the case of steel the oxygen combines with the iron to produce an iron oxide scale, which can be most undesirable. When heating hardened steel, in a tempering process, the temperature can be roughly judged by the colour of the thin film of oxide produced on the bright surface of the metal. The colours range from light straw to dark blue for the approximate temperature range of $230°C$ to $320°C$. If it is essential to avoid oxidation in a heat treatment process the furnace should have a reducing atmosphere or contain only inert gas.

As a reverse process, reduction can be applied to extract metal from an oxide ore. In the extraction of iron from iron ore (sintered iron oxide), coke which is mostly carbon combines with oxygen from an air supply to form carbon monoxide, which then reduces the iron oxide to iron and carbon dioxide, the heat of combustion of the coke being sufficient to melt the iron. For reasons which need not be discussed here this method cannot be used with every metal oxide or ore in order to extract metal and the extraction metallurgist has to use different techniques depending on the metal to be extracted and the type of ore involved.

1.5 Corrosion

Metal corrosion is the destruction of metals and alloys by oxidation or electrochemical action. Corrosion causes enormous material loss and is very costly. Some of the serious effects of corrosion are: loss of products due to leakage, blemishing of finished products, pitting of boiler tubes, and the reduction of the cross-section of a load-bearing member in a structure. The occurrence of corrosion leads designers to use higher factors of safety than would otherwise be necessary.

Because of the presence of oxygen most metals are oxidized by the atmosphere, but the extent of the corrosion will depend on the metal and the prevailing atmospheric conditions. Iron is quickly corroded to a reddish-brown rust when exposed to moist air, but will not rust in dry air or in water from which all air is excluded. When pure aluminium is in contact with the atmosphere a hard thin alumina skin is formed which provides a resistance to corrosion. The process of anodizing is carried out to increase the thickness of the alumina skin giving further protection from corrosion and to provide an improved finished appearance. There is reason to believe that pure metals are generally more able to resist corrosion than impure metals or alloys.

To prevent or reduce the occurrence of corrosion the design of structures should be such as to allow effective drainage of rain water and to avoid the collection of moisture and dirt. Corrosive effects can also be reduced or prevented by the use of protective metal coatings, enamels, lead-based paints, bituminous mixtures, plastic cladding, cement and concrete. The use of soluble oil in mixing a cutting fluid protects machined work from the corrosion which would result if water alone was used.

1.6 Combustion

The chemical combination of substances with oxygen, when accompanied by the evolution of heat and light, is called combustion. The chief combustible elements are carbon, hydrogen, and sulphur, although sulphur is regarded as an undesirable element in a fuel because of the harmful and corrosive effect of the sulphur dioxide present in the products of combustion. In addition to those elements already mentioned there are other combustible substances, such as: magnesium, calcium, phosphorus, sodium, and potassium.

The combustion of a fuel brings about the release of heat energy which may be usefully converted to doing mechanical work as in the case of petrol combustion in a motor car engine or the production of electrical power in a power station. For most practical purposes, the oxygen necessary for combustion is supplied from the air in the surrounding atmosphere. One notable exception, however, is in the case of the oxy-acetylene welding plant where the acetylene (C_2H_2) is combined with oxygen only, each gas being extracted from a steel cylinder into which it had previously been compressed.

The combustion of carbon to produce carbon dioxide can be represented by the chemical equation

$$C + O_2 = CO_2$$

substituting the molecular weights given in paragraph 1.2 we have

$$12 + 32 = 44$$

This means that 12 kg of carbon would require a theoretical minimum of 32 kg of oxygen to obtain complete combustion and this will produce 44 kg of carbon dioxide.

Example 1 (MT1)

The burning of hydrogen produces steam which condenses to water if the product of combustion is allowed to cool sufficiently.
Determine:

(a) the theoretical minimum amount of oxygen required for the complete combustion of 1 kg of hydrogen, and

(b) the mass of steam that will be produced.

Before proceeding to form the necessary chemical equation it must be noted that the atoms on both sides of the equation must be balanced, that is, the same number of atoms of each element must appear on both sides of the equation. In addition, a gas which is also an element cannot appear as one atom alone, therefore, we write H_2, not H on its own, in a chemical equation and the same will apply to oxygen. We can now start to write the required equation as $H_2 + O_2 = H_2O$ but this will not be correct since there are two atoms of oxygen on the left-hand side of the equation and only one on the right-hand side. The equation is, therefore, written as follows in order to give the same number of atoms of hydrogen and oxygen on both sides:

$$2H_2 + O_2 = 2H_2O$$

substituting the molecular weights into the equation we have

$$4 + 32 = 2(2 + 16)$$
$$4 + 32 = 36$$

Dividing through by 4 on both sides of the equation

$$1 + 8 = 9$$

This means that 8 kg of oxygen are required for the complete combustion of 1 kg of hydrogen and 9 kg of steam will be produced.

Example 2 (MT1)

Determine the theoretical minimum mass of oxygen required for the complete combustion of 1 kg of methane (CH_4). What mass of steam and carbon dioxide will be produced?
In this case the necessary equation is:

$$CH_4 + 2O_2 = CO_2 + 2H_2O$$

substituting the molecular weights in the equation we have

$$(12 + 4) + 2 \times 32 = 12 + 32 + 2(2 + 16)$$
$$16 + 64 = 44 + 36$$

dividing through by 16 on both sides of the equation

$$1 + 4 = \frac{11}{4} + \frac{9}{4}$$

This means that 1 kg of methane requires 4 kg of oxygen for complete combustion and produces $2\frac{3}{4}$ kg of carbon dioxide and $2\frac{1}{4}$ kg of steam.

Problems (MT 1)

1. What does the atomic number of an element indicate?
2. Distinguish between a chemical change and a physical change. Give an example of each case which may occur in the workshop.
3. (a) Define the terms 'atomic weight' and 'molecular weight'.
   (b) If the atomic weights of carbon, hydrogen, and oxygen are 12, 1, and 16 respectively, what are the molecular weights of:
   (i) carbon dioxide (CO_2), and (ii) pure water (H_2O)?
4. Distinguish between solid, liquid, and gaseous states. Give an example of each state which may occur in the workshop.
5. Briefly explain the differences between elements, compounds, and mixtures. Give workshop examples to illustrate the differences.
6. Classify the following as elements, compounds, or mixtures: aluminium, brass, iron, copper sulphate, acetylene, and oxygen.
7. Give the meanings of the following terms:
   (a) solvent, (b) solute, (c) alloy, (d) emulsion.
8. Classify the following as compounds, solutions or mixtures:
   (a) brine, (b) concrete, (c) lead paint, (d) carbon monoxide, (e) iron carbide.
9. What constituents of a workshop atmosphere should be excluded from the atmosphere of a gauge inspection room as far as possible? Briefly explain what harmful effects these constituents would have if allowed in the inspection room atmosphere unchecked.
10. Give at least two workshop or industrial processes in which the use of an extractor fan would be necessary and state the harmful effects which would arise if no fans were used.
11. Why is it sometimes undesirable for oxygen to be present in a furnace atmosphere during a heat treatment process?

BASIC CHEMISTRY 9

12. State how it is sometimes possible to judge the approximate temperature of a hardened steel component during a tempering operation, and state the chemical process involved.

13. State the chemical process involved in the rusting of plain carbon steel. Under what conditions would rusting not take place?

14. Why does aluminium appear to have a good resistance to corrosion? State the process that is sometimes used to improve this resistance.

15. What steps should be taken in the design of steel structures to reduce the effects of corrosion?

16. State some of the more serious effects of corrosion and give a brief outline of some of the methods which may be employed to reduce or prevent corrosion.

17. State the chief combustible elements likely to be present in a fuel and briefly explain why sulphur is regarded as an undesirable element in a fuel.

18. State two workshop processes which require the combustion of a fuel. In each case name the fuel burned and the method by which the oxygen is supplied.

19. State which of the following elements or compounds are combustible:

    (a) carbon, (b) carbon dioxide (CO_2), (c) carbon monoxide (CO), (d) acetylene (C_2H_2), (e) phosphorus, (f) sulphur dioxide (SO_2), (g) nitrogen, and (h) hydrogen.

20. State the product of combustion obtained in the complete and efficient burning of the following:

    (a) carbon, (b) hydrogen, and (c) sulphur.

    Are these products elements, compounds or mixtures?

21. Determine:
    (a) the theoretical minimum mass of oxygen required for the complete combustion of 1 kg of sulphur, and
    (b) the mass of sulphur dioxide produced.
    Ans: (a) 1 kg of O_2 (b) 2 kg of SO_2.

22. Write down the chemical equation for the partial combustion of carbon to carbon monoxide (CO) and then determine the theoretical

minimum mass of oxygen required for 1 kg of carbon in this combustion process. Also determine the mass of carbon monoxide produced from 1 kg of carbon.

Ans: $1\frac{1}{3}$ kg of O_2, $2\frac{1}{3}$ kg of CO from the equation $2C + O_2 = 2CO$.

23. Write down the chemical equation for the complete combustion of acetylene (C_2H_2) and determine:

    (a) the minimum mass of oxygen required for the complete combustion of 1 kg of acetylene, and
    (b) the mass of CO_2 and H_2O produced.

    Ans: $2C_2H_2 + 5O_2 = 4CO_2 + 2H_2O$,

    (a) $\frac{40}{13}$ kg of O_2,

    (b) $\frac{44}{13}$ kg of CO_2 and $\frac{9}{13}$ kg of H_2O.

2. Electricity

2.1 The effects of an electric current

In chapter 1 it was explained that the structure of an atom consisted of a nucleus surrounded by electrons, the nucleus containing protons and neutrons. The proton has a positive electric charge and an electron has a negative electrical charge. The surrounding electrons rotate in different orbits about the nucleus just as the planets orbit the sun. Materials consist of a huge number of atoms and in some solids electrons may break away from their original atoms and pass in random directions from one atom to another. In doing this they displace other electrons as they pass from one atom to another. When a solid in which this happens is connected to an electric cell, battery, or other means of electricity supply, the electrons which have broken free will all move in one general direction. We can say that there is an electric current in the solid, but there must be a closed loop (or circuit) including the source of electricity supply for this to happen. The nature of electricity is perhaps better understood when we see its effects.

Heating effect

If an electric fire is connected to an electricity supply the element will warm up and begin to glow. If the electric current could be increased, the heating will also be increased because the displacement of electrons become more frequent. The amount of heating effect also depends on the cross-sectional area, the smaller the area the greater the heating effect. This knowledge is applied in the use of a simple fuse which is a safety device, since if the current is too great the fuse wire is heated to the extent that it will melt and break the circuit. Some other examples of the use of this effect are: electric furnaces, electric arc welders, soldering irons, and immersion heaters.

Chemical effect

If two carbon rods are connected to an electricity supply (a battery) and are kept apart while being immersed in a solution of copper sulphate, then bubbles of gas appear on one rod and copper is deposited on the other. This demonstrates the chemical effect of an electric current. The copper sulphate solution is called an electrolyte. The carbon rods are called electrodes, the rod through which the current enters the electrolyte being called the anode and that through which the electric current leaves the electrolyte being called the cathode. This sort of process is used in the electro-plating industry with suitably chosen electrolytes and provides a means of preventing corrosion and/or giving a decorative effect, for example, chromium plating, copper plating, nickel plating, and so on.

Magnetic effect

When a bar magnet is suspended so that it can rotate in a horizontal plane it will always come to rest in the same place eventually, so that the ends point towards the magnetic poles of the earth which is itself a huge magnet. This principle is made use of when using a simple compass needle. This consists of a magnetized steel needle, which is pivotted so that it will rotate freely in a horizontal plane. The north pole of the compass needle will always point towards the magnetic north pole of the earth.

When an electric current is passed through a wire, the immediate surroundings are affected magnetically. This can be detected by placing a compass needle in the vicinity of the wire, the magnetic effect being shown by the deflection of the needle. A magnetic field is said to be set up. Thus if there is an electric current in the wire a force is exerted on the needle and mechanical work is done in moving the needle. Lines of such force are shown in paragraph 2.9, together with a brief description of an electro-magnet. Use is made of the magnetic effect of an electric current where energy is required to drive machinery in the workshop by the use of electric motors, in addition to the obvious uses such as electro-magnets for lifting iron or steel scrap and for magnetic chucks.

2.2 Conductors and insulators

The number of electrons which break away from their original atoms varies with different materials, the greater the number, the more easily will an electric current be set up in the material. Materials in which large numbers of electrons break free from their original atoms are good conductors of electricity, and are generally simply called conductors. Sub-

ELECTRICITY

stances in which relatively few electrons break free are therefore poor conductors of electricity and are called insulators. Nearly all metals are good conductors, copper, brass, and aluminium being the most commonly used. Substances such as porcelain, rubber, and bakelite are poor conductors and are used as insulating materials, they are used to prevent the electric current from following along any other path than its intended circuit.

2.3 Electric current, voltage, and resistance

Electric current

We can now see that if a number of components, made from conducting materials, are connected to a suitable electricity supply so that there is a complete circuit there will be a flow of electrons in a particular direction round the circuit. This flow is called an electric current. Originally scientists did not know in which direction the electricity flowed and a conventional direction was assumed. According to this convention current leaves the battery or cell through the positive terminal, so that in the external circuit the direction was assumed to be from positive to negative. It is now known that the flow of electrons in an external circuit is from negative to positive. Since each electron has an electric charge or quantity of electricity a unit will be needed in order to measure this charge. Another unit will also be needed to measure the flowrate of this quantity when there is an electric current. The unit of electric charge is the 'coulomb' (C) and therefore the flowrate is measured in coulombs per second (C/s) and these units are called 'amperes' (A).

$$1 \text{ ampere} = 1 \text{ coulomb per second}$$

If
Q = quantity of electricity in coulombs
I = the flowrate (electric current in amperes)

and
t = time of transfer for the quantity Q in seconds

then
$$\text{electric current } I = \frac{Q}{t} \text{ amperes}$$

and
$$Q = It \text{ coulombs}$$

The electric current in a circuit can be measured with an instrument known as an ammeter.

Voltage

When there is an electric current in a conductor, forced motion of electrons is taking place in a particular direction. In order to bring about this motion some work will have to be done. In view of this a source of energy will be needed. Although work and energy will be defined later in chapter 8 it will be helpful to try to understand the meaning of these two terms before proceeding further.

Work is done when the application of a force produces motion, and the amount of work is equal to the product of the force and the distance moved in the direction of the force and is measured in joules, where one joule (J) is equal to one newton metre (Nm).

Energy is the capacity for doing work, or in other words is a store of work and is, therefore, also measured in joules. When work is done energy will be changed from one form to another.

Electromotive force

Some device must be used to generate the energy needed to move the electrons around the circuit and this is referred to as a generator of which there are a number of different types. In the case of a cell or battery the energy is obtained by means of chemical action. An electric current can also be set up by rotating coils of conducting material through lines of magnetic force. The amount of energy made available by a generator is called electromotive force and this is usually abbreviated to e.m.f. and its quantity is indicated by the letter E. The unit of e.m.f. is called the volt where the number of volts is the number of joules of energy supplied to each coulomb of electric charge, that is,

$$1 \text{ volt} = 1 \text{ joule per coulomb}$$

Note that electromotive force is not actually a force but energy.

Example 1 (MT1)

Calculate the energy supplied per minute by a generator having an e.m.f. of 240 V in order to maintain a current of 10 A in a circuit.

$$\text{e.m.f.} = 240 \text{ V}$$

but $\quad$ 240 V = 240 joules per coulomb (J/C)

and $\quad$ 10 A = 10 coulombs per second (C/s)

ELECTRICITY

$$\text{energy supply} = 240 \times 10 \text{ joules per second (J/s)}$$
$$= 2400 \text{ J/s}$$
$$= 2400 \times 60 \text{ J/min}$$
$$= 144\,000 \text{ J/min}$$
$$= 1.44 \times 10^5 \text{ J/min}$$

Potential difference

The movement of electrons round a circuit may be likened to the flow of a liquid through a pipe, in each case some energy is required to produce motion. As the liquid flows through a pipe the friction between the liquid and the walls of the pipe will cause a loss of this type of energy. Similarly with electron flow, there will be a loss of electrical energy as the flow proceeds round the circuit. The difference between the quantities of energy (volts) between two different parts of a circuit is called the potential difference (often abbreviated to p.d.) and is denoted by the letter V and is also measured in volts (V).

Example 2 (MT1)

If an electrical heating appliance converts 3.6×10^6 joules of electrical energy to heat in one hour calculate the potential difference across the terminals of the heater, given that the current is 4 A.

$$4 \text{ A} = 4 \text{ C/s}$$

$$3.6 \times 10^6 \text{ J/h} = \frac{3.6 \times 10^6}{60 \times 60} \text{ J/s}$$

$$= 10^3 \text{ J/s}$$

Now more precisely, potential difference is energy loss per coulomb of electric charge

$$\therefore \quad \text{potential difference} = \frac{\text{loss of electrical energy per second}}{\text{number of coulombs per second}}$$

$$= \frac{10^3}{4} \left(\frac{\text{J}}{\text{s}} \times \frac{\text{s}}{\text{C}} \right)$$

$$= 250 \text{ J/C}$$

$$= 250 \text{ V}$$

Resistance

In the previous paragraph the flow of electrons was likened to the flow of liquid through a pipe. If there is a reduction in the diameter of the pipe through which the liquid flows, the resistance to this flow will increase if we try to maintain the same flowrate. The same applies to conductors of electricity, the resistance to the current is inversely proportional to the cross-sectional area of the conductor. The resistance is also directly proportional to the length of the conductor and, in addition, depends on the material, since different materials do not all provide the same resistance to an electric current. The unit of resistance is called the ohm (Ω). The letter used to denote resistance is (R).

2.4 Ohm's law

If the same flowrate (electric current) is to be maintained through a conductor the resistance will only be overcome at the expense of electrical energy. If conditions surrounding the conductor are kept constant the loss of electrical energy will be directly proportional to the electric current. This relationship is known as Ohm's law which can be stated as follows:

'the potential difference across a conductor is directly proportional to the electric current provided that the temperature of the conductor is kept constant'.

This means that the ratio

$$\frac{\text{potential difference}}{\text{electric current}} = \text{a constant}$$

and this constant will be the resistance of the conductor.

$$V \propto I$$

and
$$V = RI$$

also
$$R = \frac{V}{I} \frac{\text{volts}}{\text{amperes}}$$

hence
$$1 \text{ ohm} = 1 \text{ volt per ampere}$$

ELECTRICITY

Example 3 (MT1)

Determine the resistance of a wire which takes a current of 2 A from a voltage supply of 220 V.

$$V = RI$$
$$\therefore \quad 220 = 2R$$
$$\therefore \quad R = 110 \, \Omega$$

Example 4 (MT1)

Calculate the current carried by a heating element if its resistance is 50 Ω and the potential difference is 230 V.

$$V = IR$$
$$\therefore \quad 230 = 50I$$
$$\therefore \quad I = \frac{230}{50} \, A$$
$$= 4.6 \, A$$

Example 5 (MT1)

The potential difference across a resistor is 80 V when the current is 50 mA. Determine:

(a) the current when the potential difference is 24 V, and
(b) the potential difference when the current is 600 μA.

(a) now   50 mA = 50 milliamperes
$$= 50 \times 10^{-3} \, A$$
$$= 0.05 \, A$$

The resistance will remain constant, therefore, from Ohm's law resistance

$$R = \frac{V}{I}$$
$$= \frac{80}{0.05} \, \Omega$$
$$= 1600 \, \Omega$$

18 MECHANICAL ENGINEERING SCIENCE

now when   p.d. = 24 V
∴   24 = 1600I
∴ $I = \dfrac{24}{1600}$ A
                = 0.015 A
                = 15 mA

(b) now   600 μA = 600 microamperes
                = 600 × 10^{-6} A
since $V = RI$
                p.d. = 1600 × 600 × 10^{-6} V
                = 16 × 6 × 10^{-2} V
                = 0.96 V

Example 6 (MT1)

In a laboratory experiment to verify Ohm's law, the potential difference across a resistor was gradually increased and the following readings of voltage and current were noted for the resistor.

V volts	0	1.5	3.0	4.5	6.0	7.5	9.0
I amperes	0	0.19	0.37	0.57	0.75	0.94	1.12
V volts	10.5	12.0					
I amperes	1.3	1.5					

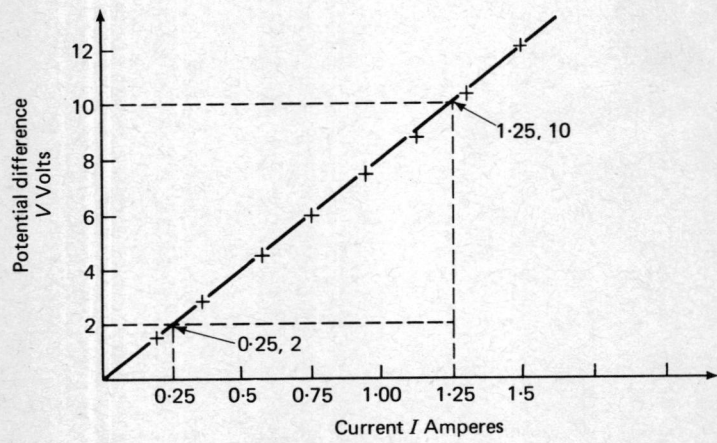

Fig. 2.1

ELECTRICITY

Plot the graph showing the relationship between voltage and current and determine the value of the resistance from the graph.

Since it is expected that the potential difference will be directly proportional to the current, the graph should result in a straight line passing through the origin. As the points do not all lie exactly on a straight line, the straight line of closest fit is drawn passing through the origin, as shown in Fig. 2.1.

Selecting a point on the straight line, say at a current of 1.25 A, we note that the potential difference reading at this point is 10 V. Since the expected law is
$$V = RI$$
then
$$10 = 1.25R$$
from which
$$R = 8 \, \Omega$$

2.5 Resistances in series and parallel

Before proceeding further it is desirable to note the standard symbols generally used to denote the various simple items which may be incorporated in an electric circuit. These are shown in Fig. 2.2.

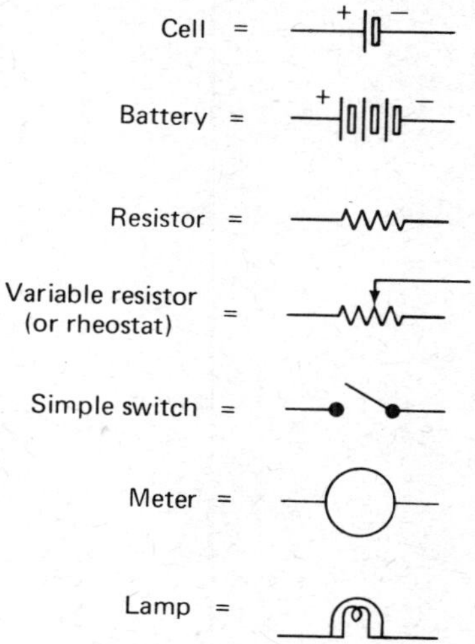

Cell =

Battery =

Resistor =

Variable resistor (or rheostat) =

Simple switch =

Meter =

Lamp =

Fig. 2.2

Resistances in series

Resistors are said to be connected in series when they are joined together consecutively to form one circuit path for the current. Consider resistances of 2 Ω, 3 Ω, and 4 Ω connected in series with a circuit current of 2 A:

$$\text{potential difference of the 2-}\Omega\text{ resistor} = 2 \times 2 \text{ V}$$
$$= 4 \text{ V}$$
$$\text{potential difference of the 3-}\Omega\text{ resistor} = 2 \times 3 \text{ V}$$
$$= 6 \text{ V}$$
$$\text{potential difference of the 4-}\Omega\text{ resistor} = 2 \times 4 \text{ V}$$
$$= 8 \text{ V}$$

The total potential difference is $(4 + 6 + 8)$ V
$$= 18 \text{ V}$$

The current will be the same at any point in a series circuit, as with a liquid flowing through one pipe line, the rate of flow is the same at any point. Applying Ohm's law to the overall circuit:

$$V = IR$$
$$18 = 2R$$

from which
$$R = 9 \text{ }\Omega$$

This is equal to the sum of the separate resistances $(2 + 3 + 4)$ Ω.

Thus if resistances R_1, R_2, and R_3 are connected in series, total resistance $R = R_1 + R_2 + R_3$.

The total resistance of a circuit should include the internal resistance of the battery or cell. However, this is sometimes ignored especially if it is small in relation to the resistances in the external circuit.

Example 7 (MT1)

Four resistors are connected in a series circuit to a battery with an e.m.f. of 24 V. If the resistances are 2 Ω, 3 Ω, 4 Ω, and 6 Ω calculate,

(a) the current in the circuit, and

(b) the potential difference across each resistor.

Neglect the internal resistance of the battery.

(a) $\quad$ total resistance $R = 2 + 3 + 4 + 6$
$$= 15 \text{ }\Omega$$

This can now be considered as a single equivalent resistance, and since the internal resistance of the battery is neglected the potential difference across the resistors will equal the e.m.f.

ELECTRICITY

Applying Ohm's law

$$E = RI$$

then

$$24 = 15I$$

from which

$$I = \frac{24}{15} \text{ A}$$
$$= 1.6 \text{ A}$$

(b) Applying Ohm's law to each resistor

$$V = IR$$

p.d. across 2-Ω resistor = 1.6 × 2 volts
= 3.2 V

p.d. across 3-Ω resistor = 1.6 × 3 volts
= 4.8 V

p.d. across 4-Ω resistor = 1.6 × 4 volts
= 6.4 V

p.d. across 6-Ω resistor = 1.6 × 6 volts
= 9.6 V

The sum of these potential differences is 24 V which is equal to the e.m.f. Since the internal resistance of the battery was ignored the potential difference across the battery terminals will also be neglected and will not appear in the calculations. However, the calculations show that the sum of all potential differences is equal to the e.m.f.

Example 8 (MT1)

Two equal resistances are connected in series with a variable resistor which can be varied from zero to 100 Ω. The e.m.f. of the battery is 12 V and its internal resistance can be neglected. If the minimum possible current in the circuit is 100 mA calculate:

(a) the value of the two equal resistances,

(b) the maximum possible current, and

(c) the current through and the potential difference across the variable resistor when it is adjusted to 30 Ω.

(a) From Ohm's law $I = \dfrac{V}{R}$, therefore, the circuit current will be at a minimum when the total resistance R is at a maximum.

Let R_1 = resistance of one of the equal resistors,

now the minimum current I = 100 mA
$$= 0.1 \text{ A}$$

since
$$E = IR$$
$$12 = 0.1(100 + 2R_1)$$

for minimum current and maximum resistance conditions

$\therefore \qquad 120 = 100 + 2R_1$

$\therefore \qquad 2R_1 = 20$

from which $\qquad R_1 = 10 \ \Omega$

(b) Maximum current occurs when the resistance of the variable resistor is zero, therefore in this case,

$$12 = 2R_1 I$$
$$= 20I$$
$\therefore \qquad I = 0.6 \text{ A}$
$\therefore \qquad$ maximum current = 600 mA

(c) When the variable resistor is at 30 Ω

$$12 = (2R_1 + 30)I$$
$$= 50I$$
$\therefore \qquad I = \dfrac{12}{50} \text{ A}$
$$= 0.24 \text{ A}$$
$$= 240 \text{ mA}$$

potential difference across the variable resistor at 30 Ω

$$= RI$$
$$= 30 \times 0.24 \text{ volts}$$
$$= 7.2 \text{ V}$$

Resistances in parallel

If a liquid flowing along a pipe reaches a place where the pipe runs into a number of parallel branch pipes, the sum of the rates of flow in each

ELECTRICITY

branch will equal the total rate of flow which existed in the single pipe. The same applies to electric current. Consider the three resistances in parallel shown in Fig. 2.3.

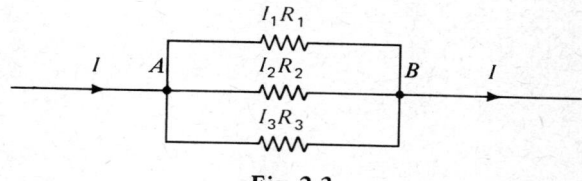

Fig. 2.3

Since each resistor joins the single main conductor at the same point at each end (A and B) the loss of electrical energy will be the same for each branch, therefore the potential difference across each resistor will be the same.

Thus
$$V = I_1 R_1 = I_2 R_2 = I_3 R_3$$

∴
$$I_1 = \frac{V}{R_1}$$

$$I_2 = \frac{V}{R_2}$$

$$I_3 = \frac{V}{R_3}$$

Now the main current $I = I_1 + I_2 + I_3$

$$I = \frac{V}{R_1} + \frac{V}{R_2} + \frac{V}{R_3}$$

Dividing both sides of the equation by V we have

$$\frac{I}{V} = \frac{1}{R_1} + \frac{1}{R_2} + \frac{1}{R_3}$$

The overall potential difference will be the same as that for each individual resistor, therefore the potential difference can be written as

$$V = IR$$

where R is the equivalent resistance for the combination of the three resistors in parallel, and I is main circuit current. Replacing V with IR we have

$$\frac{I}{IR} = \frac{1}{R_1} + \frac{1}{R_2} + \frac{1}{R_3}$$

$$\therefore \quad \frac{1}{R} = \frac{1}{R_1} + \frac{1}{R_2} + \frac{1}{R_3}$$

Example 9 (MT1)

Suppose the resistances R_1, R_2, and R_3 shown in Fig. 2.3 are 5 Ω, 8 Ω, and 10 Ω respectively, determine the value of the single equivalent resistance.

Using the formula for resistances in parallel

$$\frac{1}{R} = \frac{1}{5} + \frac{1}{8} + \frac{1}{10}$$

$$= \frac{8 + 5 + 4}{40}$$

$$= \frac{17}{40}$$

$$\therefore \quad R = \frac{40}{17} \ \Omega$$

equivalent resistance = 2.353 Ω

Example 10 (MT1)

Three resistors of 15 Ω, 30 Ω, and 40 Ω are connected in parallel to a battery with an e.m.f. of 18 V and an internal resistance of 1 Ω. Calculate:

(a) the voltage available at the terminals of the battery,

(b) the potential difference across the resistors, and

(c) the current in each resistor.

(a) In this case, the internal resistance is given; therefore, the potential difference across the battery terminals will have to be taken into consideration. Figure 2.4 shows the circuit diagram.

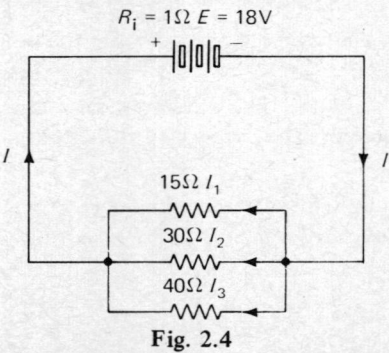

Fig. 2.4

ELECTRICITY

Let R_E be the equivalent resistance of the resistors in parallel, then

$$\frac{1}{R_E} = \frac{1}{15} + \frac{1}{30} + \frac{1}{40}$$

$$= \frac{8 + 4 + 3}{120}$$

$$= \frac{15}{120}$$

$$R_E = \frac{120}{15}\,\Omega$$

$$= 8\,\Omega$$

∴ Total circuit resistance $R = 8 + 1\,\Omega$

$$= 9\,\Omega$$

Applying Ohm's law to the complete circuit

$$E = IR$$

$$18 = 9I$$

∴ main circuit current $I = 2$ A

If R_i is the internal resistance of the battery then the potential difference across the battery terminals

$$= IR_i$$

$$= 2 \times 1 \text{ volts} = 2 \text{ V}$$

therefore, the voltage available at the battery terminals

$$= 18 - 2 \text{ volts}$$

$$= 16 \text{ V}$$

(b) p.d. across resistors $= R_E I$

$$= 8 \times 2 \text{ volts}$$

$$= 16 \text{ V}$$

Note, that since there are no other resistors in the circuit the result is, as would be expected, equal to the voltage output from the battery.

(c) To obtain the current through each resistor, Ohm's law can be applied, remembering that the potential difference across each resistor is the same at 16 V.

For the 15-Ω resistor $16 = 15I_1$

∴ $I_1 = \dfrac{16}{15}$ amperes

$= 1.067$ A

For the 30-Ω resistor $16 = 30I_2$

∴ $I_2 = \dfrac{16}{30}$ amperes

$= 0.533$ A

For the 40-Ω resistor $16 = 40I_3$

∴ $I_3 = \dfrac{16}{40}$ amperes

$= 0.4$ A

As a check $I_1 + I_2 + I_3 = 1.067 + 0.533 + 0.4$
$= 2$ A

Example 11 (MT1)

Figure 2.5 shows a circuit in which four resistors are connected in parallel in pairs at A and B as shown. The resistors in parallel at A have resistances of 15 Ω and 35 Ω and those at B are 8 Ω and 24 Ω. There is one 7-Ω resistance connected in series and the battery has an e.m.f. of 25 V and an internal resistance of 1.5 Ω.

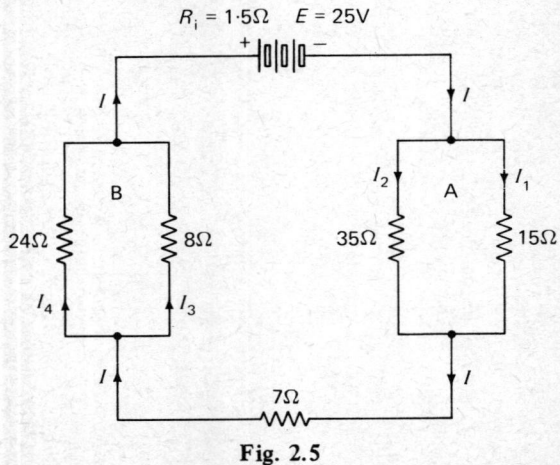

Fig. 2.5

Calculate:

(a) the potential difference across each resistor and across the battery terminals, and

(b) the current through each resistor.

(a) Let R_A be the equivalent resistance of the 15 Ω and 35 Ω parallel resistors and let R_B be the equivalent resistance of the 8 Ω and 24 Ω parallel resistors. Using the formula for resistors in parallel:

$$\frac{1}{R_A} = \frac{1}{15} + \frac{1}{35}$$

$$= \frac{35 + 15}{15 \times 35}$$

$$= \frac{50}{15 \times 35}$$

$$= \frac{2}{21}$$

∴ $$R_A = \frac{21}{2} = 10.5 \text{ Ω}$$

similarly

$$\frac{1}{R_B} = \frac{1}{8} + \frac{1}{24}$$

$$= \frac{24 + 8}{8 \times 24}$$

$$= \frac{32}{192}$$

$$= \frac{1}{6}$$

∴ $$R_B = 6 \text{ Ω}$$

The total circuit resistance $= 10.5 + 6 + 7 + 1.5$

$= 25$ Ω

Applying Ohm's law to the complete circuit

$$E = RI$$

$$25 = 25I$$

∴ main circuit current $I = 1$ A

28 MECHANICAL ENGINEERING SCIENCE

Applying Ohm's law separately to the resistors and the battery,

$$\text{p.d. across A} = IR_A$$
$$= 1 \times 10.5 = 10.5 \text{ V}$$
$$\text{p.d. across B} = IR_B$$
$$= 1 \times 6 = 6 \text{ V}$$

Note that once the equivalent resistances have been determined they may be treated in the same way as series resistors.

p.d. across the 7-Ω resistor $\quad = 1 \times 7 = 7$ V

p.d. across the battery terminals
$$= IR_i$$
$$= 1 \times 1.5 = 1.5 \text{ V}$$

(b) p.d. across the 15-Ω resistor of 10.5 V
$$= R_1 I_1$$
∴ $\quad 10.5 = 15 I_1$

∴ $$I_1 = \frac{10.5}{15} \text{ amperes}$$

∴ the current through the 15-Ω resistor
$$= 0.7 \text{ A}$$

p.d. across the 35-Ω resistor of 10.5 V
$$= I_2 R_2$$
∴ $\quad 10.5 = 35 I_2$

$$I_2 = \frac{10.5}{35} \text{ amperes}$$

∴ the current through the 35-Ω resistor
$$= 0.3 \text{ A}$$

p.d. across the 8-Ω resistor of 6 V
$$= R_3 I_3$$
∴ $\quad 6 = 8 I_3$

$$I_3 = \frac{6}{8} \text{ amperes}$$

∴ the current through the 8-Ω resistor
$$= 0.75 \text{ A}$$

p.d. across the 24-Ω resistor of 6 V
$$= R_4 I_4$$
$\therefore$
$$6 = 24 I_4$$
$\therefore$
$$I_4 = \frac{6}{24} \text{ amperes}$$
$\therefore$ the current through the 24-Ω resistor
$$= 0.25 \text{ A}$$

Note that the sum of the currents through each pair of parallel resistors adds up to the main circuit current of 1 A. The current through the 7-Ω resistor will be equal to the circuit current of 1 A since this resistor is connected in series.

2.6 Electrical power

Power is the rate of doing work, that is:
$$\text{power} = \frac{\text{work done}}{\text{time taken}} \text{ joules/second}$$

The unit of power is the watt where
$$1 \text{ watt} = 1 \text{ joule/second}$$
thus
$$1 \text{ joule} = 1 \text{ watt second}$$

When defining electromotive force in paragraph 2.3 we saw that one volt was equivalent to one joule per coulomb which is in effect a unit of work or energy. We can say that electromotive force is the energy required to transfer a unit of electric charge from one part of a circuit to another, but this takes no account of the rate at which this would be carried out. However, electric current is in effect a rate of flow, considering the basic units:
$$1 \text{ ampere} = 1 \text{ coulomb/second}$$
$$1 \text{ volt} = 1 \text{ joule/coulomb}$$
$\therefore$
$$1 \text{ ampere volt} = 1 \left[\frac{C}{s} \times \frac{J}{C} \right]$$
$$= 1 \text{ joule/second}$$
$\therefore$
$$1 \text{ ampere volt} = 1 \text{ watt (W)}$$
$\therefore$ [electrical power in watts] = [current in amperes] $\times$ [e.m.f. or p.d. in volts]

i.e., electrical power $P = IV$

MECHANICAL ENGINEERING SCIENCE

Summarizing:

$$\text{electrical charge } Q = It \text{ coulombs}$$

$$\text{electrical energy} = \text{p.d.} \times \text{electric charge}$$

$$= VQ \text{ joules}$$

$$= VIt \text{ joules}$$

$$\text{electrical power } P = \frac{VIt}{t} \text{ joules/second}$$

i.e., $\qquad P = IV$ watts as before.

By applying Ohm's law this formula for electrical power can be obtained in two other forms as follows:

since $\qquad V = IR$

then $\qquad P = I \times IR$

thus $\qquad$ electrical power $= I^2 R$ watts

also since $\qquad I = \dfrac{V}{R}$

$$P = \frac{V}{R} \times V$$

$$P = \frac{V^2}{R} \text{ watts}$$

Thus giving three alternative formulae for electrical power. A standard unit of energy used in the electrical industry is the kilowatt hour (kWh). It is developed from basic SI units as follows:

$$1 \text{ joule} = 1 \text{ watt second}$$

$$10^3 \text{ joules} = 1 \text{ kilowatt second}$$

$$60 \times 60 (10^3 \text{ joules}) = 1 \text{ kilowatt hour}$$

$$3.6 \times 10^6 \text{ J} = 1 \text{ kWh}$$

ELECTRICITY

Example 12 (MT1)

An electric heater is rated at 2 kW and takes a current of 10 A from a 240-V supply. Calculate the efficiency and the cost of using the heater for five hours at 0.6 new pence per unit (kWh).

$$\text{input power} = VI$$
$$= 240 \times 10 \text{ W}$$
$$= 2.4 \text{ kW}$$
$$\text{output power} = 2 \text{ kW}$$
$$\text{efficiency} = \frac{\text{output power}}{\text{input power}}$$
$$= \frac{2}{2.4}$$
$$= 0.8333$$
$$= 83.33\%$$

$$\text{Number of units used in 5 hours} = 5 \times 2.4 \text{ kWh}$$
$$= 12 \text{ kWh}$$
$$\text{cost} = 0.6 \times 12 \text{ new pence}$$
$$= 7.2 \text{ new pence}$$
$$= \frac{7.2}{5} \text{ shillings}$$
$$= 1.44 \text{ shillings}$$

Example 13 (MT1)

An immersion heater rated at 2 kW is connected to a 250-V supply. Assuming that the efficiency is 100% calculate the resistance of the element and the heat energy supplied in 2 hours.

In this case a formula is required which relates power, resistance and voltage, therefore using

$$P = \frac{V^2}{R}$$

and knowing that 2 kW = 2000 watts

$$2000 = \frac{250^2}{R}$$

$$R = \frac{250^2}{2000}\ \Omega$$

$$= \frac{62\,500}{2000}$$

$$= 31.25\ \Omega$$

$$\text{energy supply} = 2 \times 2 \text{ kWh}$$

$$= 4 \text{ kWh}$$

now $1 \text{ kWh} = 3.6 \times 10^6 \text{ J}$

∴ heat energy supplied in 2 hours $= 4 \times 3.6 \times 10^6 \text{ J}$

$$= 14.4 \times 10^6 \text{ J}$$

Example 14 (MT1)

An electric circuit has two resistors of 40 Ω and 60 Ω connected in parallel and two other resistors of 2 Ω and 4 Ω connected in series, the whole circuit being completed with a 120-V supply.
Calculate:

(a) the current through each resistor, and

(b) the power loss in each resistor.

Figure 2.6 shows the circuit diagram.

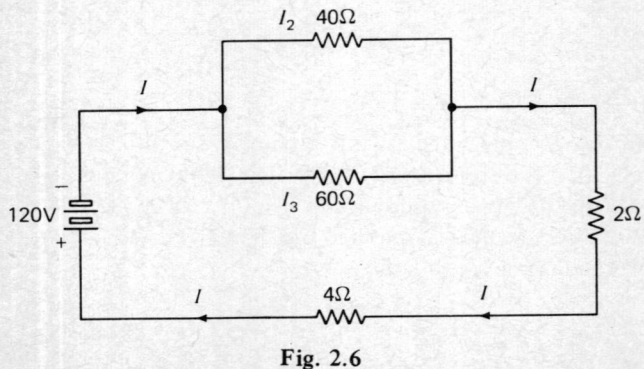

Fig. 2.6

ELECTRICITY

(a) If R_E is the equivalent resistance of the resistors in parallel

$$\frac{1}{R_E} = \frac{1}{40} + \frac{1}{60}$$

$$= \frac{60 + 40}{2400} = \frac{100}{2400}$$

$\therefore$ $\qquad R_E = 24\ \Omega$

$\therefore$ Total circuit resistance $= 24 + 2 + 4\ \Omega$

$$= 30\ \Omega$$

Applying Ohm's law to the complete circuit

$$E = IR$$

$$120 = 30I$$

$\therefore$ $\qquad$ supply current $I = 4$ A

therefore the current through the 2-Ω and 4-Ω resistors

$$= 4\ \text{A}$$

p.d. across the parallel resistors $\qquad = IR_E$

$$= 4 \times 24\ \text{V}$$

$$= 96\ \text{V}$$

This is the same for both resistors

$\therefore$ $\qquad 96 = 40I_1$

$\therefore$ $\qquad I_1 = \frac{96}{40}\ \text{A}$

$\therefore$ current through 40-Ω resistor $= 2.4$ A

also $\qquad 96 = 60I_2$

$$I_2 = \frac{96}{60}\ \text{A}$$

$\therefore$ current through 60-Ω resistor $= 1.6$ A

(b) power loss in the 40-Ω resistor

$$= I_1^2 R_1$$

$$= 2.4^2 \times 40\ \text{W}$$

$$= 5.76 \times 40\ \text{W}$$

$$= 230.4\ \text{W}$$

power loss in the 60-Ω resistor

$$= I_2{}^2 R_2$$
$$= 1.6^2 \times 60 \text{ W}$$
$$= 2.56 \times 60$$
$$= 153.6 \text{ W}$$

power loss in the 2-Ω resistor

$$= I^2 \times 2$$
$$= 16 \times 2 \text{ W}$$
$$= 32 \text{ W}$$

power loss in the 4-Ω resistor

$$= I^2 \times 4$$
$$= 16 \times 4 \text{ W}$$
$$= 64 \text{ W}$$

2.7 Magnetism and magnetic materials

Magnetism is the force of attraction which exists between a natural or artificial magnet and a piece of material, such as iron, which is attracted by a magnet. The magnetic force is at a maximum intensity at the north and south poles of a magnet. The earth itself has a magnetic north and south pole and these are slightly displaced from the geographical north and south poles.

Materials most readily attracted by a magnet are iron and steel, and to a lesser extent nickel and cobalt. Most magnetic materials are alloys containing one or more of the elements iron, cobalt, and nickel. Various alloys are used as magnetic materials, chief among these are the iron-silicon and iron-nickel alloys in addition to a number of others used to a lesser extent. It should be noted that these magnetic materials are not only attracted by another magnet but can themselves be made into magnets.

2.8 Permanent magnets and magnetic fields

A permanent magnet is one in which, as the name suggests, retains its magnetism for a very long period and without any connection to any other source of energy. Permanent magnets are usually in the bar or horseshoe forms shown in Figs. 2.7(a) to 2.8(b). A compass needle could also be called a permanent magnet.

Experiments show that the ends of a bar magnet are apparently areas of maximum magnetic effect. The end marked N would point towards the earth's magnetic north pole if the magnet was allowed to rotate freely in a horizontal plane. Likewise the end marked S would be attracted towards the earth's magnetic south pole under similar conditions. Experiments would also show that like poles repel each other and unlike poles are attracted to each other. Since unlike poles attract each other and the north pole of a magnet is attracted by the earth's north pole, the magnetic poles of the earth must be of opposite polarity to that of other magnets. Due to magnetic effect forces are set up at all positions in a magnetic field, and these forces will have magnitude and direction. Figures 2.7(a) to 2.8(b) show the approximate lines and directions of force in the vicinity of bar and horseshoe magnets.

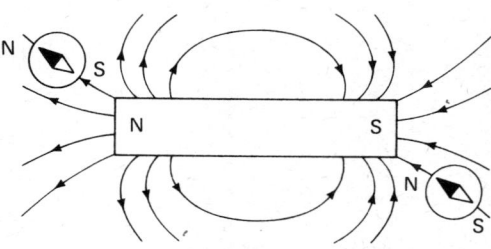

Fig. 2.7(a)

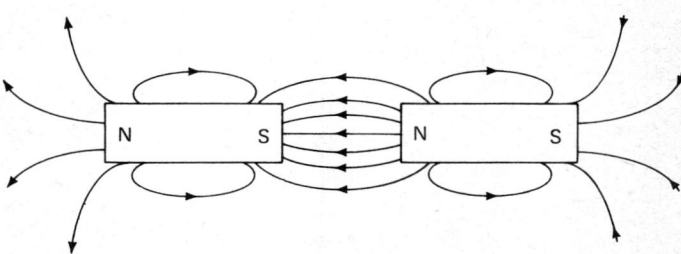

Fig. 2.7(b)

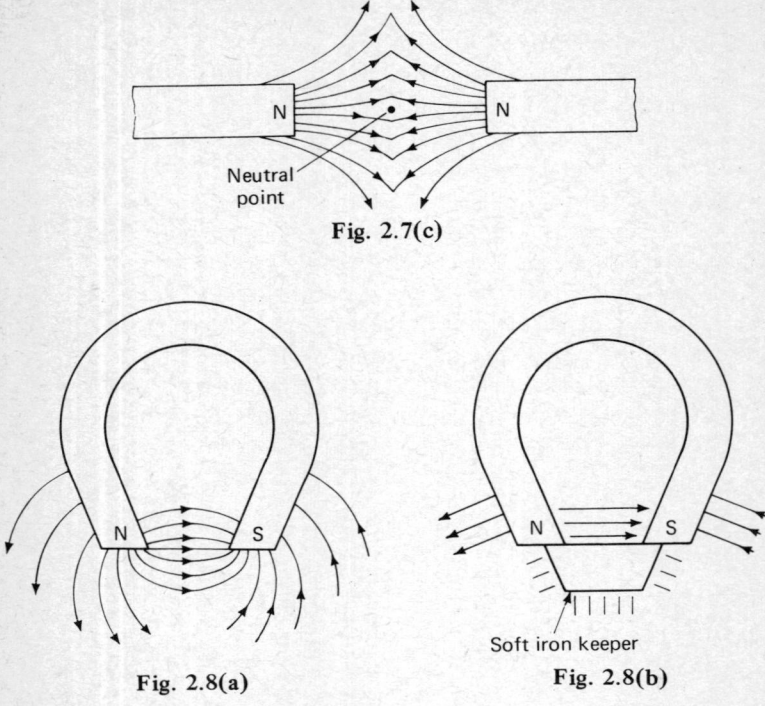

Fig. 2.7(c)

Fig. 2.8(a)   Fig. 2.8(b)

The experiments can be carried out by placing a sheet of paper over the magnets in turn and lightly sprinkling iron filings over the paper. After tapping the paper lightly, typical patterns will be observed. Alternatively, the lines of force may be plotted by placing a compass needle in various positions in the magnetic field and marking the direction of the compass needle in each case as shown in Fig. 2.7(a). The difference between the lines of force in Figs. 2.8(a) and 2.8(b) should be noted. In Fig. 2.8(b) the lines of force pass through the soft-iron keeper, thus forming a closed magnetic circuit.

2.9 Electromagnets

As stated in paragraph 2.1 a magnetic field is set up in the vicinity of a conductor when an electric current exists in the conductor. The directions of the lines of magnetic force in relation to the direction of the electric current is shown in Fig. 2.9 for a straight conductor.

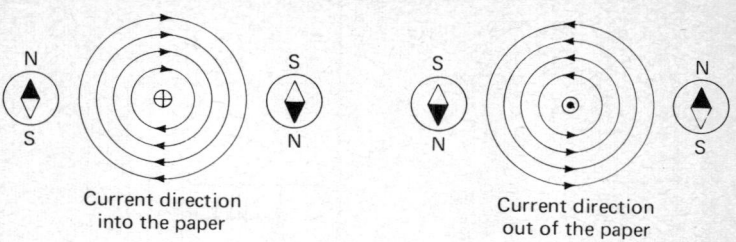

Fig. 2.9

Suppose that the straight conductor is closely wound round a circular bar, so making a closely wound coil. If an electric current is passed through the coil, the magnetic effect will be more intense than it was when electric current was passed through the conductor in its straight form. When such a coil is formed it is called a solenoid, the approximate lines of magnetic force are shown in Fig. 2.10.

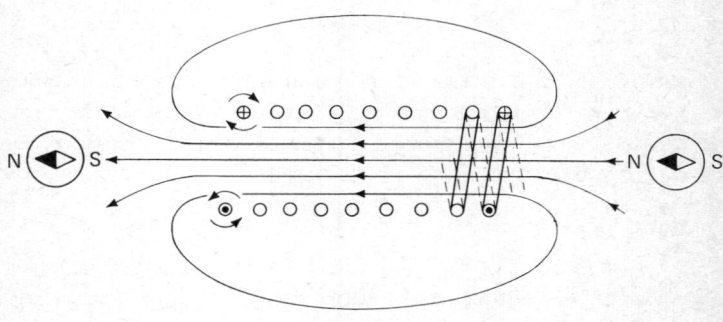

Fig. 2.10

If a soft iron core is also fitted inside the coil, the intensity of magnetic force will be even more increased while an electric current exists in the coil. A simple electromagnet can be formed by closely winding a conducting coil around a soft-iron core shaped like a horseshoe and an electric current passed through the coil. This is a particularly useful form, for the part which is attracted to the poles will complete a magnetic circuit. A simple example is seen in the operation of an electric bell (see Fig. 2.11).

When the push-button switch is closed a circuit is completed through the contact C and the electromagnet is activated. The armature is then attracted to the magnet causing the striker to hammer the gong. In doing this the contact at C is broken and the circuit is no longer complete, thus

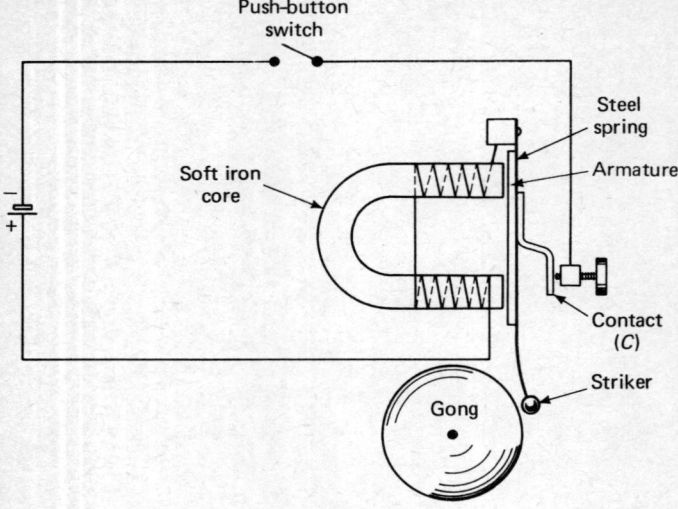

Fig. 2.11

the electromagnet is de-activated and the armature-striker unit is released and springs back to make contact at C once again, and since the circuit is completed again the whole process is repeated in quick succession for as long as the push-button switch is kept closed.

2.10 Magnetic devices in the workshop

Magnetic devices in industry generally may be operated either by permanent magnets or electromagnets. Electromagnets are used for lifting and conveying scrap iron and steel. Another application is in the breaking up of large scrap parts, a heavy steel ball being raised by the electromagnet and then allowed to fall on the scrapped parts. Other uses for electromagnets include: magnetic clutches, electric motors, dynamos, relays, and separators, the latter being used to separate iron and steel scrap from other non-magnetic material.

Magnetic devices in the workshop include: magnetic chucks, magnetic bases for scribing blocks, relays for switchgear, and electric motors for driving machinery. The magnetic chuck is used for holding work in position chiefly during surface grinding operations. The chuck may be a separate device bolted to the machine table or it may be an integral part of the machine table itself. Naturally the work being ground, if it is of a non-magnetic material, will not be held to the table. Strips are fitted at the ends of the chuck and these are raised and used as stops to hold the work from slipping if a very heavy cut is being applied.

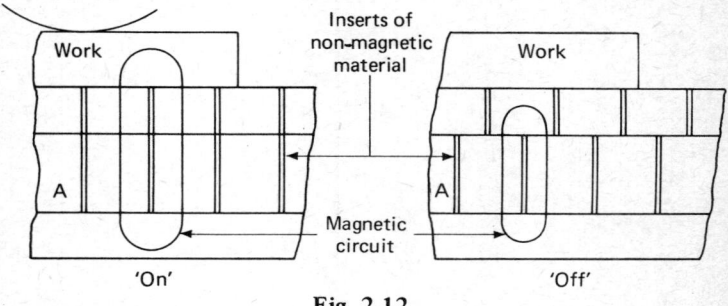

Fig. 2.12

Referring to Fig. 2.12, the part A can be moved from side to side to complete a magnetic circuit through the work, or in the 'off' position to divert the path of the magnetic circuit so that it does not pass through the work. When the work is removed from the chuck it will be magnetized to a certain extent. Now magnetism can be destroyed by hammering or by heating, but since this would distort the work an electrical device known as a demagnetizer is used to remove the unwanted magnetism.

Problems (MT1)

1. State the three main effects of an electric current, and give a practical example of each effect.
2. Explain the difference between conductors and insulators when used in connection with the passage of an electric current. Give three materials which are good conductors and three which are good insulators.
3. Briefly explain the nature of electric current, electromotive force and resistance and state the unit in which each is measured.
4. (a) Define 'potential difference'.
   (b) An electric fire converts 6.48×10^6 joules of electrical energy to heat in one hour. Calculate the potential difference across the terminals of the fire, given that the current taken is 8 A.
   Ans: 225 V.

5. (a) State the meaning of 'electric charge' and state its unit.
   (b) If an electric current of 6 A is maintained through a potential difference of 35 V for 20 min calculate the electric charge round the circuit and the electrical energy loss per minute.
   Ans: 7200 C, 12.6 kJ/min.

6. An accumulator is charged with 180 000 coulombs for 10 hours. If the e.m.f. is constant calculate the current maintained during this time.
   Ans: 5 A.

7. State Ohm's law.
   An electric furnace takes an electric current of 12 A when connected to a 240-V supply. Calculate:
   (a) the resistance of the furnace, and
   (b) the current taken by the furnace if the voltage supply is reduced to 220 V.
   Ans: (a) 20 Ω. (b) 11 A.

8. In an experiment to verify Ohm's law the following readings of potential difference V across the terminals of a resistor and electric current I were noted:

V (volts)	0	2	4	5	6	8	10	12
I (amperes)	0	0.17	0.35	0.41	0.5	0.67	0.83	1

   Plot the graph of potential difference (V) against current (I) and use the graph to estimate the probable value of the resistance.
   Ans: 12 Ω.

9. Calculate the current through a lamp which has a resistance of 150 Ω and is connected to a 240-V supply.
   Ans: 1.6 A.

10. An electric heater provides a resistance of 25 Ω to an electric current of 8.5 A. Calculate the potential difference across the terminals of the heater.
    Ans: 212.5 V.

11. The current through a moving coil meter is 0.4 mA when measuring a potential difference of 6 V. Determine:
    (a) the resistance of the meter, and
    (b) the current when measuring a potential difference of 10 V.
    Ans: (a) 15 kΩ. (b) $\frac{2}{3}$ mA.

ELECTRICITY

12. Three lamps are connected in series to a 24-V supply. Two of the lamps each have a resistance of 12 Ω, while the current is 0.6 A. Calculate:
    (a) the resistance of the third lamp, and
    (b) the potential difference across this lamp.
    Ans: (a) 16 Ω. (b) 9.6 V.

13. Three resistors of 5, 10, and 15 Ω respectively are connected in series. If the current is 4 A, determine:
    (a) the total resistance,
    (b) the potential difference across each resistor, and
    (c) the total voltage.
    Ans: (a) 30 Ω. (b) 20 V, 40 V and 60 V. (c) 120 V.

14. Two resistors and a 12-V battery are connected in series. If the resistances are 8 Ω and 40 Ω determine:
    (a) the current in the circuit, and
    (b) the potential difference across each resistor.
    Neglect the internal resistance of the battery.
    Ans: (a) 250 mA. (b) 2 V, 10 V.

15. Four coils having resistances of 10 Ω, 15 Ω, 30 Ω and 45 Ω are connected in parallel to a 24-V battery with an internal resistance of 0.5 Ω. Calculate:
    (a) the total circuit resistance,
    (b) the voltage available at the terminals of the battery,
    (c) the potential difference across the coils, and
    (d) the current in each coil.
    Ans: (a) 5 Ω. (b) 21.6 V. (c) 21.6 V. (d) 2.16 A, 1.44 A, 720 mA, 480 mA.

16. Six lamps each having a resistance of 24 Ω are to be connected to a 50-V supply. Calculate the current in each lamp if they are:
    (a) connected in series, and
    (b) connected in parallel.
    State, with reason, which circuit will give the brighter light.
    Ans: (a) 347.2 mA. (b) 2.083 A.

17. Six 40-W lamps of equal resistance are connected in parallel to a 240-V supply. Calculate:
    (a) the current in each lamp,
    (b) the main circuit current, and
    (c) the resistance of each lamp.
    Ans: (a) $\frac{1}{6}$ A. (b) 1 A. (c) 1440 Ω.

18.

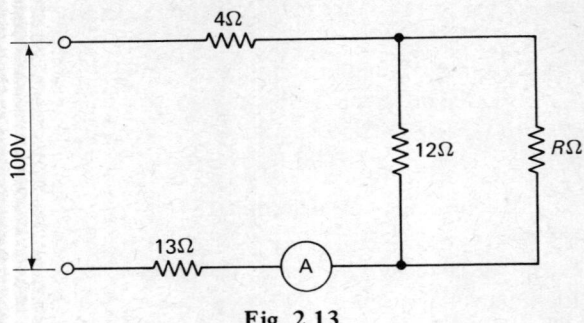

Fig. 2.13

If the ammeter reading A in the circuit shown in Fig. 2.13 is 5 A determine the coil resistance R and the potential difference across each coil.

Ans: 4 Ω, 20 V across 4 Ω, 65 V across 13 Ω, 15 V across coils in parallel.

19. In a laboratory test to determine the calorific value of a sample of coal, a fuse wire was passed through the sample and connected to terminals in an electric circuit. A 6-W, 12-V lamp, a push-button switch, and the sample were connected in series to a 25-V output from a transformer.
  (a) When the push-button switch is closed determine:
      (i) the circuit current,
      (ii) the potential difference across the sample, and
      (iii) the power dissipated at the sample.
  (b) If the push-button switch is kept closed for 30 seconds calculate the energy converted to heat by the combustion of the sample during this time.

Ans: (a) (i) 0.5 A, (ii) 13 V, (iii) 6.5 W. (b) 195 J.

20. A small electric motor is rated at 400-W and takes a current of 1.8 A from a 240-V supply. Calculate:
  (a) the efficiency of the motor, and
  (b) the cost of running the motor for 100 hours at 0.64 new pence per unit.

Ans: (a) 92.59%. (b) 27.61 new pence.

21.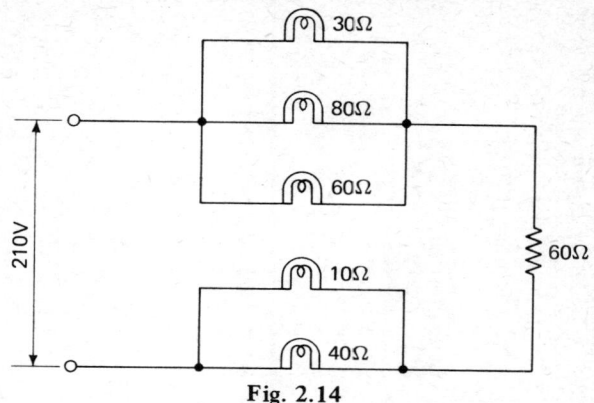

Fig. 2.14

Five lamps and a heating element are connected in a circuit as shown in Fig. 2.14. Calculate:
(a) the power loss across each lamp,
(b) the power loss across the heating element,
(c) the energy converted to heat at the element in one hour.
Ans: (a) $53\frac{1}{3}$ W across 30 Ω, 20 W across 80 Ω, $26\frac{2}{3}$ W across 60 Ω, 10 W across 40 Ω, 40 W across 10 Ω.
(b) 375 W.
(c) 1.35×10^6 J.

22. An electric furnace rated at 2.89 kW has an efficiency of 85%. A certain heat treatment operation requires 4.25×10^6 J of energy. Determine:
(a) the time required for the heat treatment operation, and
(b) the resistance of the heating element if the furnace is connected to a 240-V supply.
Ans: (a) 20 min 50 s. (b) 19.93 Ω.

23. The power of the heating element in an electric iron is 875 W when connected to a 225-V supply. Calculate the current taken by the iron and the resistance of its heating element.
Ans: 3.889 A, 57.86 Ω.

24. A lathe is provided with a small electric motor for driving a coolant pump. If the efficiency of the motor is 90% calculate the power output when a current of 50 mA is taken at 420 V. Also determine the energy provided by the motor during a continuous run of one hour.
Ans: 18.9 W, 68.04 kJ.

3. Effects of heat

3.1 Common changes due to heat application

Since heat is a form of energy transfer a definition of energy at this point would not appear to be out of place.

Briefly, we may say that energy is a store of work; if a substance possesses energy it has the ability to perform some work.

It follows, therefore, that if a substance gains or loses heat there will be some energy changes giving rise to the following possibilities:

(a) the temperature of the substance may rise as it gains heat or the temperature may fall as heat is lost,

(b) there may be a change of state, that is, the substance may melt or evaporate on heating, condense or freeze on cooling, there may also be some internal structural changes in a material which are not visible to the naked eye,

(c) there may be chemical changes, for example, oxidation may take place giving rise to an oxide scale on the outer skin of a material sometimes appearing as a change of colour in the case of steel for example, a phenomenon made use of in obtaining an approximate tempering temperature,

(d) there may be a change of size; substances nearly always expand on heating and contract when cooling,

(e) the resistance to an electric current generally increases when the substance is heated,

(f) if two different metals are joined at one end, and fixed to terminals at the other end such that a complete circuit is formed then an electric current may be set up if the joint is heated.

EFFECTS OF HEAT 45

3.2 Thermometers and temperature measurement

Some accurate method is needed to estimate how hot or cold a substance may be, that is we estimate its degree of hotness and this is known as its temperature. One of the commonest devices for measuring temperature is the mercury-in-glass thermometer which consists of a glass tube of narrow uniform bore sealed at its ends. One of the ends is enlarged to become a bulbous container of mercury. On heating the mercury expands readily and evenly and thus can be made to give an indication of temperature by suitably calibrating the glass stem of the thermometer. The standard of comparison used is the range from freezing to boiling point of water at atmospheric pressure.

The SI unit for temperature is the kelvin (K). A Kelvin temperature is the Celsius temperature plus 273.15, that is, ($^\circ$C + 273.15)K. On the Celsius scale at atmospheric pressure the freezing point of water is 0°C and the boiling point of water is 100°C. The Kelvin scale is used for thermodynamic work and since 1 K = 1°C the Celsius scale may also be used, particularly for temperature changes.

For very high temperatures a thermocouple pyrometer is used. This makes use of the effect (f) mentioned in paragraph 3.1. Other methods used are: seger cones, mercury in steel thermometers, optical pyrometers and constant volume thermometers. The student will find descriptions of some of these temperature measuring devices in books covering the subject of workshop processes for mechanical technicians.

3.3 Coefficient of linear expansion

As previously explained in this chapter, most substances expand when heated whether they are in a solid, liquid, or gaseous state (there are exceptions such as the melting of ice). In some cases this expansion can be a serious disadvantage, since if the expansion were to be forcibly prevented in a solid material it would eventually become distorted or even fracture if heating continues. In the case of a gas being kept in a containing vessel it will exert a pressure on that vessel. If the gas is heated it will be prevented from expanding and thus exert a greater pressure. Eventually, if heating is continued, the pressure exerted will become so great that the containing vessel will burst. If a framed structure is prevented from expanding during a rise of temperature forces will be exerted on the members in the structure which could cause a failure of the framework. A method for allowing expansion is

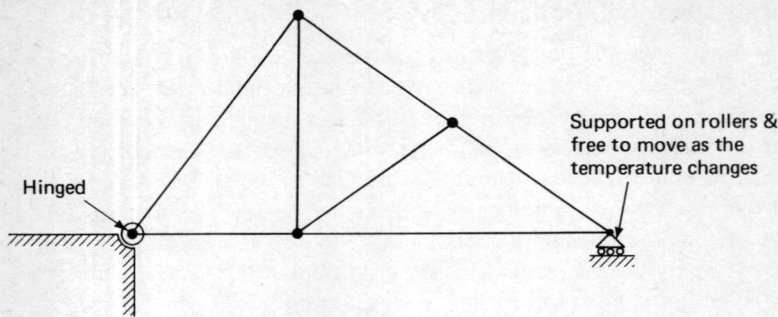

Fig. 3.1

shown in Fig. 3.1. Another disadvantage incurred by a change of temperature is that it affects accurate measurement, hence inspection departments and metrology laboratories must have conditions of constant standard temperature otherwise accuracy of measurement is affected. On the other hand, expansion and contraction due to temperature changes can be used to advantage.

Expansion and contraction fits. Suppose that it is required to fit a steel cylindrical core into a brass tube so that they are rigidly fixed together. This could be done by heating the brass tube until the steel core will slide into the tube and then allowing the brass tube to cool and shrink onto the core. This is called a shrink fit. A bush or liner can be fitted by cooling the bush well below the freezing point of water and allowing it to expand into its housing which would remain undistorted since no heating would be necessary. This is called an expansion fit. Another useful device is the bimetal strip. This can be used in thermostatic controls and consists of two strips of different metals rigidly fixed together. The metals used must have different rates of expansion, so that bending

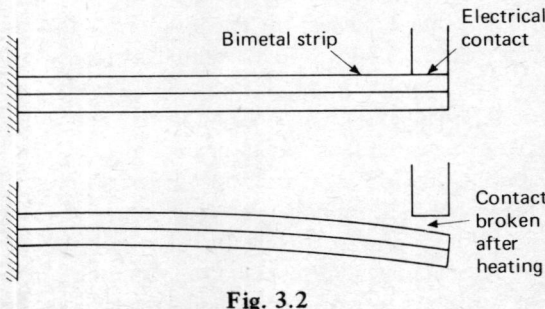

Fig. 3.2

EFFECTS OF HEAT

will take place when the temperature is increased. Figure 3.2 shows a steel strip rivetted to a brass strip. The bimetal strip will only bend when heated because one of the metals expands more than the other, that is, each material has its own coefficient of linear expansion.

As the temperature of the bimetal strip increases it bends, the metal on the upper side expanding more than the lower strip. When the contact shown is broken, heating from the element stops because the circuit is broken, hence the bimetal strip cools and straightens again until contact is made once more.

Although expansion takes place in all directions, that is, in volume, many practical problems are concerned only with expansion in one particular direction, that is, linear expansion or expansion in length. The coefficient of linear expansion of a material is the increase in length over a unit length when its temperature is increased by one degree, for example, a coefficient of linear expansion of 17×10^{-6} per degree celsius means that one metre will expand by 17×10^{-6} metres when the temperature is increased by one degree celsius. Suppose that

$$\text{amount of expansion} = x \text{ mm}$$
$$\text{original length} = l \text{ mm}$$
$$\text{initial temperature} = t_1 \,°\text{C}$$
$$\text{final temperature} = t_2 \,°\text{C}$$
$$\text{coefficient of linear expansion} = \alpha$$

By definition

$$\text{coefficient of linear expansion} = \frac{\text{increase of length}}{\left[\begin{array}{c}\text{original length} \\ \times \text{ increase of temperature}\end{array}\right]}$$

$$\alpha = \frac{x}{l(t_2 - t_1)}$$
$$x = \alpha l(t_2 - t_1)$$
$$\text{final length} = l + x$$
$$= l + \alpha l(t_2 - t_1)$$

If the material is cooling and contraction is taking place

$$\text{contraction } x = \alpha l(t_1 - t_2)$$

and

$$\text{final length} = l - x$$
$$= l - \alpha l(t_1 - t_2)$$

The important point to remember, is that a change of length (x) brought about by a change of temperature (t) is given by
$$x = \alpha l t$$

Example 1 (MT1)

A rule is made to measure 0.5 m exactly when it is at a temperature of 16°C. If the rule is made from steel with a coefficient of linear expansion of $11 \times 10^{-6}/°C$ calculate the percentage error in measurement when the temperature has increased to 26°C.

increase of 0.5 metre length $(x) = \alpha l(t_2 - t_1)$
$\qquad = 11 \times 10^{-6} \times 0.5(26 - 16)\text{m}$
$\qquad = 11 \times 10^{-6} \times 5\text{m}$
$\qquad = 55 \times 10^{-6}\text{m}$

$\%\text{ error} = \dfrac{\text{increase of length}}{\text{original length}} \times 100\%$

$\qquad = \dfrac{55 \times 10^{-6} \times 10^2}{0.5}\%$

$\qquad = 11 \times 10^{-3}\%$

$\qquad = 0.011\%$

Example 2 (MT1)

A length of steam pipe is 4 m long at a temperature of 15°C. Calculate the length of the pipe under working conditions when the temperature is 265°C. Take the coefficient of linear expansion to be $11.6 \times 10^{-6}/°C$.

increase of length $x = \alpha l(t_2 - t_1)$
$\qquad = 11.6 \times 10^{-6} \times 4(265 - 15)\text{ m}$
$\qquad = 11.6 \times 10^{-6} \times 1000\text{ m}$
$\qquad = 11.6 \times 10^{-3}\text{ m}$

new length $= 4 + 11.6 \times 10^{-3}\text{ m}$
$\qquad = 4.0116\text{ m}$

EFFECTS OF HEAT

Example 3 (MT1)

In an experiment to determine the coefficient of linear expansion for brass, steam was passed through a brass tube. An expansion of 0.75 mm was measured over a length which was 0.5 m at 20°C. Assuming that the temperature of the tube was 100°C when the expansion was measured calculate the coefficient of linear expansion for brass.

Now coefficient of linear expansion α

$$= \frac{\text{expansion }(x)}{\text{original length }(l) \times \text{temperature rise }(t)}$$

$$= \frac{0.75}{500 \times 80}/°C \quad (l = 500 \text{ mm})$$

$$= \frac{0.75}{40\,000}/°C$$

$$= 75 \times 10^{-2} \times \tfrac{1}{4} \times 10^{-4}$$

$$= \tfrac{1}{4} \times 75 \times 10^{-6}$$

$$= 18.75 \times 10^{-6}/°C$$

The temperature of wet steam at atmospheric pressure would be 100°C but this is no guarantee that the tube in this experiment will be quite at this temperature, therefore, the actual temperature rise may be a little lower than 80°C, thus the value of α obtained is probably a little lower than the true value.

Example 4 (MT1)

A phosphor bronze bush is to be expansion fitted into a steel housing bored to 55 mm diameter at 15°C to receive the bush. Calculate the outside diameter of the bush at 15°C if it is to just fit into the steel housing when its temperature has been reduced to −85°C. Take the coefficient of linear expansion for phosphor bronze to be $17 \times 10^{-6}/°C$.

Since the change of diameter is directly proportional to the change of circumference, the original length can be taken as the original diameter in this type of problem. Thus change of length will be taken as change of diameter.

$$\text{temperature reduction }(t) = 15 - (-85)°C$$

$$= 15 + 85$$

$$= 100°C$$

now
$$x = \alpha l t$$
$$= 17 \times 10^{-6} \times 55 \times 100 \text{ mm}$$
$$= 935 \times 10^{-4} \text{ mm}$$

∴ required diameter $= 55 + 935 \times 10^{-4}$ mm
$$= 55.0935 \text{ mm}$$

Example 5

A steel shaft runs in a phosphor bronze bush. The diameter of the fit is nominally 100 mm and when assembled at room temperature of 20°C, the diametral clearance is 0.08 mm. The coefficients of linear expansion of the steel and the phosphor bronze can be taken as $11 \times 10^{-6}/°C$ and $19 \times 10^{-6}/°C$ respectively.

Calculate:

(a) the diametral clearance at the normal running temperature of 70°C, and

(b) the sub-zero temperature at which the clearance disappears.

C.G.L.I.

(a) The expansion of the bronze
$$x_B = \alpha_B l(t_2 - t_1)$$

where
$$l = 100 \text{ mm}$$
$$x_B = 19 \times 10^{-6} \times 100 \times (70 - 20)$$
$$= 19 \times 10^{-6} \times 5000 \text{ mm}$$
$$= 95 \times 10^{-3} \text{ mm}$$
$$= 0.095 \text{ mm}$$

Similarly, the expansion of the steel
$$x_S = 11 \times 10^{-6} \times 100 \times 50 \text{ mm}$$
$$= 55 \times 10^{-3} \text{ mm}$$
$$= 0.055 \text{ mm}$$

Increase of clearance $(x_B - x_S) = 0.095 - 0.055$
$$= 0.04 \text{ mm}$$

total diametral clearance $= 0.08 + 0.04$
$$= 0.12 \text{ mm}$$

EFFECTS OF HEAT

Note that the original diameter was taken to be the same for both the steel and the bronze although there was an original difference of 0.08 mm. This does not matter since the effect of this on the answer is so small that it can be ignored.

(b) For no clearance:

$$\text{reduction of clearance} = \text{original clearance}$$

that is $\qquad x_B - x_S = 0.08 \text{ mm}$

If $\qquad t = \text{reduction of temperature}$

then $\quad 19 \times 10^{-6} \times 100t - 11 \times 10^{-6} \times 100t$

$$= 0.08$$

$\therefore \qquad 800 \times 10^{-6} t = 0.08$

$\therefore \qquad 100 \times 10^{-6} t = 0.01$

$\therefore \qquad 10^{-4} t = 10^{-2}$

$\therefore \qquad t = 10^2 = 100°C$

the temperature must be reduced by 100°C

$$\text{the final temperature} = 20 - 100°C$$
$$= -80°C$$

Problems (MT1)

1. A large vernier caliper is used for the accurate measurement and checking of the lengths of sheet metal panels. If the vernier is set to measure 1.5 m exactly when the temperature is 15°C calculate the error in measurement when the temperature has increased to 27°C. Take the coefficient of linear expansion to be $11.5 \times 10^{-6}/°C$.
   Ans: 0.207 mm.

2. A thin-walled brass cylinder has an internal diameter of 80 mm at 15°C. In order to carry out a turning operation on its exterior curved surface the cylinder is to be shrink fitted on to a steel mandrel which has a diameter of 80.1 mm at 15°C. Calculate the temperature to which the brass cylinder must be heated so that it just fits over the steel mandrel.
   Take the coefficient of linear expansion for brass to be $18.8 \times 10^{-6}/°C$.
   Ans: 81.5°C.

3. In an experiment to determine the coefficient of linear expansion for aluminium the results showed that an aluminium tube of length 0.5 m at 15°C expanded by 1.07 mm when heated to 100°C. Calculate the value of the coefficient of linear expansion for aluminium from these results.
   Ans: $25.18 \times 10^{-6}/°C$.

4. A steel shaft, nominally 50 mm diameter at 15°C, runs in a bronze bearing with a clearance of 0.1 mm when the temperature is 15°C. Taking the coefficients of linear expansion for steel and bronze to be $11.6 \times 10^{-6}/°C$ and $17 \times 10^{-6}/°C$ respectively, calculate:

   (a) the clearance, correct to 3 decimal places, when the temperature is 65°C, and

   (b) the temperature when the clearance has been reduced to 0.08 mm.
   Ans: (a) 0.114 mm. (b) −58.6°C.

5. The tubes in a fire-tube boiler are 2.5 m long at a temperature of 17°C. Calculate the length of the tubes:

   (a) when surrounded only by feed water at 12°C, and

   (b) when the boiler is operating and the mean temperature of the tubes is 267°C.

   Take the coefficient of linear expansion for the tube material to be $17 \times 10^{-6}/°C$.
   Ans: (a) 2.4998 m. (b) 2.5106 m.

6. An aluminium piston is to operate in a cast iron cylinder with a clearance of 0.016 mm at the working temperature of 315°C. Calculate the diameter to which the piston must be turned at 15°C given that the cylinder diameter is 88 mm at this temperature. Take the coefficients of linear expansion for cast iron and aluminium to be $10.2 \times 10^{-6}/°C$ and $25.5 \times 10^{-6}/°C$.
   Ans: 87.7 mm.

7. A stainless steel spindle is to be turned in a lathe to a finished diameter of not less than 48 mm at 15°C. At the end of a turning operation the diameter was found to be 48.01 mm, but due to the heat generated during the cutting of the metal the temperature of the spindle was 62°C.
   Taking the coefficient of linear expansion for stainless steel to be $11 \times 10^{-6}/°C$ calculate the error on diameter at 15°C correct to three decimal places. How could this error be avoided?
   Ans: 0.015 mm too small.

EFFECTS OF HEAT

8. A brass collar of bore diameter 100 mm is to be shunk on to a steel shaft 100.4 mm diameter, both of these dimensions being measured at 16°C. Calculate the temperature to which the collar must be heated so that it slides on to the shaft with a diametral clearance of 0.1 mm.
Take the coefficient of linear expansion for brass to be $18.9 \times 10^{-6}/°C$.
Ans: 280.5°C.

9. Lead weights are to be formed by pouring molten lead into moulds 320 mm long. If the solidification temperature of lead is 327°C, calculate the length of an ingot when it has cooled to a temperature of 17°C.
Take the coefficient of linear expansion of lead as $29.1 \times 10^{-6}/°C$.
Ans: 317.1 mm.

10. A dimension of 54.14 mm is to be checked by using slip gauges which are correct at 20°C. Calculate the error in the slip gauge build up if the gauges are used at a temperature of 12°C.
Take the coefficient of linear expansion for the slip gauge material to be $11.5 \times 10^{-6}/°C$.
Ans: 4.98×10^{-3} mm.

11. A temperature control system is operated by the expansion of a brass rod which is 200 mm long at 18°C. If the system is set so that the source of heat supply is cut off when the rod has expanded by 0.25 mm, calculate the temperature to which the system is limited.
Take $\alpha = 18.9 \times 10^{-6}/°C$.
Ans: 84.13°C.

12. An aluminium bronze tube of external diameter 25.08 mm is to be shrunk into a steel plate which has a receiving hole 25 mm diameter, both diameters being measured at 22°C. The process is to be carried out by cooling the tube to 0°C and heating the steel plate until there is a diametral clearance of 0.08 mm between the tube and the hole in the steel plate. Calculate the temperature to which the steel plate must be heated.
Take the coefficients of linear expansion for steel and aluminium bronze to be $11.6 \times 10^{-6}/°C$ and $17 \times 10^{-6}/°C$ respectively.
Ans: 541.3°C.

13. The assembly of a framed structure is to be secured by the insertion and fixing of a tie-bar 3 m long between two members of the frame. At a temperature of 15°C the tie-bar was found to be 1.4 mm short of the required length of 3 m.

Calculate:
(a) the temperature to which the tie-bar must be heated to attain the length of 3 m, and
(b) the contraction from 3 m of the tie-bar when the temperature of the assembled frame falls to −5°C and the members of the structure yield by 1 mm less than the free contraction of the tie-bar.

Take the coefficient of linear expansion to be $11.5 \times 10^{-6}/°C$.
Ans: (a) 55.6°C. (b) 1.09 mm.

14. A composite tube consists of an aluminium outer tube 250 mm long with an internal diameter of 100 mm and an inner bronze tube 250.5 mm long with an external diameter of 100 mm, all of these dimensions being correct at 20°C. Determine:

    (a) the temperature at which the tubes are the same length, and

    (b) the diametral clearance between the tubes at this temperature.

    Take the coefficient of linear expansion for aluminium and bronze to be $25.5 \times 10^{-6}/°C$ and $16.8 \times 10^{-6}/°C$ respectively.
    Ans: (a) 251°C (b) 0.2 mm.

15. A brass bar 400 mm long is being turned between centres in a lathe to a diameter of 40 mm both of these dimensions being correct at a temperature of 20°C. Due to the heat generated by cutting the temperature of the bar rises to 45°C and at this temperature the bar was found to be 400.1 mm long.

    (a) Calculate the amount of expansion prevented by the tailstock.

    (b) Determine the diameter required at the higher temperature in order to ensure its accuracy at the lower temperature correct to four significant figures.

    Assume that the coefficient of linear expansion for brass is $19 \times 10^{-6}/°C$.
    Ans: (a) 0.09 mm. (b) 40.02 mm.

16. In an experiment to determine the coefficient of linear expansion of a particular nickel steel a rod of the metal, one metre long at 20°C, expanded by 0.96 mm when the temperature reached 100°C. Calculate the coefficient of linear expansion for this particular alloy steel from the given information.
    Ans: $12 \times 10^{-6}/°C$.

17. A phosphor bronze bush has external and internal diameters of 100 mm and 60 mm respectively at 20°C. The bush is to be shrunk into a steel housing which is bored to 99.83 mm diameter at 20°C to receive the bush. Calculate the temperature to which the bush must be reduced so that it will just enter the housing, and determine the internal diameter of the bush at this temperature.
Take the coefficient of linear expansion for phosphor bronze to be $17 \times 10^{-6}/°C$.
Ans: −80°C. 59.9 mm.

4. Quantity of Heat

4.1 Changes of state

A change of state is one of the effects of heat mentioned in the previous chapter (paragraph 3.1(b)). If a substance such as a solid piece of metal is heated its energy will be increased, since heat is a form of energy transfer. This increase of energy will be accompanied by a rise in temperature which will continue until the metal begins to melt. When melting starts the energy gained by continued heating is offset by the energy needed for the change of state and the temperature remains constant even though heating is continued. As soon as the metal is completely liquid the change of state is complete and the temperature begins to rise again while heating continues. Eventually the liquid metal will begin to vaporize, that is, it becomes partly liquid and partly gaseous. At this point the temperature rise is again arrested even with continued heating and would only rise again if all of the liquid is converted to a gas. Thus during the changes, solid to liquid, liquid to gas, gas to liquid, and liquid to solid the temperature will always remain constant even though heat energy may be flowing to or from the substance.

4.2 Sensible heat

The heat energy which flows to a substance and brings about a rise of temperature is called sensible heat. Similarly, the heat energy which flows from a substance while the temperature is falling is also called sensible heat. Since heat is energy transfer we may say that sensible heat is an energy transfer which can be 'sensed', for example, by using a thermometer it can be detected by observing a change of temperature.

4.3 Specific heat

The amount of heat energy required to raise the temperature of a substance depends on the mass, temperature, and the type of material of which the substance comprises. Considering, for example, equal masses of steel and aluminium at the same temperature it is known that the aluminium will require approximately twice the heat energy needed for the steel in order to bring about the same temperature rise for both masses. In order to make this comparison, other than by experiment, we would need to know the specific heat of each metal.

The specific heat of a substance is the amount of heat energy required to raise the temperature of unit mass of the substance by one degree and is denoted by the symbol 'c'. In the use of SI units mass is measured in kilogrammes (kg), and all types of energy (including heat energy) are measured in joules (J) or kilojoules (kJ).

The temperature change may be measured in degrees Celsius (°C). A more exact scale adopted in SI units is the Kelvin scale. This measures degrees of temperature above absolute zero ($-273°C$ to the nearest whole number). One degree on this scale is called a kelvin (K). Thus Kelvin temperature (K) is the Celsius temperature (°C) + 273 approximately. However, a change of temperature is the same on both scales, that is, $1°C = 1 K$.

Note,
$$1 \text{ kJ} = 10^3 \text{ J}$$
$$1 \text{ MJ} = 10^6 \text{ J}$$
$$1 \text{ GJ} = 10^9 \text{ J}$$

The units of specific heat will generally be kJ/kg K, for example, the specific heat of water at 20°C and at atmospheric pressure is approximately 4.182 kJ/kg K. This means that 1 kg of the water would require 4.182 kJ of heat energy to increase the temperature by 1°C, or to be more exact, from 20°C to 21°C. It should be noted that although constant values are given for the specific heat of various materials for convenience, the specific heat of any substance does change and depends on pressure and temperature conditions.

4.4 Measurement of heat quantity

From the previous paragraph it follows that 4.182 x 2 kJ would be required to raise the temperature of 2 kg of water by 1°C and that 4.182 x 2 x 2 kJ would be required to raise the temperature of 2 kg of water by 2°C. From this we can make the general statement applicable to all heat quantity calculations, that is:

$$\begin{bmatrix} \text{heat flow to} \\ \text{or from the} \\ \text{substance} \end{bmatrix} = \begin{bmatrix} \text{mass} \\ \text{of the} \\ \text{substance} \end{bmatrix} \times \begin{bmatrix} \text{specific} \\ \text{heat} \end{bmatrix} \times \begin{bmatrix} \text{temperature} \\ \text{change} \end{bmatrix}$$

58   MECHANICAL ENGINEERING SCIENCE

If
Q = heat flow (kJ)
c = specific heat (kJ/kg K)
m = mass (kg)
t = temperature change (°C)

then $Q = mct$ kJ

Quantities of heat energy are normally measured above 0°C for convenience, but this does not mean that there is no heat energy in a substance when its temperature is below 0°C, however this need not concern us since our calculations will invariably be concerned with differences of heat quantities which are unaffected by choice of datum.

Example 1 (MT1)

Calculate the heat energy required to raise the temperature of 5 kg of copper from 15°C up to its melting point temperature of 1083°C. Take the specific heat of copper to be 0.4 kJ/kg K.

Thus
heat flow $Q = mct$ (kJ)
mass m = 5 kg
specific heat c = 0.4 kJ/kg K
temperature rise t = 1083 − 15°C
= 1068°C

∴ Q = 5 × 0.4 × 1068 kJ
= 2136 kJ

Example 2 (MT1)

An aluminium kettle of mass 0.8 kg contains 1.5 litres (l) of water at 20°C. Calculate the heat energy required to raise the temperature of the water to boiling point assuming that there are no heat losses. Take the specific heats of aluminium and water to be 0.9 kJ/kg K and 4.18 kJ/kg K respectively. One litre of water has a mass of one kilogramme.

The heat energy required for the water

= 1.5 × 4.18 × (100 − 20) kJ

= 1.5 × 4.18 × 80 kJ

= 4.18 × 120 kJ

= 501.6 kJ

QUANTITY OF HEAT 59

The heat energy required for the aluminium kettle

$$= 0.8 \times 0.9 \times (100 - 20) \text{ kJ}$$
$$= 0.72 \times 80 \text{ kJ}$$
$$= 57.6 \text{ kJ}$$

∴   Total heat energy = 501.6 + 57.6 kJ
$$= 559.2 \text{ kJ}$$

Example 3 (MT1)

A number of steel springs of total mass 250 g are to be heated in a furnace to a temperature of 350°C for the purpose of tempering. If the springs were initially at a temperature of 26°C calculate the heat energy required from the furnace.
Take the specific heat of the steel to be 0.5 kJ/kg K.
Thus   the mass m = 250 g
$$= 0.25 \text{ kg}$$
specific heat c = 0.5 kJ/kg K
temperature rise t = 350 − 26°C
$$= 324°C$$
heat energy required $Q = mct$
$$= 0.25 \times 0.5 \times 324 \text{ kJ}$$
$$= \tfrac{1}{8} \times 324 \text{ kJ}$$
$$= 40.5 \text{ kJ}$$

4.5 Latent heat and dryness fraction

The heat energy which flows to or from a substance while the temperature remains constant is called latent heat, and this occurs during a change of state as previously explained. The heat energy gained or lost during melting or solidification is called the latent heat of fusion, for example, the latent heat of fusion for aluminium is approximately 387 kJ/kg. This means that 387 kJ of heat energy are required to melt 1 kg of aluminium completely.

In changing a substance from its liquid state to a gas a certain amount of heat energy is again required and this energy is called the latent heat of vaporization.

Consider a quantity of water initially at 0°C being heated in a vessel fitted with a movable piston in such a manner that a constant atmospheric pressure can be maintained in the vessel. If the water is heated continuously until it has all been converted to steam then the graph of temperature against time would be similar to that shown in Fig. 4.1.

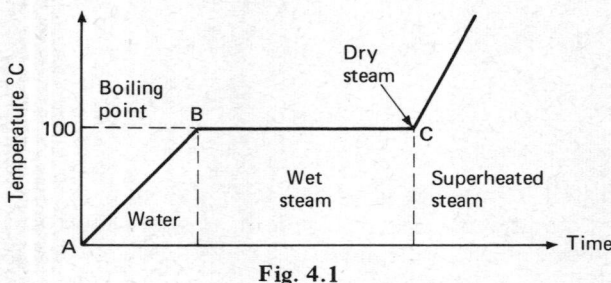

Fig. 4.1

During the stage A to B sensible heat energy flows to the water accompanied by a rise of temperature. At B the water boils at a temperature sometimes referred to as the saturation temperature. This temperature depends on the pressure in the vessel and at atmospheric pressure will be 100°C. During the stage B to C steam is formed while the temperature remains constant, the contents of the vessel during this time will be a mixture of water and steam known as wet steam. At the point C the steam will have received all the heat energy necessary to convert the water completely to dry steam. While the steam is wet only part of the water has received its latent heat and changed into steam. That fraction of the initial quantity of water which has received its latent heat is called dryness fraction (symbol x).

$$\text{dryness fraction} = \frac{\text{mass of dry steam}}{\begin{bmatrix}\text{total mass of steam}\\\text{and moisture}\end{bmatrix}}$$

When heating is continued beyond the point C the temperature begins to rise again and the steam is now known as superheated steam and behaves as a gas.

Strictly speaking the quantities of heat energy involved are a combination of energies called enthalpy, so that the latent heat of vaporization is more exactly known as the enthalpy of vaporization. However, for the conditions considered at this stage the enthalpy quantities will equal the heat energies involved. Special tables are available (known as steam tables) which give specific enthalpy values for the generation of steam at various pressures. Summarizing:

QUANTITY OF HEAT

If a mass m kg of solid metal of specific heat c kJ/kg K at a temperature of $t\,°C$ is to be completely melted then the total heat energy required

$$Q = \text{sensible heat} + \text{latent heat}$$
$$= mc(t_m - t) + mL \text{ kJ}$$

where
L = latent heat of fusion (kJ/kg)
t_m = melting point temperature

If a mass m kg of water (not boiling) at $t\,°C$ is to be heated to its boiling point temperature $t_c\,°C$ and then converted to wet steam of dryness fraction x, the total heat energy required

$$Q = 4.19m(t_c - t) + xLm \text{ kJ}$$

where L = latent heat of vaporization in kJ/kg

and the specific heat of water is taken to be 4.19 kJ/kg K. If the steam is to be superheated the dryness fraction will be unity and the heat energy required $Q = 4.19m(t_c - t) + mL + mc_p(t_s - t_c)$ kJ

where t_s = temperature of superheated steam (°C)
and c_p = specific heat of superheated steam in kJ/kg K.

Example 4 (MT1)

Given that aluminium has a specific heat of 0.9 kJ/kg K, a melting point of 660°C and a latent heat of fusion of 387 kJ/kg calculate the heat energy required to melt a 10-kg ingot starting from a room temperature of 20°C.

$$\text{sensible heat required} = mct$$
$$= 10 \times 0.9 \times (660 - 20) \text{ kJ}$$
$$= 9 \times 640 \text{ kJ}$$
$$= 5760 \text{ kJ}$$

$$\text{latent heat required} = \text{mass} \times \text{latent heat of fusion}$$
$$= 10 \times 387 \text{ kJ}$$
$$= 3870 \text{ kJ}$$

$$\text{total heat required} = 5760 + 3870 \text{ kJ}$$
$$= 9630 \text{ kJ}$$

Example 5 (MT1)

Calculate the heat energy required to convert 10 l of water at 20°C to wet steam with a dryness fraction of 0.8
Take the specific heat of water to be 4.19 kJ/kg K and its latent heat of vaporization to be 2260 kJ/kg. One litre of the water has a mass of 1 kg and its boiling point is 100°C.

$$\text{Heat energy required} = \text{sensible heat} + \text{latent heat}$$

$$\begin{aligned}
\text{sensible heat} &= 4.19 m(t_c - t) \\
&= 4.19 \times 10 \times (100 - 20) \text{ kJ} \\
&= 41.9 \times 80 \text{ kJ} \\
&= 3352 \text{ kJ}
\end{aligned}$$

$$\begin{aligned}
\text{latent heat} &= xmL \\
&= 0.8 \times 10 \times 2260 \text{ kJ} \\
&= 18\,080 \text{ kJ}
\end{aligned}$$

$$\begin{aligned}
\text{total energy required} &= 3352 + 18\,080 \text{ kJ} \\
&= 21\,432 \text{ kJ}
\end{aligned}$$

Example 6 (MT1)

Steam at atmospheric pressure and with a dryness fraction of 0.9 enters a condenser at the rate of 2000 kg/h, and leaves as water at 50°C. Assuming that the pressure remains constant calculate the heat energy given up by the steam per hour.
Take the latent heat of vaporization to be 2260 kJ/kg and the specific heat of water as 4.19 kJ/kg K.

The total heat energy given up per hour will be equal to the loss of sensible and latent heat.
That is

$$\begin{aligned}
Q &= 4.19 m(t_c - t) + xmL \text{ kJ/h} \\
&= 4.19 \times 2000 \times (100 - 50) \ldots \\
&\quad \ldots + 0.9 \times 2000 \times 2260 \text{ kJ/h} \\
&= 8380 \times 50 + 2 \times 10^3 \times 2034 \\
&= 419 \times 10^3 + 4068 \times 10^3 \text{ kJ/h} \\
&= 419 + 4068 \text{ MJ/h} \\
&= 4487 \text{ MJ/h}
\end{aligned}$$

Example 7 (MT1)

Calculate the heat energy required to convert 20 kg of water at 20°C to superheated steam at 200°C, the whole process taking place at atmospheric pressure.

Take the latent heat of vaporization to be 2260 kJ/kg and the specific heats of water and steam to be 4.19 kJ/kg K and 2.1 kJ/kg K respectively.

$$\text{Heat energy required} = \text{sensible heat} + \text{latent heat} \ldots$$
$$\ldots + \text{superheat}$$

Assuming that the boiling point of water at atmospheric pressure is 100°C:

$$\begin{aligned}
\text{sensible heat} &= 4.19m(t_c - t) \text{ kJ} \\
&= 4.19 \times 20 \times (100 - 20) \text{ kJ} \\
&= 83.8 \times 80 \text{ kJ} \\
&= 6704 \text{ kJ}
\end{aligned}$$

$$\begin{aligned}
\text{latent heat} &= mL \\
&= 20 \times 2260 \text{ kJ} \\
&= 45\ 200 \text{ kJ}
\end{aligned}$$

$$\begin{aligned}
\text{superheat} &= mc_p(t_s - t_c) \\
&= 2.1 \times 20 \times (200 - 100) \text{ kJ} \\
&= 42 \times 100 \text{ kJ} \\
&= 4200 \text{ kJ}
\end{aligned}$$

$$\begin{aligned}
\therefore \text{ total heat energy required} &= 6704 + 45\ 200 + 4200 \text{ kJ} \\
&= 56\ 104 \text{ kJ} \\
&\simeq 56.1 \text{ MJ}
\end{aligned}$$

4.6 Heat transfer

Heat energy may flow from one substance to another, or from one part of a substance to another part of the same substance in three possible ways namely:

(a) by conduction,
(b) by convection, or
(c) by radiation.

Conduction Heat energy can only be transferred by conduction from one part of a substance to another, or from one substance to another, provided that they are in contact. If hot tea is poured into a mug some of the heat energy in the tea will be transferred by conduction to the mug, and the mug becomes warm to hold. In general, metals are good conductors of heat. When using a soldering iron heat energy flows from the soldering iron to the work which is initially at a lower temperature. Eventually the temperature of the work will reach the melting point of the solder which then flows around the joint. The conducting property of a material is indicated by its thermal conductivity which is given as a rate of heat energy transference in J/m s °C, that is, the number of joules of energy required per second to transfer the heat energy by one metre for each degree Celsius rise of temperature.

Convection For heat energy to be transferred by convection the substance must be in motion and be in a liquid or gaseous form. If a kettle of water is heated with the source of heat energy at the bottom, the water nearest the source of heat energy will expand and become reduced in density, thus causing it to rise to the top, its place being taken by colder water. The circulation thus set up is called convection.

Radiation When heat energy is transferred by radiation the substances or objects are not in contact. A person sitting in front of an electric fire receives heat by radiation because of the fact that the heat of the element is reflected by a highly polished reflector situated behind the element. Heat energy is also received from the sun by radiation.

In any plant which makes direct use of a source of heat energy, some of the energy is diverted from its true purpose by conduction, convection, or radiation. This means that such thermal plants as furnaces, internal combustion engines, steam engines, and steam plants can be very inefficient and this problem will be referred to again in paragraph 4.8. For the time being we will consider problems involving heat transfer on the assumption that there are no heat losses. On this assumption if two substances at different temperatures are mixed together, then the mixture will eventually arrive at a common temperature, and

$$\begin{bmatrix} \text{heat energy gained by} \\ \text{the cold substance} \end{bmatrix} = \begin{bmatrix} \text{heat energy lost by} \\ \text{the hot substance} \end{bmatrix}$$

Such interchange of heat energy can occur in a number of different operations, for example, when hot steel is quenched in oil for hardening or tempering purposes, or when coolant is applied in a cutting opera-

QUANTITY OF HEAT

tion such as milling, grinding or turning, where the heat generated by cutting is partly transferred to the coolant.

Example 8 (MT2)

Twenty steel drilling jig bushes each having a mass of 80 g are to be heated to 220°C and quenched in water for tempering purposes. If there are initially 20 l of water at 20°C calculate the final temperature of the water and the steel bushes. Assume that there are no heat losses to the surroundings or to the containing vessel.

Take the specific heats of water and steel to be 4.19 kJ/kg K and 0.5 kJ/kg K respectively. The mass of one litre of water is one kilogramme.

As it is assumed that there will be no heat losses:
[heat energy gained by the water] = [heat energy given up by the steel bushes]

$$20 \times 4.19 \times (t - 20) = 20 \times 0.08 \times 0.5 \times (220 - t)$$

∴ $$83.8(t - 20) = 0.8(220 - t)$$

where t = the final temperature

∴ $$83.8t - 1676 = 176 - 0.8t$$

$$84.6t = 176 + 1676$$

$$t = \frac{1852}{84.6} \,°C$$

$$= 21.9°C$$

Example 9 (MT2)

A steel component having a mass of 2 kg is to be hardened by heating it to a temperature of 800°C and quenched in oil. The initial temperature of the oil is 30°C. Neglecting the effect of the oil container and ignoring heat losses to the surroundings, calculate the minimum mass of oil required if the final temperature of the oil and steel is to be limited to 50°C. Take the specific heats of steel and oil to be 0.5 kJ/kg K and 1.55 kJ/kg K respectively.

[heat energy gained by the oil] = [heat energy lost by the steel]

$$1.55 \times m \times (50 - 30) = 0.5 \times 2 \times (800 - 50)$$

where m = mass of oil required (kg)

$$20 \times 1.55 \times m = 750$$

$$m = \frac{750}{31} \text{ kg}$$

$$= 24.2 \text{ kg}$$

Example 10 (MT2)

During an experiment to determine the specific heat of copper the following results were noted:

Mass of copper calorimeter	50 g
Mass of water in calorimeter	150 g
Initial temperature of water and calorimeter	20°C
Mass of copper rod	100 g

The copper rod was heated to 100°C and placed in the water contained in the calorimeter. The final temperature of the water and copper was 24.5°C. Taking the specific heat of water to be 4.19 kJ/kg K and ignoring heat losses calculate the specific heat of copper.

Let the specific heat of copper be c kJ/kg K. The temperature rise of the calorimeter and the water

$$= 24.5 - 20°C$$
$$= 4.5°C$$

The temperature drop of the copper rod

$$= 100 - 24.5°C$$
$$= 75.5°C$$

Since the units of specific heat are kJ/kg K the masses will have to be converted to kg:

∴ mass of calorimeter = 0.05 kg

mass of water = 0.15 kg

mass of copper rod = 0.1 kg

∴ the heat energy gained by the water and the calorimeter

$$= 0.05 \times 4.5c \ldots$$
$$\ldots + 0.15 \times 4.19 \times 4.5 \text{ kJ}$$

QUANTITY OF HEAT

the heat energy lost by the copper rod

$$= 0.1 \times 75.5c$$

Ignoring heat losses to the surroundings:

the heat energy lost by the copper rod will equal the heat energy gained by the water and the calorimeter

$$\therefore \qquad 7.55c = 0.225c + 0.15 \times 4.19 \times 4.5$$

$$\therefore \qquad 7.55c = 0.225c + 2.828$$

$$7.325c = 2.828$$

$$c = \frac{2.828}{7.325} \text{ kJ/kg K}$$

$$= 0.3861 \text{ kJ/kg K}$$

Example 11 (MT2)

A lead ingot of mass 100 kg is to be cast by pouring molten lead at its melting point temperature of 327°C into a steel mould of mass 10 kg initially at a temperature of 40°C. Ignoring all heat losses calculate the amount of lead which will have solidified at the instant the temperature of the steel mould reaches 327°C.

Take the latent heat of fusion for lead to be 21 kJ/kg and the specific heat of steel to be 0.5 kJ/kg K.

The heat energy
gained by the steel = mct

$$= 10 \times 0.5 \times (327 - 40) \text{ kJ}$$

$$= 5 \times 287 \text{ kJ}$$

$$= 1435 \text{ kJ}$$

let $\qquad m$ = mass of lead solidified (kg)

then the latent heat
energy given up by the lead = $21m$ kJ

All heat losses to the surroundings are to be ignored therefore the heat energy gained by the steel will be equal to the latent heat energy given up by the lead,

$$\therefore 21m = 1435$$

$$m = \frac{1435}{21} \text{ kg}$$

$$= 68.33 \text{ kg}$$

4.7 Calorific value and combustion

In chapter 1 it was pointed out that combustion is the chemical combination of oxygen with the combustible elements of a fuel. Combustion of a fuel brings about the release of heat energy and the amount of this energy released when a unit mass of fuel is efficiently burned is known as the calorific value of the fuel. The calorific value of a typical fuel oil is 45 MJ/kg, this means that when 1 kg of this oil is efficiently burned, it will release 45×10^6 joules of heat energy.

4.8 Heat losses and thermal efficiency

As previously explained furnaces, petrol engines, marine engines, steam engines, and any other power plants obtaining energy directly from a source of heat are bound to waste some of the heat energy. This is because heat energy is lost to the surroundings by conduction, convection, or radiation. Such losses are unavoidable, although they can be reduced by suitable lagging with a material of a low thermal conductivity Also efficiency may sometimes be improved by making use of the heat energy in waste or exhaust gases, for example, the feed water in some steam plants is pre-heated by the hot flue gases. Briefly we may state:

$$\begin{bmatrix} \text{heat energy supplied} \\ \text{from a fuel} \end{bmatrix} = \begin{bmatrix} \text{useful heat} \\ \text{energy} \end{bmatrix} + \begin{bmatrix} \text{unavoidable} \\ \text{losses} \end{bmatrix}$$

$$\text{thermal efficiency} = \frac{\text{useful heat energy}}{\text{heat energy supplied}}$$

QUANTITY OF HEAT

Alternatively, thermal efficiency

$$= \frac{\left[\begin{array}{c}\text{heat energy required for heat}\\ \text{treatment operation}\end{array}\right]}{\text{heat energy supplied}}$$

Example 12 (MT2)

During a hardening process a press tool of mass 4 kg and specific heat 0.5 kJ/kg K is to be heated from 15°C to 840°C. In order to bring about the necessary temperature rise the furnace uses 0.35 m³ of gas with a calorific value of 17.5 MJ/m³. Calculate the thermal efficiency of the furnace.

now   furnace efficiency = $\dfrac{\text{heat energy required}}{\text{heat energy supplied}}$

heat energy required to raise the temperature of the steel

$$= 4 \times 0.5 \times (840 - 15) \text{ kJ}$$
$$= 2 \times 825 \text{ kJ}$$
$$= 1650 \text{ kJ}$$

heat energy supplied by the gas

$$= \text{volume used} \times \text{calorific value per m}^3$$
$$= 0.35 \times 17.5 \text{ MJ}$$
$$= 6.125 \text{ MJ}$$
$$= 6125 \text{ kJ}$$

furnace efficiency = $\dfrac{1650}{6125}$

$$= 0.2694$$
$$= 26.94\%$$

that is,   73.06% of the fuel is wasted.

Example 13 (MT2)

An electric furnace is rated at 5 kW and is known to have an efficiency of 75%. Calculate the time taken for the furnace to melt 10 kg of copper, if it is placed in the furnace at a temperature of 30°C. For copper take the melting point temperature to be 1083°C, the specific heat as 0.4 kJ/kg K and the latent heat of fusion as 180 kJ/kg.

The required increase of heat energy

$$= \text{sensible heat} + \text{latent heat}$$

$$\text{sensible heat} = mct$$
$$= 10 \times 0.4 \times (1083 - 30) \text{ kJ}$$
$$= 4 \times 1053 \text{ kJ}$$
$$= 4212 \text{ kJ}$$

$$\text{latent heat} = mL$$
$$= 10 \times 180 \text{ kJ}$$
$$= 1800 \text{ kJ}$$

total heat energy increase required

$$= 4212 + 1800 \text{ kJ}$$
$$= 6012 \text{ kJ}$$

Since the furnace is only 75% efficient the heat energy required from the furnace

$$= \frac{100}{75} \times 6012 \text{ kJ}$$

$$= \frac{4}{3} \times 6012 \text{ kJ}$$

$$= 4 \times 2004 \text{ kJ}$$

$$= 8016 \text{ kJ}$$

The furnace rating is 5 kW, and since 1 W is equal to 1 J/s,

$$1 \text{ kW} = 1 \text{ kJ/s}$$

$$\therefore \quad 5 \text{ kW} = 5 \text{ kJ/s}$$

QUANTITY OF HEAT

therefore, the furnace supplies 5 kJ of heat energy every second

$$\text{time taken} = \frac{\text{heat energy required}}{\text{energy supplied per second}}$$

$$= \frac{8016}{5} \text{ s}$$

$$= 1603 \text{ s}$$

$$= 26.7 \text{ min}$$

Problems

Section A (MT1)

1. A large steel casting of mass 160 kg is to be heated from its initial temperature of 30°C to 900°C in an annealing process.
   Taking the specific heat of steel to be 0.5 kJ/kg K calculate the heat absorbed by the casting.
   Ans: 69.6 MJ (69 600 kJ).

2. Calculate the heat energy required to raise the temperature of 20 kg of aluminium scrap up to its melting point temperature of 660°C from an initial temperature of 20°C.
   Take the specific heat of aluminium to be 0.92 kJ/kg K.
   Ans: 11.78 MJ (11 780 kJ).

3. In a cooling process 190 kg of water at 16°C are required to absorb 8 MJ of heat energy.
   Taking the specific heat of water to be 4.18 kJ/kg K, calculate the final temperature of the water.
   Ans: 26°C.

4. A copper hot-water storage tank of mass 12 kg contains 550 l of water. Ignoring heat losses to the surroundings, calculate the total heat energy absorbed by the tank and its contents when the temperature is raised from 14°C to 74°C.
   Take the specific heats of water and copper to be 4.19 kJ/kg K and 0.4 kJ/kg K respectively. One litre of water has a mass of one kilogramme.
   Ans: 138.6 MJ.

5. A quenching bath is in the form of a small steel tank of mass 2 kg. In a hardening operation the quenching oil and the steel tank absorb 1000 kJ of heat energy from the component being quenched. Calculate the minimum quantity of quenching oil in litres required to keep the temperature rise to 10°C.
Take the specific heats of oil and steel to be 1.5 kJ/kg K and 0.5 kJ/kg K respectively. One litre of the quenching oil has a mass of 0.95 kg.
Ans: 69.5 l.

6. In a particular turning operation the coolant has to absorb 4.8 kJ of heat energy per minute. Calculate the necessary rate of flow of the coolant in litres per minute if its temperature increase is to be limited to 3°C.
Take the specific heat of the coolant to be 3.85 kJ/kg K. One litre of the coolant has a mass of 0.96 kg.
Ans: 0.4329 l/min.

7. (a) Define: (i) sensible heat, (ii) latent heat.
   (b) Calculate the heat energy required to melt 40 kg of lead initially at a temperature of 20°C. For lead assume that the melting point temperature = 327°C, the specific heat = 0.13 kJ/kg K, and the latent heat of fusion = 22 kJ/kg.
   Ans: 2476 kJ.

8. A steel crucible of mass 3 kg contains 5 kg of scrap pieces of tin. Taking the melting point of tin to be 232°C and its latent heat of fusion as 62 kJ/kg calculate the heat energy required to raise the temperature of the crucible and its contents to the melting point of tin and to melt the tin given that the initial temperature was 32°C. Take the specific heats of steel and tin to be 0.5 kJ/kg K and 0.23 kJ/kg K respectively.
Ans: 840 kJ.

9. An electric furnace rated at 3 kW is required to melt 12 kg of zinc from an initial temperature of 20°C.
Taking the specific heat of zinc to be 0.42 kJ/kg K and its latent heat of fusion as 111 kJ/kg, calculate the time required to melt the zinc. The melting point of zinc is 420°C.
Ans: 18 min 36 s.

10. Calculate the amount of heat energy required to raise the temperature of 20 kg of tin from 22°C to 242°C given that the latent heat of fusion for tin is 62 kJ/kg.

Take the specific heat of tin to be 0.23 kJ/kg K when solid and 0.27 kJ/kg K when molten. The melting point of tin can be taken as 232°C.
Ans: 2260 kJ.

11. Calculate the heat energy required to convert 50 kg of water at 13°C to wet steam with a dryness fraction of 0.85 and at a temperature of 100°C.
Take the latent heat of vaporization to be 2260 kJ/kg and the specific heat as 4.19 kJ/kg K.
Ans: 114.3 MJ.

12. Wet steam with a dryness fraction of 0.8 passes through a heat exchanger at the rate of 5000 kg/h and at atmospheric pressure. If the steam loses heat energy at the rate of 11 GJ/h calculate the temperature of the condensed steam (water) leaving the heat exchanger.
Take the specific heat of water as 4.19 kJ/kg K and the latent heat of vaporization as 2260 kJ/kg.
Ans: 6.44°C.

13. (a) Explain the meaning of the terms 'dryness fraction' and 'superheated steam'.
   (b) Calculate the heat energy required to convert 500 kg of steam 0.75 dry to superheated steam at 140°C.
   Assume that the process takes place at atmospheric pressure and use the following information:

Latent heat of vaporization	2260 kJ/kg
Saturation (boiling) temperature	100°C
Specific heat of superheated steam	2.09 kJ/kg K

   Ans: 324.3 MJ.

14. A bar of aluminium of mass 10 kg and at 35°C is placed in an electric furnace rated at 4 kW. If the bar is left in the furnace for 20 min determine the condition of the aluminium (solid or molten) at the end of this time and calculate its final temperature.
Take the melting point of aluminium to be 660°C and its latent heat of fusion to be 386 kJ/kg.
Assume that the specific heat of aluminium is 0.92 kJ/kg K when solid and 1.2 kJ/kg K when molten.
Ans: Molten at 690.4°C.

15. A piece of copper of mass 4 kg and at 23°C is placed in an electric furnace rated at 2 kW. Calculate the amount of copper which will have melted after 15 min.
Take the melting point of copper to be 1083°C, its specific heat 0.395 kJ/kg K and its latent heat of fusion as 180 kJ/kg.
Ans: 0.6944 kg.

Section B (MT2)

16. A plain carbon steel component of mass 1.4 kg is to be hardened by heating it to a temperature of 820°C and quenching in 20 l of brine at 20°C.
Taking the specific heats of brine and plain carbon steel to be 3 kJ/kg K and 0.5 kJ/kg K respectively determine the final steady temperature of the brine and steel. Neglect heat losses to the surroundings and assume that one litre of brine has a mass of 1.2 kg.
Ans: 27.7°C.

17. A press tool die made from tool steel and of mass 4 kg is to be heated to 800°C and quenched in oil with an initial temperature of 25°C. If the final temperature of the oil and the die is 45°C calculate the mass of oil used.
Assume that there are no heat losses and that the specific heats of tool steel and quenching oil are 0.5 kJ/kg K and 1.5 kJ/kg K respectively.
Ans: 50⅓ kg.

18. Steam at atmospheric pressure and with a dryness fraction of 0.8 enters a condenser at a rate of 20 kg/min and leaves as water at 60°C. Assuming that there are no heat losses and that the steam pressure remains constant calculate the rate of flow of the condenser cooling water in kg/min if it enters the condenser at 20°C and leaves at 40°C.
Assume that the latent heat of steam is 2260 kJ/kg and that the specific heat of water is 4.18 kJ/kg K.
Ans: 472.6 kg/min.

19. Batches of steel components are to be hardened by heating to a temperature of 828°C and quenching in 100 kg of oil held in a steel tank of mass 5 kg. The maximum temperature of the oil is not to exceed 48°C. If the initial temperature of the oil and container is 18°C determine the number of batches that can be quenched in

QUANTITY OF HEAT

quick succession before the limiting temperature is reached given that each batch has a mass of 2.5 kg, and that the temperature of the oil does not fall after each quenching.

Assume that there are no heat losses and that the specific heats of steel and oil are 0.48 kJ/kg K and 1.54 kJ/kg K respectively.

Ans: 5.

20. In order to reduce the temperature of the oil and the tank in question 19 from 48°C to 18°C they are subjected to a blast of cold air which is directed through pipes which pass through the oil. The initial temperature of the air blast is 10°C. Assuming that there are no heat losses to the surroundings and that the specific heat of air is 1 kJ/kg K, calculate the volume of air (in cubic metres) which must pass through the pipes in order to make the required temperature reduction.

Take the mean density of air to be 1.22 kg/m^3.

Ans: 480.7 m^3.

21. During an experiment to determine the specific heat of aluminium, a piece of aluminium was heated to 100°C and placed in water contained in a lagged copper calorimeter. The following observations were also noted:

Mass of copper calorimeter	64 g
Mass of water in the calorimeter	160 g
Initial temperature of the water and calorimeter	16°C
Mass of aluminium	80 g
Final temperature of water, aluminium, and the calorimeter	24°C

Taking the specific heat of copper to be 0.394 kJ/kg K use these results to calculate an approximate value for the specific heat of aluminium.

Assume that the specific heat of water is 4.185 kJ/kg K.

Ans: 0.9145 kJ/kg K.

22. (a) A factory uses waste steam to heat a liquid used for a plating process. The steam enters a heat exchanger at atmospheric pressure, its dryness fraction being 0.9. The steam leaves the heat exchanger converted to water at 40°C. How many heat units are available for the process per kilogramme of wet steam?

Take the latent heat of vaporization at atmospheric pressure to be 2260 kJ/kg.

76   MECHANICAL ENGINEERING SCIENCE

(b) The process consists of heating a quantity of liquid having a specific heat of 3.77 kJ/kg K and a mass of 227 kg. The container for the liquid has a mass of 91 kg and has a specific heat of 0.5 kJ/kg K. The temperature of the liquid has to rise from 12°C to 24°C. Neglecting heat losses how many kilogrammes of wet steam are required for the process?
Take the specific heat of water to be 4.2 kJ/kg K.
C.G.L.I. (modified).
Ans: (a) 2286 kJ. (b) 4.731 kg.

23. (a) Tin has a melting point of 230°C, a specific heat of 0.23 kJ/kg K, and a latent heat of 58.7 kJ/kg. What quantity of heat is required to melt 22.7 kg of tin originally at 30°C?

(b) Steel has a specific heat of 0.46 kJ/kg K. What quantity of heat is necessary to raise 1.6 kg of steel from 30°C to 230°?

(c) If the steel object referred to in (b) at its original temperature of 30°C is plunged into the molten tin referred to in (a), what mass of tin solidifies when the steel object and the tin both acquire a temperature of 230°C?
C.G.L.I. (modified).

Ans: (a) 2376 kJ. (b) 147.2 kJ. (c) 2.508 kg.

24. An oil-fired furnace is required to melt 60 kg of copper, the initial temperature of the copper being 33°C. The furnace uses oil with a calorific value of 43 MJ/kg and 30% of the heat energy released from the fuel is used to melt the copper.
Taking the specific heat of the copper to be 0.4 kJ/kg K and its latent heat of fusion to be 180 kJ/kg, calculate the mass of oil used by the furnace. The melting point of copper is 1083°C.
Ans: 2.79 kg.

25. An electric furnace is rated at 5 kW and takes 8 min to melt two 10 kg ingots, one of lead and the other of tin. If the initial temperature of the ingots was 22°C, calculate:

(a) the heat energy required to melt the lead ingot,

(b) the heat energy required to melt the tin ingot, and

(c) the efficiency of the furnace.

Assume the following information for lead;
melting point = 327°C, specific heat = 0.13 kJ/kg K, and latent heat of fusion = 21 kJ/kg;

and for tin:
melting point = 232 °C, specific heat = 0.23 kJ/kg K, and latent heat of fusion = 60 kJ/kg.
Ans: (a) 606.5 kJ. (b) 1083 kJ. (c) 70.42%.

26. A gas-fired furnace is known to have an efficiency of 30% and it uses gas with a calorific value of 18.7 MJ/m^3. Calculate the volume of gas needed to raise the temperature of four steel billets from 20°C to 900°C.
Each billet has a mass of 100 kg and a specific heat of 0.48 kJ/kg K.
Ans: 30.15 m^3.

27. In a particular case-hardening operation the steel components are placed inside a cast iron container. The cast iron container has a mass of 20 kg and a specific heat of 0.53 kJ/kg K, the steel components have a mass of 25 kg and a specific heat of 0.48 kJ/kg K. The container and its components are placed in a furnace and the temperature is increased from 25 °C to 925 °C.

   (a) Calculate the heat energy absorbed by the cast iron container and the steel components.

   (b) Ignoring the effect of the carburizing material, determine the efficiency of the furnace if it burns 4 m^3 of gas with a calorific value of 18.5 MJ/m^3 in bringing about the required temperature rise.
   Ans: (a) 20.34 MJ. (b) 27.5%.

28. An aluminium alloy has a specific heat of 0.88 kJ/kg K, it melts at 660°C, and the latent heat of melting being 402 kJ/kg.

   (a) Calculate the amount of heat required to melt an ingot of the alloy which has a mass of 5.44 kg, starting from a room temperature of 20°C.

   (b) If the heating is performed by an electric furnace rated at 10 kW, having an overall efficiency of 80%, how long does it take to melt the ingot?
   C.G.L.I. (modified).
   Ans: (a) 5251 kJ. (b) 10.94 min.

5. Forces in equilibrium

5.1 Vector representation of forces

A force can be defined by stating its effects; for example, the application of force may produce motion, or it may cause some distortion. In view of these effects it can be said that force is that which produces (or tends to produce) motion from rest, or change of motion, or change of shape. The SI unit of force is the newton (N). It should be noted at this stage that the weight of an object is the force exerted upon it by the earth's gravitational pull. The mass of an object, on the other hand, is constant and to obtain the gravitational pull acting on the object it is necessary to multiply the mass by the gravitational acceleration (g). Both the gravitational pull (weight) and the gravitational acceleration vary slightly according the position of the object on the earth's surface. The average value of 9.81 m/s^2 is generally taken to be the gravitational acceleration, but the convenient value of 10 m/s^2 may be taken if the resulting small error is acceptable. Thus gravitational pull (weight) is equal to the mass in kilogrammes multiplied by 9.81 m/s^2, the resulting unit being newtons.

Equilibrium If a number of forces act on an object and it remains at rest, the whole system is said to be in equilibrium.

Vectors A line drawn to a suitable scale in order to represent a force in magnitude and direction is called a vector.

Resultant and equilibrant A single force which can replace a number of other separate forces and have the same effect as those forces is called the resultant force. The equal and opposite balancing force is called the equilibrant. Figure 5.1 shows a motor car on a level road. In order to start the car from rest the propulsive force must exceed the forces due to road and wind resistances.

Suppose road resistances amounted to 100 N, and the propulsive force applied is 1000 N then the resultant force in the direction of motion

FORCES IN EQUILIBRIUM

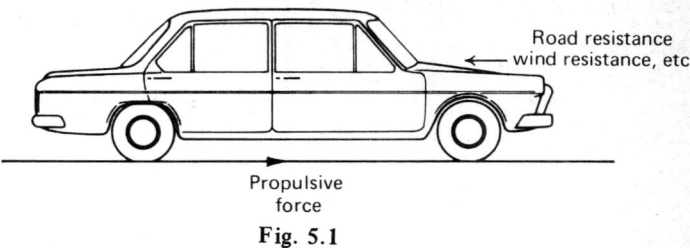

Fig. 5.1

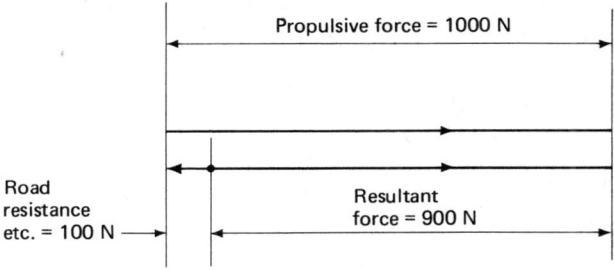

Fig. 5.2

would be the algebraic sum 1000 − 100 newtons or 900 N. The forces involved could be represented by vectors, that is, they could be drawn to scale in the appropriate directions and the resultant obtained as shown in Fig. 5.2.

5.2 Triangle and parallelogram of forces

Suppose that the car shown in Fig. 5.1 is now subjected to a cross-wind force in addition to the resultant force of 900 N as shown in Fig. 5.3.

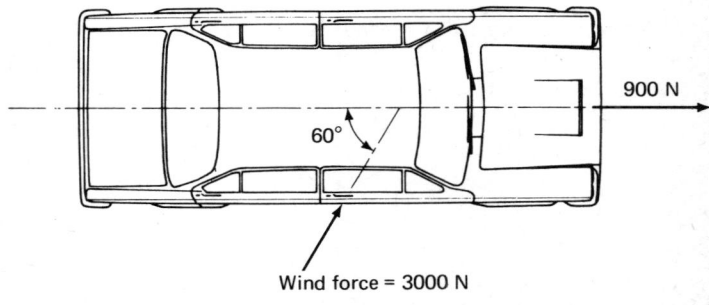

Fig. 5.3

In this case, a simple algebraic addition will not obtain the resultant force on the car because the forces involved are not parallel, however they can be drawn to scale as shown in Fig. 5.4.

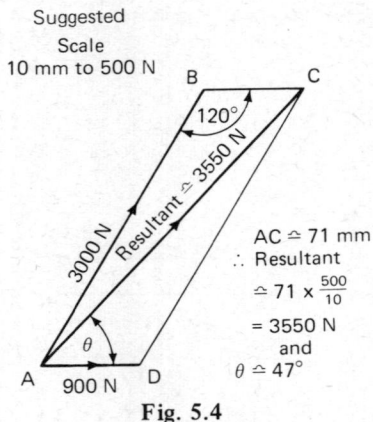

Fig. 5.4

Choosing a suitable scale (say 20 mm to 1000 N) draw AD horizontally as shown 18 mm long to represent 900 N and AB at 60° to the horizontal 60 mm long to represent 3000 N. Complete the parallelogram ABCD and draw in the diagonal AC as shown in Fig. 5.4. The resultant force can be obtained by measuring the length of AC and using a protractor to measure its angle to the horizontal. From the diagram in Fig. 5.4

$$AC \simeq 71 \text{ mm and}$$

$$\text{angle BAD} \simeq 47°$$

$$\text{resultant force} = \frac{71}{20} \times 1000 \text{ N}$$

$$= 3550 \text{ N at } 47° \text{ to the 900 N force}$$

The diagram used in this problem is called a parallelogram of forces.

The parallelogram of forces law This states that if two forces are represented by the sides of a parallelogram, then the diagonal which meets the point of intersection of the two forces will represent the resultant force in magnitude and direction.

Example 1 (MT1)

Determine, by means of a suitable scale diagram, the magnitude and direction of the resultant of the axial and radial forces acting on the lathe tool shown in Fig. 5.5. In this case the parallelogram of forces becomes a rectangle because the applied forces are at right angles to each other. Choosing a suitable scale, say 10 mm to 100 N, the rectangle can be completed as shown in Fig. 5.6. The length of the diagonal is

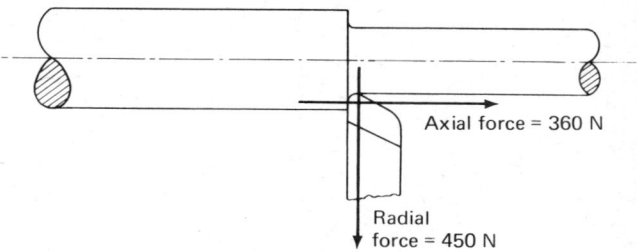

Fig. 5.5

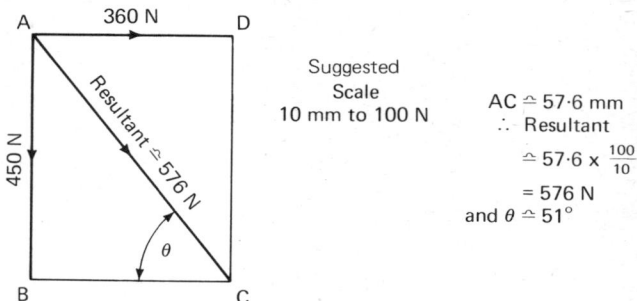

Fig. 5.6

57.6 mm and its angle to the horizontal is approximately 51°. From these measurements the resultant is approximately 576 N acting at approximately 51° to the centre line of the work.

The triangle of forces law This law states that if three non-parallel forces act in the same plane and are in equilibrium, they may be represented by the sides of a closed triangle, each side representing the appropriate force both in magnitude and direction as shown in Fig. 5.7. The three forces must also be concurrent, that is, their lines of action must intersect each other at the same point. In the space diagram the forces are merely drawn in their correct directions but not to scale. In the vector diagram the forces are drawn in their correct directions and to scale in order to represent their magnitudes.

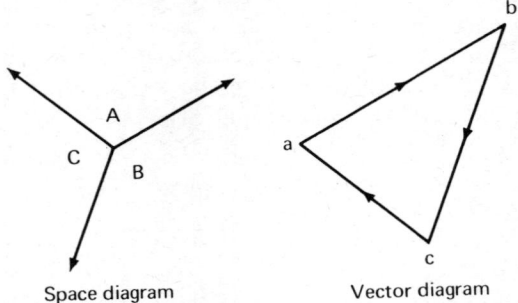

Space diagram   Vector diagram

Fig. 5.7

In general it is preferable to use the parallelogram of forces method when two forces are known both in magnitude and direction, and the resultant or equilibrant is required, remembering that the equilibrant is equal and opposite to the resultant. When the direction of all three forces are known but only the magnitude of one of the forces is given, it is preferable to use the triangle of forces method to determine the magnitudes of the other two forces.

Bow's notation This is a method of referring to forces by means of letters. In this system the forces are referred to by capital letters in the spaces on either side of the force, in the example shown in Fig. 5.7 this is done in a clockwise direction. The corresponding vectors representing the forces are given lower-case letters of the same character as the force. Direction is indicated by the order of the letters in addition to arrows, as shown in Fig. 5.7. Note that the arrows should follow each other round the vector diagram.

Example 2 (MT1)

Figure 5.8 shows a bar of steel with a cross-section in the form of a segment of a circle clamped in an assymetrical vee. If the normal forces P and Q are each 200 N determine, graphically, the magnitude and direction of the clamping force.

The question requests a graphical solution. This means that space and vector diagrams are to be drawn. Figure 5.9 shows these two diagrams.

FORCES IN EQUILIBRIUM

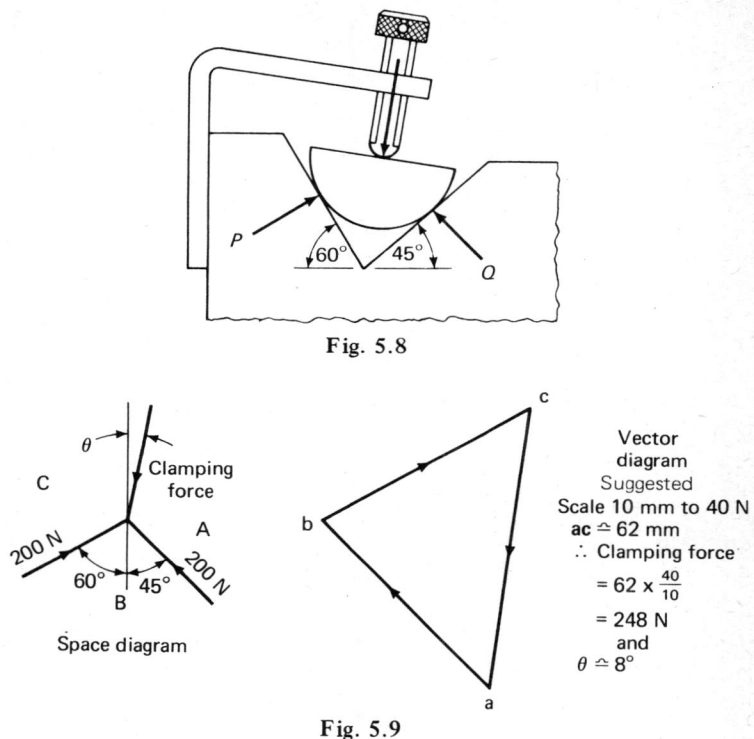

Fig. 5.8

Fig. 5.9

Taking the first known force AB in a clockwise direction, a vector **ab** is drawn to scale 200 units long at 45° to the horizontal. A vector **bc** is then drawn to scale starting from b and 200 units long, in order to represent the force BC. The angle between AB and BC is 105° and this represents an exterior angle of the triangle being formed, the angle between **ab** and **bc** is, therefore, 180-105° which is 75°. The closing line **ca** represents the clamping force and this is approximately 248 units long and 8° to the vertical, therefore, the clamping force is approximately 248 N at approximately 8° to the vertical.

Example 3 (MT1)

A casting of mass 200 kg is suspended horizontally in a sling as shown in Fig. 5.10. Determine, graphically, the tension in the two chains. Assume that the gravitational acceleration g is 10 m/s².

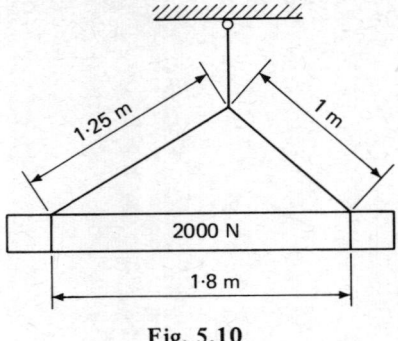

Fig. 5.10

The gravitational pull on the casting = mass × g newtons
$$= 200 \times 10 \text{ N}$$
$$= 2000 \text{ N}$$

In this problem no angles are given, therefore, the space diagram must be drawn to a suitable distance scale and the angles measured with a protractor. Figure 5.11 shows the space and vector diagrams for the solution of this problem.

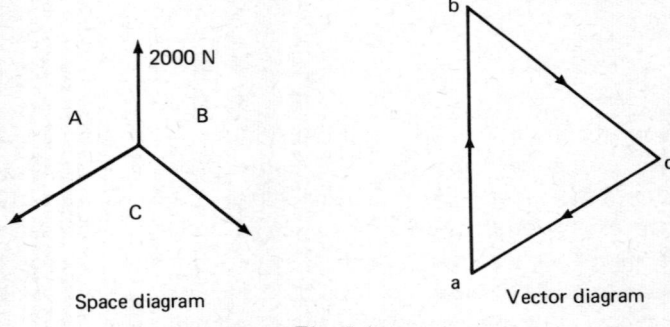

Fig. 5.11

In this case the only known force is the equal and opposite reaction to the gravitational pull on the casting of 2000 N. A vector **ab** can be drawn 2000 units long to represent this force. The forces BC and AC are known only in direction. A vector can be drawn starting from b running parallel to the force BC and in the same direction. Since the magnitude is not known the length will have to be indefinite until a vector is drawn from the point 'a' parallel to AC until it meets the line

FORCES IN EQUILIBRIUM 85

from b. The point of intersection of these two vectors will be the point 'c' thus completing the vector diagram. By measuring vector **bc** to scale the force

$$BC \simeq 1760 \text{ N}$$

By measuring the vector **ac** to scale the force

$$AC \simeq 1560 \text{ N}$$

Example 4 (MT1)

A small wall jib-crane carries a load of 200 N as shown in Fig. 5.12. Determine, graphically, the forces acting in the jib and tie.

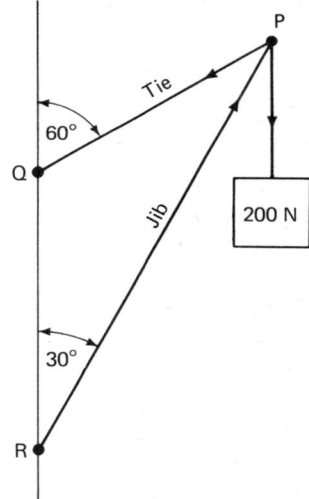

Fig. 5.12

In order to support the load, the force in the tie must pull in a direction towards the wall away from the point of concurrency P. The force in the jib must act in an upward direction to support the load. This means that the jib force acts towards the point of concurrency while the other two forces pull away from this point. However, when drawing the space diagram, it is quite permissible to draw the jib force line through to the other side of the point of concurrency as shown in Fig. 5.13.

7

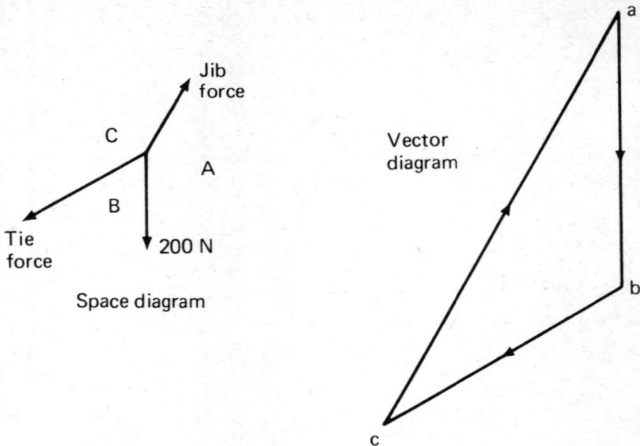

Fig. 5.13

From the vector diagram shown in Fig. 5.13 measuring the vector **bc** to scale the force in the tie

= 200 N

By measuring vector **ac** to scale the force in the jib

= 346 N

Example 5 (MT1)

In order to have one of its faces machined by turning, a casting of unsymmetrical shape is bolted to the face-plate of a lathe. Two balance weights are also bolted to the face-plate to ensure that no out-of-balance force will be exerted on the machine spindle. When the lathe is running at a particular speed the casting alone exerts an out-of-balance force of 90 N and the balance weights each exert out-of-balance forces of 60 N and 100 N. Determine, graphically, the required angular positions of the balance weights relative to the casting in order to create complete balance. Details are shown in Fig. 5.14.

From the vector diagram shown in Fig. 5.15 the angle **bac** is approximately 80° 30′, therefore, the angle of the 60 N force is 180° − 80° 30′ anticlockwise from the casting, that is 99° 30′ from the casting. The angle **abc** is approximately 36°, therefore, the angle of the 100 N force is 180° + 36° or 216° anticlockwise from the casting.

FORCES IN EQUILIBRIUM

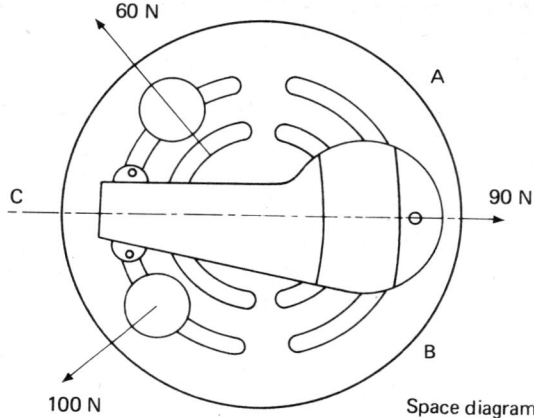

Fig. 5.14

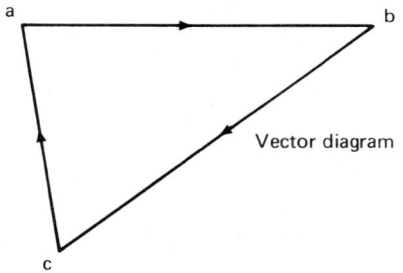

Fig. 5.15

In this case, all three forces are known only in magnitude. The force of 90 N is taken to be horizontal to the right, since the angles of the other two forces are to be relative to this. To complete the vector diagram, as shown in Fig. 5.15, draw a horizontal line ab 90 units long. Set a pencil bow to strike an arc for the vector **ac** 60 units long and repeat this process for the vector **bc** 100 units long. The point of intersection of these two arcs will be the point 'c' in the vector diagram and the angles can now be measured and estimated in relation to the 90 N force as previously explained.

5.3 Resolution of forces into vertical and horizontal components

Example 1 in this chapter showed how two forces acting at right angles to each other could be combined together to give one force known as the resultant which would have the same effect as the two original forces. This was done by using the parallelogram of forces method (see paragraph 5.2 and example 1). If, on the other hand, a single force F newtons inclined at an acute angle θ to the horizontal is given as shown in Fig. 5.16 and it is required to know the effect of this force in vertical and horizontal directions, this could be done by completing a parallelogram of forces by a reverse process as shown in Fig. 5.17

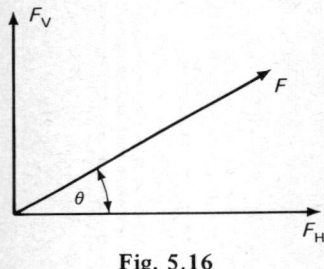
Fig. 5.16

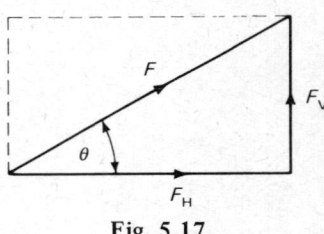
Fig. 5.17

Since the components are vertical and horizontal the parallelogram becomes a rectangle. The vertical and horizontal components can now be determined by calculation as follows:

Since the actual vector diagram forms a right-angled triangle

$$\frac{F_V}{F} = \sin \theta$$

∴ $F_V = F \sin \theta$

also $\frac{F_H}{F} = \cos \theta$

∴ $F_H = F \cos \theta$

Example 6 (MT2)

A component is clamped in position in a right-angled corner by a clamping force of 120 N inclined at 40° to the horizontal as shown in Fig. 5.18. By resolving the clamping force into vertical and horizontal components determine the thrust exerted by the work on the vertical and horizontal surfaces.

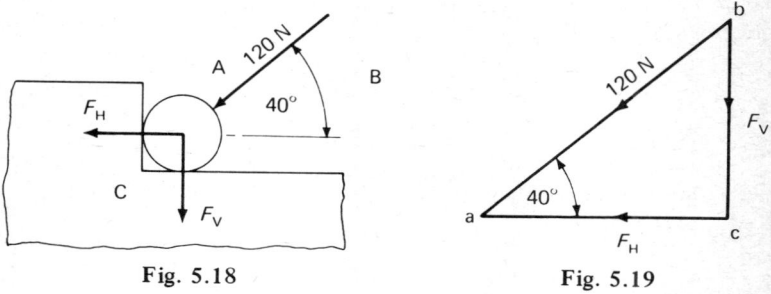

Fig. 5.18 Fig. 5.19

The vector diagram is shown in Fig. 5.19, from which

$$F_V = 120 \sin 40°$$
$$= 120 \times 0.6428$$
$$= 77.14 \text{ N}$$

and
$$F_H = 120 \cos 40°$$
$$= 120 \times 0.7660$$
$$= 91.92 \text{ N}$$

The vertical and horizontal thrusts are 77.14 N and 91.92 N respectively.
   The problem could also be solved by drawing the vector diagram to scale as in Fig. 5.19, treating AB as if it was an equilibrant force and reversing the arrow direction on the vector ab. Note that the vector diagram shown is the lower half of the parallelogram (rectangle) of forces.

Example 7 (MT2)

The toggle mechanism PQR shown in Fig. 5.20 is used to apply a horizontal force at right angles to the relatively small vertically applied effort. The links are 200 mm long and pin-jointed at P, Q, and R. Determine the horizontal force exerted and the force in each link when an effort of 220 N is applied in the position shown.

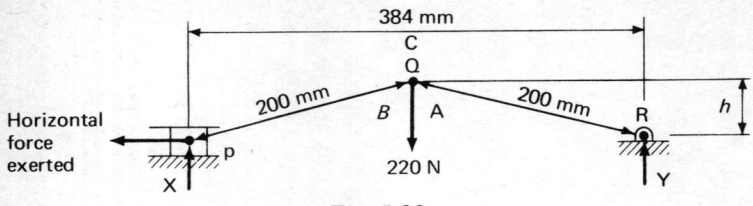

Fig. 5.20

Using the theorem of Pythagoras to obtain the vertical height of the toggle (h)

$$200^2 = 192^2 + h^2$$
$$\therefore \quad h^2 = 200^2 - 192^2$$
$$\therefore \quad h = \sqrt{(200^2 - 192^2)}$$
$$= \sqrt{(40000 - 36864)}$$
$$= \sqrt{3136}$$
$$\therefore \quad h = 56 \text{ mm}$$

This dimension, together with the length of each link 200 mm, will enable us to evaluate $\sin \theta$ and $\cos \theta$.

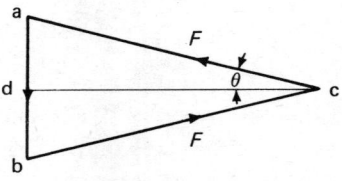

Fig. 5.21

Figure 5.21 shows the vector diagram for the joint Q. This forms an isosceles triangle because the system is symmetrical and, therefore, the line **cd** perpendicular to **ab** will bisect the triangle.

$$\therefore \quad \frac{110}{F} = \sin \theta$$

but
$$\sin \theta = \frac{56}{200} \text{ from Fig. 5.20}$$
$$= \frac{7}{25}$$

∴ $\dfrac{110}{F} = \dfrac{7}{25}$

∴ $F = \dfrac{25 \times 110}{7}$

$= 392.9 \text{ N}$

The force in each link is, therefore, 392.9 N. Again, since the system is symmetrical the vertical supports at X and Y are equal and each 110 N. Figure 5.22 shows the vector diagram for the joint P. From this diagram it can be seen that the horizontal force exerted can be taken as the horizontal component of the force in the link of 392.9 N.

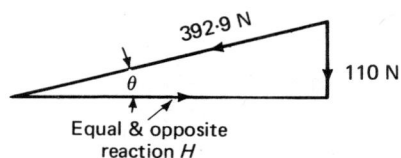

Fig. 5.22

Horizontal force $H = 392.9 \cos \theta$

but $\cos \theta = \dfrac{192}{200}$ from Fig. 5.20

$= \dfrac{24}{25}$

$H = 392.9 \times \dfrac{24}{25}$

$= 377.1 \text{ N}$

Example 8 (MT2)

A wedge has an included angle of 10°. Determine the normal force exerted by a side of the wedge when a wedging force of 200 N is applied in the same direction as the line which bisects the angle of 10°.

The normal force F exerted by a side of the wedge means that the direction of this force will be at right angles to the side of the wedge. Figure 5.23 shows the three forces involved.

For equilibrium the three forces must be concurrent and, therefore, they intersect at O. Figure 5.24 shows the vector diagram; the triangle abc is isosceles and the line **cd** bisects **ab** and the angle **bca**.

92 MECHANICAL ENGINEERING SCIENCE

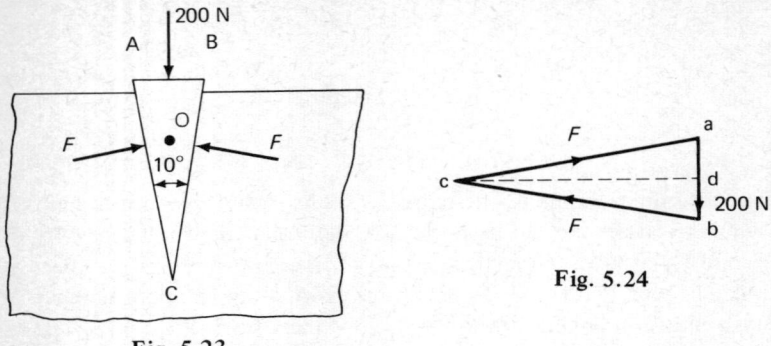

Fig. 5.23

Fig. 5.24

$$\therefore \quad \frac{100}{F} = \sin 5°$$

$$\therefore \quad F = \frac{100}{\sin 5°}$$

$$= \frac{100}{0.0872}$$

$$= 1147 \text{ N}$$

The problem can also be solved by drawing the vector diagram to scale.

5.4 The Principle of Moments

A moment is exerted by a force which produces, or tends to produce, turning about a fixed point. The magnitude of this twisting or turning effect can be measured as indicated by the following definition: 'the moment of a force is the product of the force (in newtons) and the perpendicular distance (in metres) from the fulcrum to the line of action of the force'. The SI unit used for measuring moments is the newton metre (Nm). The fulcrum is the name given to the fixed point about which turning takes place. In the workshop there are many occasions when a moment is applied, the following few examples will suffice to show this: using a spanner to tighten a nut and bolt, using a pair of tinman's snips to cut a piece of sheet metal, applying a force to a vice handle to grip a piece of work, using a tap and wrench to cut an internal

FORCES IN EQUILIBRIUM

screw-thread. The tools mentioned are all types of simple levers. Figure 5.25 shows the outline of an arbor press mechanism in which the operator exerts a moment when applying a press force on the work. Note that the operator can exert a greater moment when applying the hand force at right angles to the handle than he would if the hand force

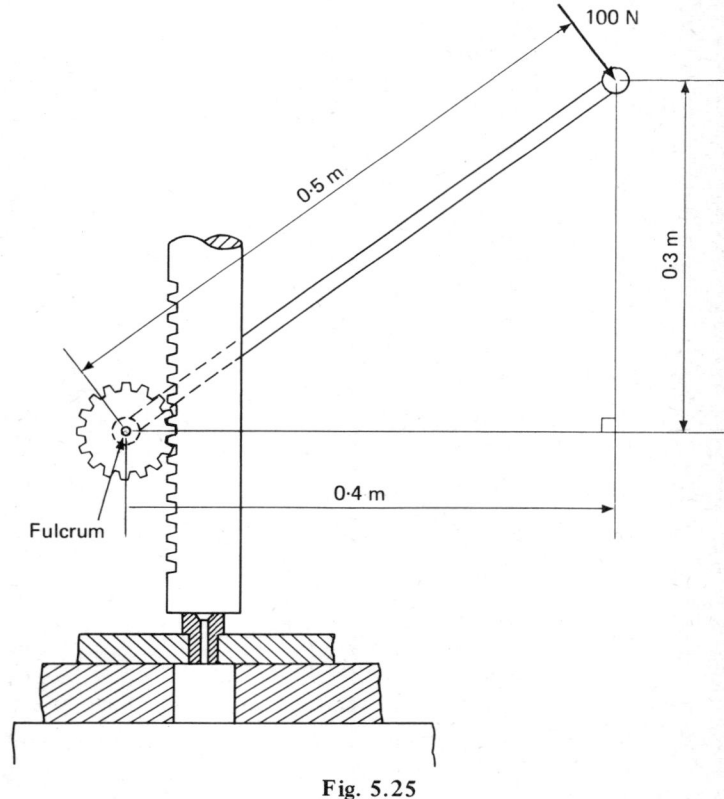

Fig. 5.25

is vertical in the given position. The diagram in Fig. 5.25 shows the position at the end of the operation of forcing home a hardened steel drill-bush into a drilling jig plate. In this final position no more motion takes place and all of the applied forces are said to be in equilibrium. For the operator-force and dimensions shown the operator is applying a moment of 100 x 0.5 Nm or 50 Nm. If the hand force of 100 N is applied vertically the moment is only 100 x 0.4 Nm or 40 Nm.

94 MECHANICAL ENGINEERING SCIENCE

The Principle of Moments states that the sum of the clockwise moments must equal the sum of the anticlockwise moments when the system of forces is in equilibrium.

If the pinion of the arbor press shown in Fig. 5.25 has an effective radius of 40 mm, the force F exerted on the bush can be determined from the principle of moments as follows: the moment 100×0.5 Nm will equal the moment $0.04F$ Nm, therefore,

$$0.04F = 100 \times 0.5$$

$$F = \frac{50}{0.04} \text{ N}$$

$$= 1250 \text{ N}$$

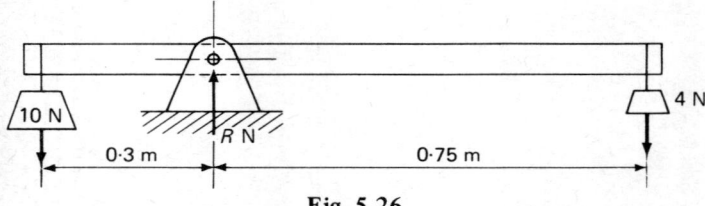

Fig. 5.26

In the simple see-saw system shown in Fig. 5.26

the clockwise moment = 4×0.75 Nm

= 3 Nm

the anticlockwise moment = 10×0.3 Nm

= 3 Nm

the clockwise moment = the anticlockwise moment

therefore, the see-saw is at rest (in equilibrium), that is, there is no out-of-balance moment. For equilibrium to be complete the upward reaction

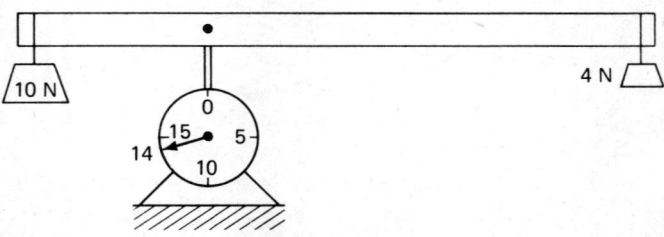

Fig. 5.27

FORCES IN EQUILIBRIUM   95

R must equal the sum of the downward forces 10 + 4 N or 14 N so that there will be no resultant out of balance force. As a simple experiment this can be verified by replacing the fulcrum by a spring balance as shown in Fig. 5.27.

5.5 Simply supported beams

An important application of the principle of moments occurs when calculating the reactions at the supports of a horizontal simply supported beam. These reactions are the upward forces exerted by the supports of beams which are subjected to vertical loads. Apart from the obvious uses of beams in construction work, there are many other examples in engineering where certain arrangements, fixtures, clamping devices, and various mechanisms may be regarded as simply supported beams.

Example 9 (MT1)

A light uniform steel bar is supported on knife-edges 0.5 m apart as shown in Fig. 5.28. If the bar is subjected to vertical downward forces of 16 N and 12 N, 125 mm and 250 mm respectively from the left-hand support, calculate the reactions at the knife-edge supports, neglecting the weight of the steel bar.

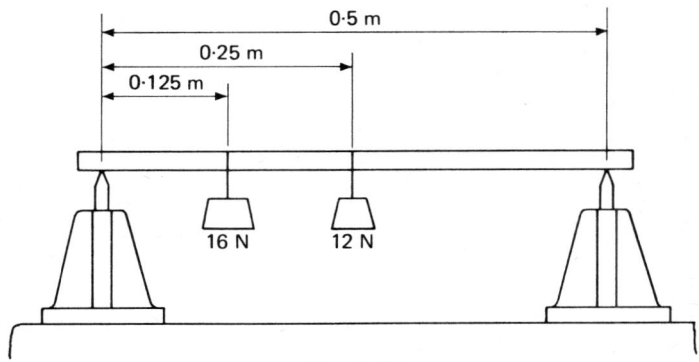

Fig. 5.28

This set up can be reduced to the skeleton beam diagram shown in Fig. 5.29.

Let R_1 and R_2 equal the reactions at the left- and right-hand supports respectively. This type of problem can be solved by a simple application of the principle of moments, that is, the sum of the anticlockwise moments is made equal to the sum of the clockwise moments about a fixed point, the position of this point may be placed at any convenient spot. If the line of action of a force passes through the fulcrum, it will exert no moment about that point, therefore it will be convenient to imagine that the fulcrum is situated at either R_1 or R_2 so that, if moments are taken about either of these two points, one of the unknown

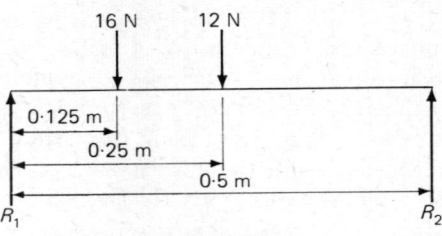

Fig. 5.29

forces will be eliminated from the calculations. Let the fulcrum be at the point where the beam rests on the knife-edge support R_1, that is, we imagine that it is possible to turn the beam about this point. There are two clockwise moments due to the 16 N and 12 N forces and one anticlockwise moment due to the reaction force R_2.

The sum of the clockwise moments about R_1

$$= 16 \times 0.125 + 12 \times 0.25 \text{ Nm}$$
$$= 2 + 3 \text{ Nm}$$
$$= 5 \text{ Nm}$$

the anticlockwise moment about R_1

$$= 0.5 R_2$$

For equilibrium anticlockwise moments

$$= \text{clockwise moments}$$

∴
$$0.5 R_2 = 5 \text{ Nm}$$
$$R_2 = \frac{5}{0.5} \text{ N}$$
$$= 10 \text{ N}$$

Also, for equilibrium, the sum of the vertical downward forces must equal the sum of the vertical upward forces

∴
$$16 + 12 = R_1 + R_2$$

FORCES IN EQUILIBRIUM

$$\therefore \quad 28 = R_1 + 10$$
$$\therefore \quad R_1 = 18 \text{ N}$$

As an additional check we may take moments about R_2

$$\text{clockwise moment} = 0.5R_1 \text{ Nm}$$
$$\text{anticlockwise moments} = 12 \times 0.25 + 16 \times 0.375 \text{ Nm}$$
$$= 3 + 6 \text{ Nm}$$
$$= 9 \text{ Nm}$$

$$\therefore \quad 0.5R_1 = 9 \text{ Nm}$$
$$R_1 = \frac{9}{0.5} \text{ N}$$
$$= 18 \text{ N as before.}$$

Example 10 (MT1)

A uniform steel shaft, 1 m long, has a mass of 15 kg, and is supported in bearings, one at its left-hand end and the other 0.2 m from the right-hand end. The shaft carries gear wheels of mass 0.4 kg and 1.6 kg, 0.2 m and 0.6 m respectively from the left-hand end. A pulley of mass 3.2 kg is fixed at the right-hand end. Calculate the reaction forces at the support bearings.
Assume that gravitational acceleration $g = 10$ m/s^2.

Since the gravitational acceleration is to be taken as 10 m/s^2 it is only necessary to multiply all the masses by 10 to obtain all the forces due to gravity. The gravitational force due to the shaft can be taken to act at its mid-point since the shaft is uniform. Figure 5.30 shows the skeleton beam diagram.

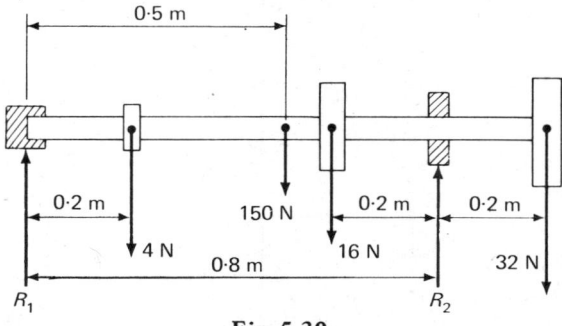

Fig. 5.30

R_1 will be the most convenient point about which to take moments, since it is situated at one end and it has no overhanging loads. Therefore, taking moments about R_1:

$$\text{anticlockwise moment} = 0.8R_2 \text{ Nm}$$

The sum of the clockwise moments

$$= 4 \times 0.2 + 150 \times 0.5 \ldots$$
$$\ldots + 16 \times 0.6 + 32 \times 1 \text{ Nm}$$
$$= 0.8 + 75 + 9.6 + 32 \text{ Nm}$$
$$= 117.4 \text{ Nm}$$

$\therefore \quad 0.8R_2 = 117.4 \text{ Nm}$

$\therefore \quad R_2 = \dfrac{117.4}{0.8} \text{ N}$

$\therefore \quad R_2 = 146.75 \text{ N}$

$$\text{Total downward force} = 4 + 150 + 16 + 32$$
$$= 202 \text{ N}$$

$\therefore \quad R_1 = 202 - 146.75$
$$= 55.25 \text{ N}$$

Example 11 (MT1)

A beam 8 m long is simply supported 1.5 m from its left-hand end and 0.5 m from its right-hand end. Forces of 20 kN and 40 kN are applied at the left- and right-hand ends respectively, and a further force of 50 kN is applied midway between the supports. Calculate the reactions at the beam supports, neglecting the weight of the beam itself. Figure 5.31 shows the relative positions of the forces and support reactions.

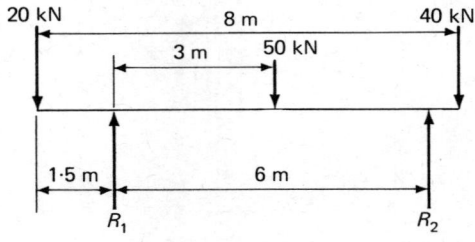

Fig. 5.31

Taking moments about R_1

$$\text{clockwise moments} = 50 \times 3 + 40 \times 6.5 \text{ kNm}$$
$$= 150 + 260 \text{ kNm}$$
$$= 410 \text{ kNm}$$
$$\text{anticlockwise moments} = 6R_2 + 20 \times 1.5 \text{ kNm}$$
$$= 6R_2 + 30 \text{ kNm}$$
$$6R_2 + 30 = 410 \text{ kNm}$$
$$\therefore \quad 6R_2 = 380 \text{ kNm}$$
$$\therefore \quad R_2 = 63.33 \text{ kN}$$
$$\text{The sum of the downward forces} = 20 + 50 + 40 \text{ kN}$$
$$= 110 \text{ kN}$$
$$\text{The sum of the upward forces} = 63.33 + R_1$$
$$\therefore \quad R_1 = 110 - 63.33 \text{ kN}$$
$$= 46.67 \text{ kN}$$

5.6 Simple and cranked levers

A lever is a device which may be used to lift a load or overcome a resistance by the application of a relatively small effort. This is made possible by positioning the fulcrum much nearer to the load than the effort.

First order lever In this type of lever the fulcrum is placed between the effort and the load as, for example, in a pair of pliers.

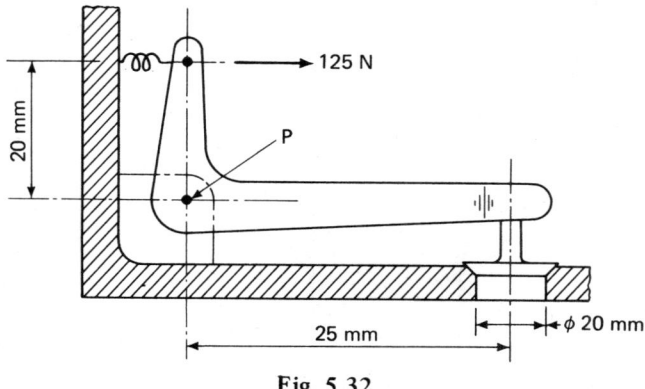

Fig. 5.32

100   MECHANICAL ENGINEERING SCIENCE

Second order lever In this type of lever the load is placed between the effort and the fulcrum as, for example, in the arbor press set up shown in Fig. 5.25.

Third order lever In this type of lever the effort is placed between the fulcrum and the load as, for example, in a safety valve of the type shown in Fig. 5.32 (see the following example).

Example 12 (MT1)

A safety valve is kept closed by the spring-loaded bell-crank lever mechanism shown in Fig. 5.32. If a spring force of 125 N keeps the valve shut, calculate the pressure which will cause the valve to open, given that the valve port is 20 mm diameter.

Taking moments about the pivot P

$$25F = 20 \times 125 \text{ Nmm}$$

$$F = 100 \text{ N}$$

where F is the force keeping the valve shut.

now   force F = pressure × area of port

now   area of port = $\pi \times 10^2$

$$= 314.2 \text{ mm}^2$$

$$\text{pressure} = \frac{\text{force}}{\text{area}}$$

$$= \frac{100}{314.2} \text{ N/mm}^2$$

$$= \frac{100 \times 10^6}{314.2} \text{ N/m}^2$$

$$= \frac{100 \times 10^3}{314.2} \text{ kN/m}^2$$

$$= 318.3 \text{ kN/m}^2$$

The valve will open if the pressure exceeds 318.3 kN/m^2.

FORCES IN EQUILIBRIUM

Example 13 (MT1)

The mechanism for operating the exhaust valve of an oil engine is shown in Fig. 5.33.

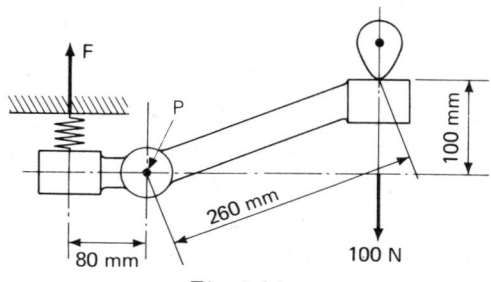

Fig. 5.33

(a) If the force operated by the cam in the position shown is 100 N, determine the force F newtons exerted on the spring.

(b) Determine the stiffness of the spring if it is compressed 20 mm by the force F.

Before taking moments it will be necessary to determine the perpendicular distance x from the line of action of the 100-N force to the fulcrum (pivot P).

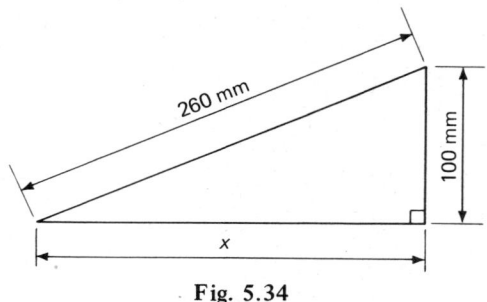

Fig. 5.34

(a) Figure 5.34 shows a skeleton triangle of the situation. Using the theorem of Pythagoras:

$$x^2 = 260^2 - 100^2$$
$$= 67600 - 10000$$
$$x^2 = 57600$$
$$x = 240 \text{ mm}$$

Alternatively, a skeleton diagram could be drawn to scale and the distance x can then be scaled from this drawing.

Taking moments about the pivot P

$$80F = 100 \times 240 \text{ Nmm}$$
$$F = 300 \text{ N}$$

(b) The stiffness:
$$S = \frac{\text{force applied}}{\text{compression}}$$
$$= \frac{300}{20} \text{ N/mm}$$
$$= 15 \text{ kN/m}$$

Example 14 (MT2)

Figure 5.35(a) shows a small hand-guillotine adapted for cutting metal rod of circular cross-section. If the shearing strength of the rod being cut is 300 MN/m² and its diameter is 4 mm calculate the minimum force F required at the handle to shear the rod.

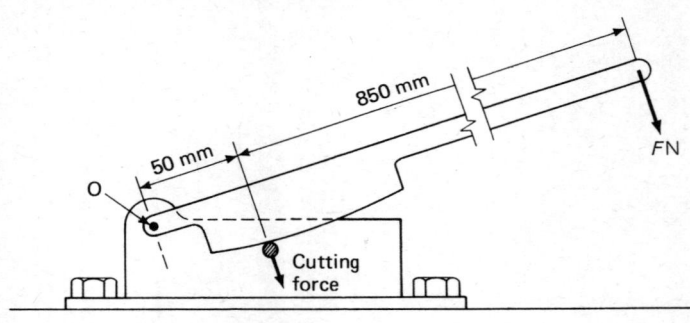

Fig. 5.35(a)

cutting force = shearing strength × area
(see example 4, chapter 6)
cross-sectional area of the rod
being sheared = $\pi \times 2^2$ mm²
$= 12.57$ mm²
cutting force = $300 \times 12.57 \times 10^{-6}$ MN
$= 300 \times 12.57$ N
$= 3771$ N

Taking moments about O

$$900F = 3771 \times 50 \text{ Nmm}$$

$$F = \frac{3771 \times 50}{900} \text{ N}$$

$$= 209.5 \text{ N}$$

Example 15 (MT2)

The cranked lever shown in Fig. 5.35(b) is in equilibrium in part of a remote control system. Determine the force E newtons required to keep the lever in equilibrium and also the magnitude and direction of the force exerted on the pivot P.

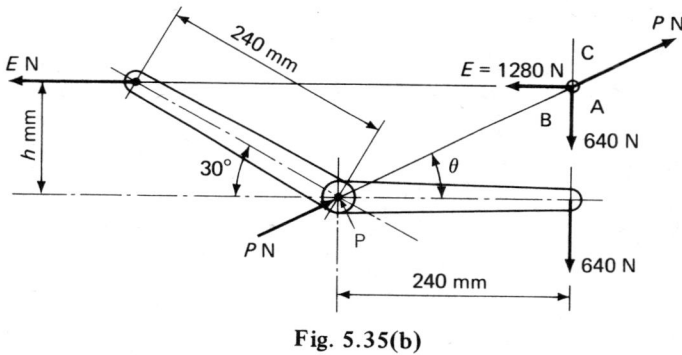

Fig. 5.35(b)

First, it will be necessary to determine the perpendicular distance h from

$$\frac{h}{240} = \sin 30°$$

$$= 0.5$$

∴ $$h = 0.5 \times 240 \text{ mm}$$

$$= 120 \text{ mm}$$

Taking moments about the pivot P

$$120E = 240 \times 640$$

$$E = 2 \times 640 \text{ N}$$

$$= 1280 \text{ N}$$

To determine the magnitude and direction of the force on the pivot, continue the lines of action of the 640 N and 1280 N forces until they intersect at O as shown in Fig. 5.35(b). The line of action of the force on the pivot must also pass through O and the space diagram can be drawn around this point. The vector diagram is shown in Fig. 5.35(c).

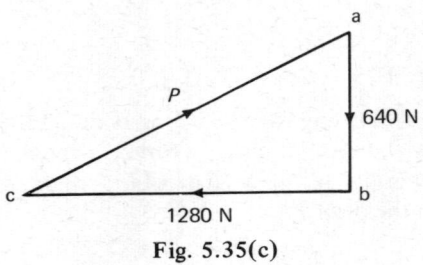

Fig. 5.35(c)

Measuring **ca** to scale the force P is approximately 1430 N at approximately 26° 30′ to the horizontal.

5.7 Couples and torque

A torque is exerted by a force which causes (or tends to cause) twisting. Torque is sometimes called a turning moment and is a term generally used in connection with such things as: rotating shafts, work being turned in a lathe, and rotating machine tools such as milling cutters. When turning a steel bar on a lathe the cutting tool exerts a tangential cutting force on the bar and there is a tendency to twist the bar, it can be said that a torque is exerted on the bar. Turning moment or torque

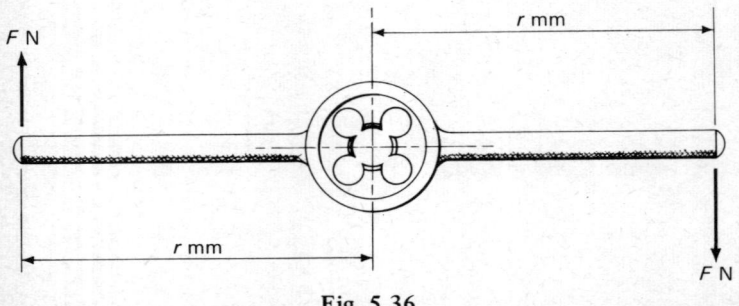

Fig. 5.36

FORCES IN EQUILIBRIUM

(T) is obtained by multiplying the tangential force (F) by the radius of rotation (r). If the force is in newtons and the radius in metres then

$$T = Fr \text{ newton metres}$$

A couple is exerted when two parallel forces cause (or tend to cause) turning or twisting both in the same direction. A typical example of a couple being exerted is in the case of screwing a metal rod using a stock and die as shown in Fig. 5.36.

$$\text{couple} = 2Fr \text{ newton metres}$$

If the applied hand force F newtons is 40 N and the radius is 150 mm then the couple exerted

$$= 2 \times 40 \times 150 \text{ Nmm}$$
$$= 12\ 000 \text{ Nmm (12 Nm)}$$

Example 16 (MT1)

The effective pull in a belt drive is 350 N and the pulley diameter is 240 mm. Calculate:

(a) the torque transmitted, and

(b) the effective belt pull when transmitting the same torque and using a 150-mm diameter belt pulley.

(a) Torque = tangential force × radius
$$= 350 \times 120 \text{ Nmm}$$
$$= 350 \times 0.12 \text{ Nm}$$
$$= 42 \text{ Nm}$$

(b) Tangential force = $\dfrac{\text{torque}}{\text{radius}}$

$$= \dfrac{84}{0.15} \text{ N}$$
$$= 560 \text{ N}$$

Note that the smaller the pulley the greater the effective pull when transmitting the same torque.

5.8 Centre of gravity

The force of gravity acting on an object is due to the attractive pull of a very large mass (the earth) on a relatively very small mass (the object). The centre of gravity of an object is the point through which the line of action of the force of gravity passes. In other words, the gravitational pull on an object (its weight) may be considered to be concentrated at its centre of gravity, and this is very often a convenient simplification in the solution of engineering problems, such as in example 10 in paragraph 5.5. If an object could be supported at its centre of gravity it would balance because the mass of the object would be distributed in such a way that if moments are taken about the centre of gravity, the moment of that part on one side of the centre of gravity would be equal and opposite to the moment of the other part.

Example 17 (MT1)

Determine the position of the centre of gravity for the turned steel pin shown in Fig. 5.37.

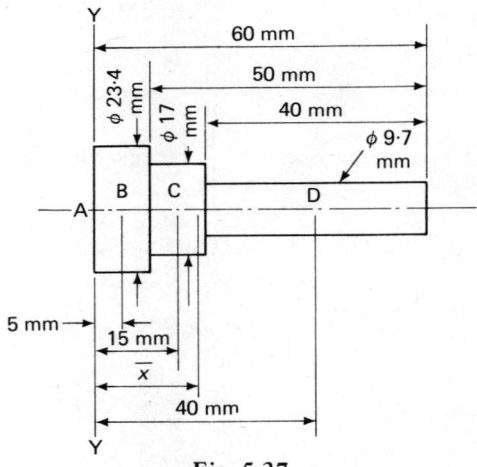

Fig. 5.37

In order to solve this type of problem it is necessary to take moments about a vertical line (say YY) passing through one end (say A). These moments are exerted by the forces of gravity acting on each of the parts B, C, and D and the sum total of these moments must equal the moment of the force of gravity acting on the whole object about the same line YY. Since the density of the material can be assumed to be the same

FORCES IN EQUILIBRIUM

throughout in this case, the volume of each part of the pin will be directly proportional to the force of gravity acting upon it, therefore it will only be necessary to take moments of volume and not forces.

Now the volume of a cylinder

$$= \frac{\pi d^2 l}{4}$$

where $\quad d =$ the diameter
and $\quad l =$ the length

$$\text{volume of cylinder B} = \frac{\pi \times 23.4^2 \times 10}{4} \text{ mm}^3$$

$$= 430 \times 10 \text{ mm}^3$$

$$= 4300 \text{ mm}^3$$

$$\text{volume of cylinder C} = \frac{\pi \times 17^2 \times 10}{4} \text{ mm}^3$$

$$= 227 \times 10 \text{ mm}^3$$

$$= 2270 \text{ mm}^3$$

$$\text{volume of cylinder D} = \frac{\pi \times 9.7^2 \times 40}{4} \text{ mm}^3$$

$$= 73.9 \times 40 \text{ mm}^3$$

$$= 2956 \text{ mm}^3$$

$$\text{total volume} = 4300 + 2270 + 2956$$

$$= 9526 \text{ mm}^3$$

Now the moment of the whole volume must equal the sum of the moments of the separate cylindrical parts. The mass, and hence the volume of each cylindrical part can be considered concentrated at their own centres of gravity. Thus:

$$9526\bar{x} = 4300 \times 5 + 2270 \times 15 + \ldots$$
$$\ldots + 2956 \times 40$$

$$= 21\,500 + 34\,050 + 118\,240$$

$$= 173\,790$$

$$\therefore \quad \bar{x} = \frac{173\,790}{9526} \text{ mm}$$

$$= 18.24 \text{ mm}$$

The centre of gravity is on the centre line 18.24 mm from the end A.

Example 18 (MT1)

A metal spindle 100 mm long and 40 mm diameter has a flat-bottomed hole 20 mm diameter bored centrally along its axis to a depth of 70 mm from one of its ends. Determine the position of its centre of gravity. Details of the bored metal spindle are shown in Fig. 5.38.

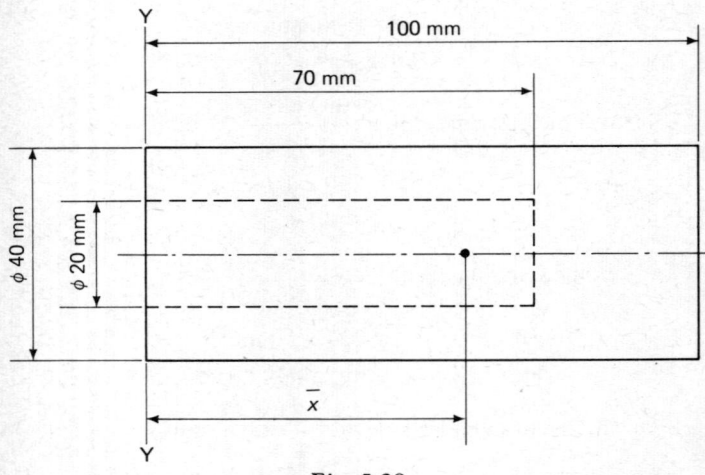

Fig. 5.38

In this case, since metal has been removed, the moment of the metal removed must be subtracted from the moment of the whole cylinder as it was before boring. The volume of the complete cylinder before boring

$$= \frac{\pi \times 40^2}{4} \times 100 \text{ mm}^3$$

$$= 1257 \times 100 \text{ mm}^3$$

$$= 125\,700 \text{ mm}^3$$

the volume of hole $= \dfrac{\pi \times 20^2}{4} \times 70 \text{ mm}^3$

$$= 314.2 \times 70 \text{ mm}^3$$

$$= 22\,000 \text{ mm}^3$$

∴ net volume $= 125\,700 - 22\,000 \text{ mm}^3$

$$= 103\,700 \text{ mm}^3$$

FORCES IN EQUILIBRIUM

Now the moment of the bored cylinder about YY must equal the difference between the moment of the original cylinder and the moment of the metal removed.

$\therefore$
$$103\,700\bar{x} = 125\,700 \times 50 - 22\,000 \times 35$$
$$= 6.285 \times 10^6 - 0.77 \times 10^6$$
$$= 5.515 \times 10^6$$

$\therefore$
$$\bar{x} = \frac{5.515 \times 10^6}{103\,700} \text{ mm}$$
$$= 53.19 \text{ mm}$$

The centre of gravity lies on the centre line, 53.19 mm from the line YY.

5.9 Centre of area

The centre of area, or centroid, as it is sometimes called, is the point which coincides with the centre of gravity of a thin flat sheet, the thickness of which is negligible. Such a flat sheet is sometimes referred to as a lamina.

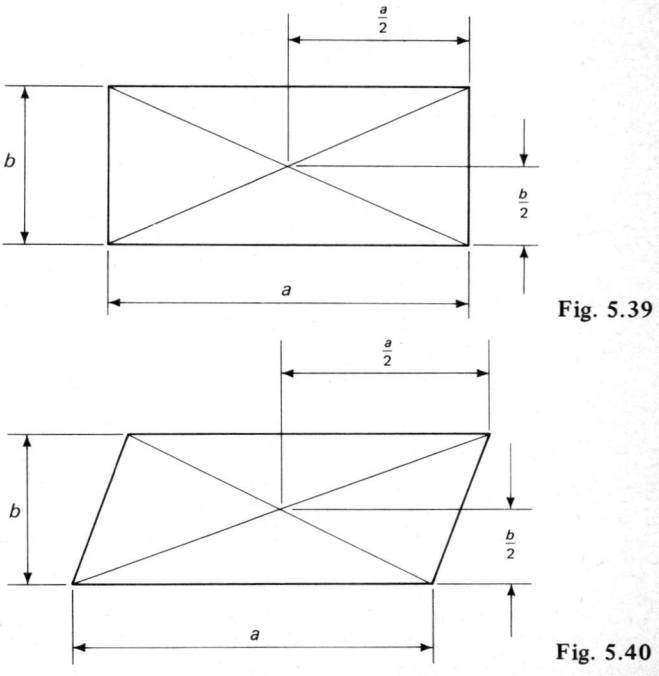

Fig. 5.39

Fig. 5.40

The centre of area of a rectangle or parallelogram lies on the intersection of the diagonals, as shown in Figs. 5.39 and 5.40.

The centroid of a triangle lies on the intersection of its medians, a median being a line which joins a corner with the mid-point of the opposite side. This position is always one-third of the distance between a corner and its opposite side measured from the side as shown in Fig. 5.41.

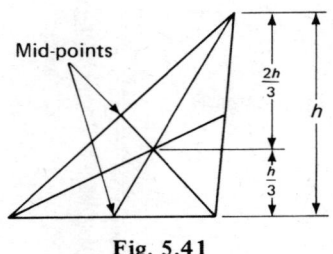

Fig. 5.41

The centroid of a semicircle of radius R lies at a distance of $\dfrac{4R}{3\pi}$ measured from the diameter, as shown in Fig. 5.42.

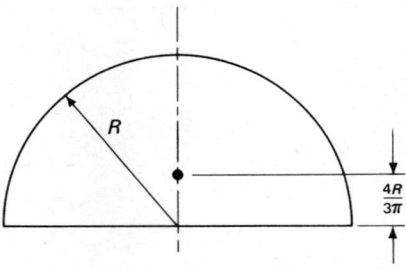

Fig. 5.42

To determine the position of the centre of area it will only be necessary to take moments of area about a given reference line, because the thickness is negligible and, therefore, ignored.

Example 19 (MT1)

Determine the position of the centre of area for the symmetrical tee-shaped lamina shown in Fig. 5.43.

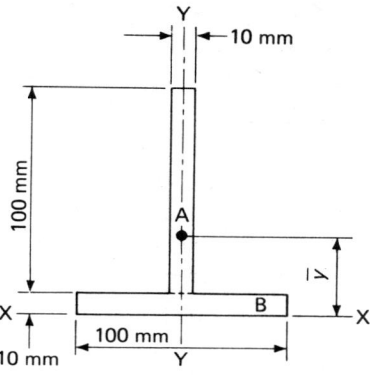

Fig. 5.43

Since the tee-shape is symmetrical the centre of area must lie on the centre line YY.

$$\text{area of A} = 1000 \text{ mm}^2$$
$$\text{area of B} = 1000 \text{ mm}^2$$
$$\text{total area} = 2000 \text{ mm}^2$$

Now the moment of the whole area about XX must equal the sum of the moments of the areas A and B about XX.

The moment of area A about XX
$$= 1000 \times (10 + 50)$$
$$= 1000 \times 60 = 60\,000$$

The moment of area B about XX
$$= 1000 \times 5$$
$$= 5000$$

∴
$$2000\bar{y} = 60\,000 + 5000$$
$$= 65\,000$$
$$\bar{y} = \frac{65\,000}{2000}$$
$$= 32.5 \text{ mm}$$

The centroid lies on the centre line YY 32.5 mm from the base XX.

Example 20 (MT1)

Figure 5.44 shows details of the cross-section of a bar of unequal steel angle. Calculate the position of the centre of area for this cross-section measured from the lines XX and YY:

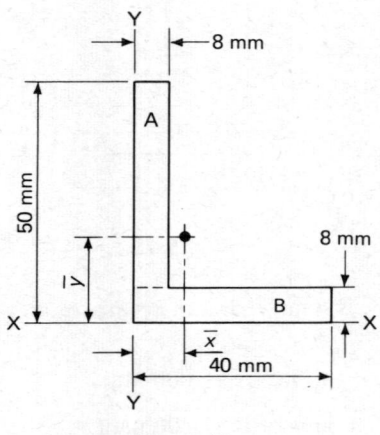

Fig. 5.44

$$\text{Area of A} = 42 \times 8 \text{ mm}^2$$
$$= 336 \text{ mm}^2$$

$$\text{Area of B} = 40 \times 8 \text{ mm}^2$$
$$= 320 \text{ mm}^2$$

$$\text{Total area} = 336 + 320 \text{ mm}^2$$
$$= 656 \text{ mm}^2$$

The moment of area A about YY

$$= 336 \times 4$$
$$= 1344$$

The moment of area B about YY

$$= 320 \times 20$$
$$= 6400$$

FORCES IN EQUILIBRIUM

The moment of the whole area about YY must equal the sum of the moments of areas A and B about YY

$\therefore$
$$656\bar{x} = 1344 + 6400$$
$$= 7744$$
$$\bar{x} = \frac{7744}{656} \text{ mm}$$
$$= 11.8 \text{ mm}$$

The moment of area A about XX
$$= 336 \times (8 + 21)$$
$$= 336 \times 29$$
$$= 9744$$

The moment of area B about XX
$$= 320 \times 4$$
$$= 1280$$

The moment of the whole area about XX must equal the sum of the moments of areas A and B about XX:

$$656\bar{y} = 9744 + 1280$$
$$= 11\,024$$
$$\bar{y} = \frac{11\,024}{656} \text{ mm}$$
$$= 16.81 \text{ mm}$$

The centroid lies at a point outside the cross-section 11.8 mm from YY and 16.81 mm from XX.

Example 21 (MT1)

A stiffening plate is in the form of a square of 200 mm side and is cut from steel sheet of uniform thickness. The stiffener has a hole of 70 mm diameter punched through in the position shown in Fig. 5.45. Calculate the position of the centroid for the stiffener.
Assume that $\pi = 22/7$.

114   MECHANICAL ENGINEERING SCIENCE

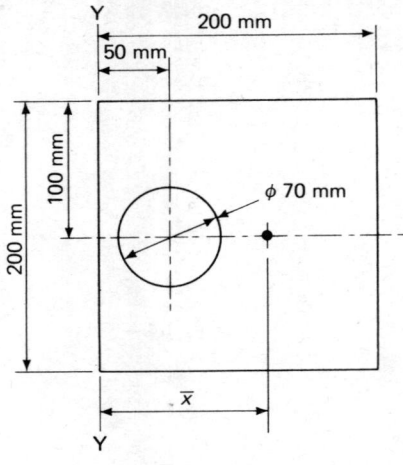

Fig. 5.45

As in example 17, metal has been removed, in this case by punching a hole of 70 mm diameter; the moment of the metal removed must be subtracted from the moment of the whole square.

$$\text{Area of square} = 200^2 \text{ mm}^2$$
$$= 40\,000 \text{ mm}^2$$

$$\text{Area of hole} = \pi \times 35^2$$
$$= \frac{22}{7} \times 35^2$$
$$= 3850 \text{ mm}^2$$

$$\text{Net area} = 40\,000 - 3850$$
$$= 36\,150 \text{ mm}^2$$

The moment of the hole about YY

$$= 3850 \times 50$$
$$= 192\,500$$

The moment of the complete square about YY

$$= 40\,000 \times 100$$

FORCES IN EQUILIBRIUM

The moment of the net area of the stiffening plate must equal the difference between the moment of the complete square and the moment of the hole, all about YY

$$\therefore \quad 36\,150\bar{x} = 40\,000 \times 100 - 192\,500$$
$$\therefore \quad 361.5\bar{x} = 40\,000 - 1925$$
$$= 38\,075$$
$$\therefore \quad \bar{x} = \frac{38\,075}{361.5} \text{ mm}$$
$$= 105.3 \text{ mm}$$

Example 22 (MT1)

Calculate the position of the centre of area for the gusset plate shown in Fig. 5.46.

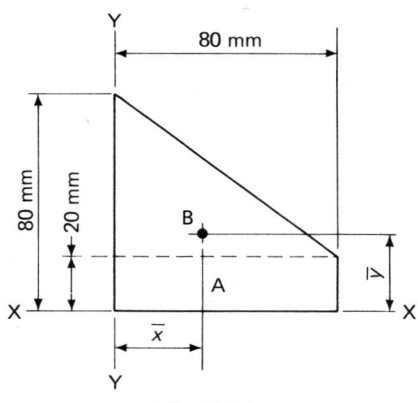

Fig. 5.46

$$\text{Area of rectangle A} = 80 \times 20 \text{ mm}^2$$
$$= 1600 \text{ mm}^2$$
$$\text{Area of triangle B} = \tfrac{1}{2} \times 80 \times 60 \text{ mm}^2$$
$$= 2400 \text{ mm}^2$$
$$\text{Total area} = 1600 + 2400 \text{ mm}^2$$
$$= 4000 \text{ mm}^2$$

116 MECHANICAL ENGINEERING SCIENCE

The moment of area A about the line XX
$$= 1600 \times 10$$
$$= 16\,000$$

The moment of area B about the line XX
$$= 2400 \times (20 + \tfrac{1}{3} \times 60)$$
$$= 2400 \times 40$$
$$= 96\,000$$

The moment of the whole area must equal the sum of the moments of the rectangle and the triangle, all about XX

$\therefore$ $\quad 4000\bar{y} = 16\,000 + 96\,000$

$\therefore$ $\quad \bar{y} = 4 + 24$ mm
$$= 28 \text{ mm}$$

The moment of area A about the line YY
$$= 1600 \times 40$$
$$= 64\,000$$

The moment of area B about the line YY
$$= 2400 \times \frac{80}{3}$$
$$= 800 \times 80$$
$$= 64\,000$$

The moment of the whole area about the line YY must equal the sum of the moments of the rectangle and the triangle about the same line

$\therefore$ $\quad 4000\bar{x} = 64\,000 + 64\,000$

$\therefore$ $\quad \bar{x} = 16 + 16$ mm
$$= 32 \text{ mm}$$

The centre of area is 32 mm from the left-hand side and 28 mm from the base.

Example 23 (MT1)

Calculate the position of the centre of area for the sheet metal template shown in Fig. 5.47. Take the position of the centroid of a semicircle to be $\frac{4R}{3\pi}$ from the diameter where R is the radius of the semicircle. Assume that $\pi = \frac{22}{7}$.

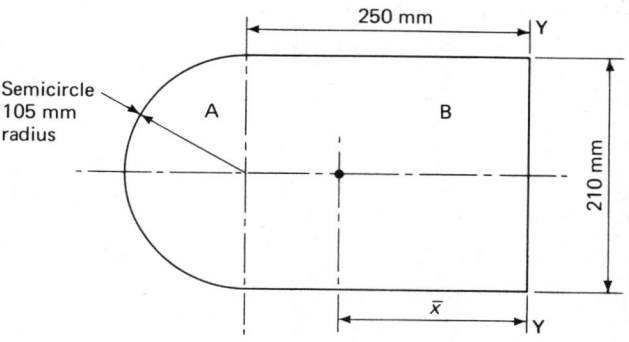

Fig. 5.47

Area of semicircle A = $\frac{\pi R^2}{2}$

$= \frac{22}{7} \times \frac{105 \times 105}{2}$ mm²

$= 11 \times 1575$ mm²

$= 17\,325$ mm²

Area of rectangle B $= 250 \times 210$ mm²

$= 52\,500$ mm²

Total area $= 17\,325 + 52\,500$ mm²

$= 69\,825$ mm²

The moment of A about YY $= \frac{\pi R^2}{2}(250 + \frac{4R}{3\pi})$

$= 125\pi R^2 + \frac{2R^3}{3}$

$= 125 \times \frac{22}{7} \times 105^2 + \frac{2 \times 105^3}{3}$

$= 125 \times 330 \times 105 + 70 \times 105^2$

The moment of B about YY $= 52\,500 \times 125$

Equating moments about YY

$$69\,825\bar{x} = 52\,500 \times 125 + \ldots$$
$$\ldots 125 \times 330 \times 105 + 70 \times 105^2$$
$$133\bar{x} = 125 \times 66 + 125 \times 100 + \ldots$$
$$\ldots + 70 \times 21$$
$$= 8250 + 12\,500 + 1470$$
$$= 22\,220$$
$$\bar{x} = \frac{22\,220}{133}\ \text{mm}$$
$$= 167\ \text{mm}$$

The centroid lies on the centre line of symmetry, 167 mm from the right-hand end.

Problems

Section A (MT1)

1. A steel bar of circular cross-section is clamped in a vee block which has a symmetrical included angle of 90°. If the clamping force is 250 N and is applied in a direction in line with the bisector of the angle of 90°, determine the normal force exerted by the steel bar on the side of the vee.
   Ans: 176.8 N.

2. Figure 5.48 shows a uniform steel shaft of mass 80 kg being raised by a sling. For the symmetrical configuration shown determine the force in each side of the sling.
   Assume that $g = 10$ m/s^2.

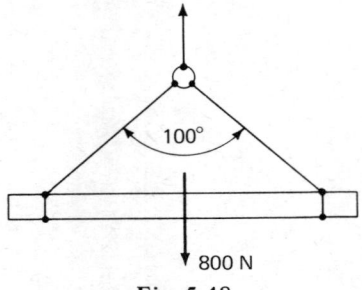

Fig. 5.48

Ans: 622.3 N

FORCES IN EQUILIBRIUM 119

3. A casting, having a mass of 270 kg, is suspended horizontally in a sling as shown in Fig. 5.49. Determine the tension in the chains A and B for the configuration shown. Assume that $g = 10$ m/s^2.

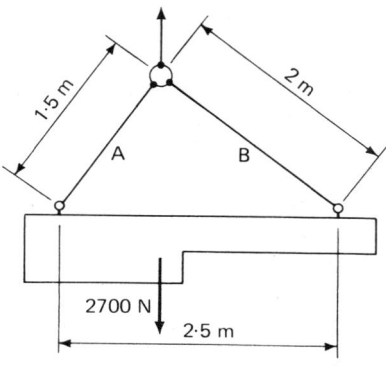

Fig. 5.49

Ans: 1620 N in A, 2160 N in B.

4. Determine the magnitude and direction of the resultant force exerted on a parting tool being used on a capstan lathe when the tool is being fed into the work with a force of 900 N and the vertical tangential cutting force is 2000 N.
Ans: 2193 N, 24° 14' to the verticle.

5. Figure 5.50 shows part of a framework at its hinged end. For the given forces, determine the magnitude and direction of the force on the hinge.

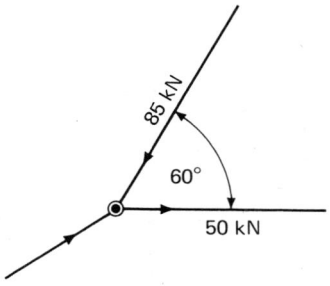

Fig. 5.50

Ans: 74 kN, 84° 10' to the horizontal member.

6. Determine the forces in the jib PQ and the tie QR for the wall jib crane shown in Fig. 5.51.

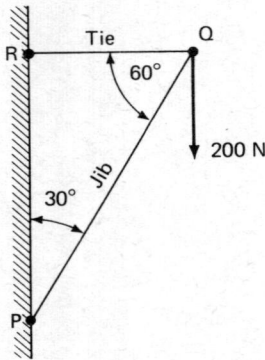

Fig. 5.51

Ans: Jib 231 N, tie 115.5 N.

7. Determine the forces in the jib and tie of the jib crane shown in Fig. 5.52.

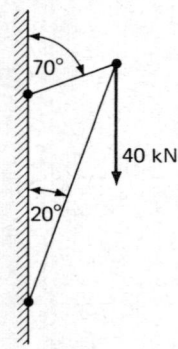

Fig. 5.52

Ans: Jib 49.07 kN, tie 17.86 kN.

8. Determine the forces in the jib and tie of the jib crane shown in Fig. 5.53.

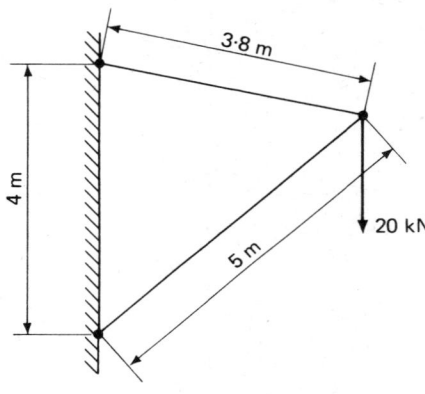

Fig. 5.53

Ans: Jib 25 kN, tie 19 kN.

9. Determine the reaction at the supports of the uniform beams shown in Figs. 5.54(a) to 5.54(d).

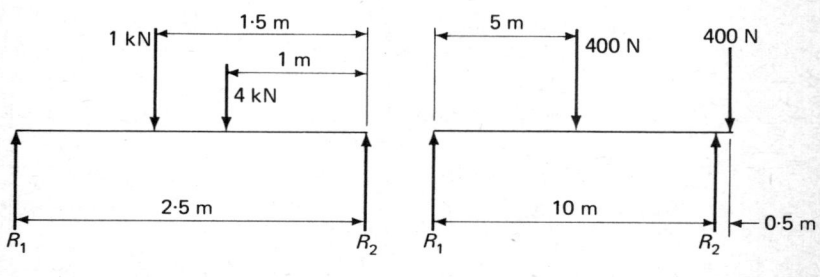

Fig. 5.54(a) Fig. 5.54(b)

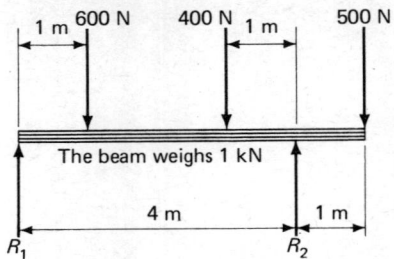

Fig. 5.54(c)

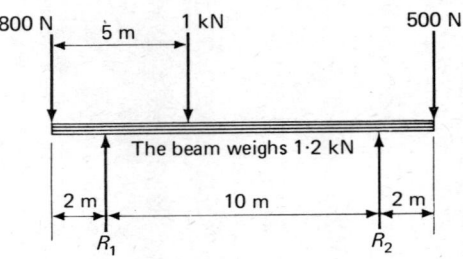

Fig. 5.54(d)

Ans: (a) $R_1 = 2.2$ kN, $R_2 = 2.8$ kN.
(b) $R_1 = 180$ N, $R_2 = 620$ N.
(c) $R_1 = 800$ N, $R_2 = 1700$ N.
(d) $R_1 = 2160$ N, $R_2 = 1340$ N.

10. A uniform steel shaft 1.6 m long has a mass of 20 kg and is supported in bearings 0.2 m from the left-hand end and 0.3 m from the right-hand end. The shaft is subjected to downward forces of 800 N and 200 N 0.4 m from the left-hand end and at the right-hand end respectively. Calculate the reactions at the support bearings.
Assume that $g = 10$ m/s^2.
Ans: $R_2 = 509$ N, $R_1 = 691$ N.

11. Calculate the reactions at the supports A and B in the shaping machine tool set up shown in Fig. 5.55.

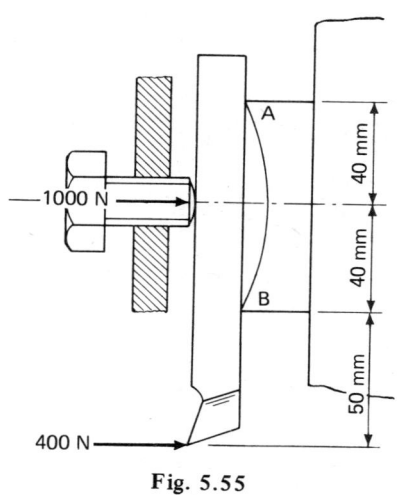

Fig. 5.55

Ans: R_A = 250 N, R_B = 1150 N.

12. Figure 5.56 shows details of a bell-crank lever in a mechanism. In the equilibrium position shown determine the force F.

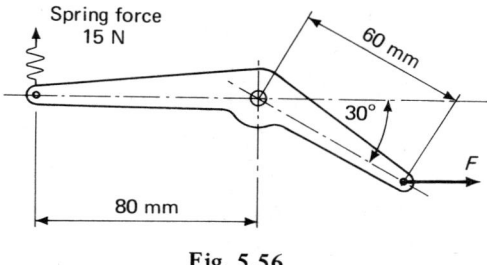

Fig. 5.56

Ans: 40 N.

13. Figure 5.57 shows details of part of the operating mechanism for a treadle-operated guillotine. Determine the force in the link to the blade when the force exerted by the operator is 700 N. Note that this force is shared by two sides of the treadle mechanism shown.

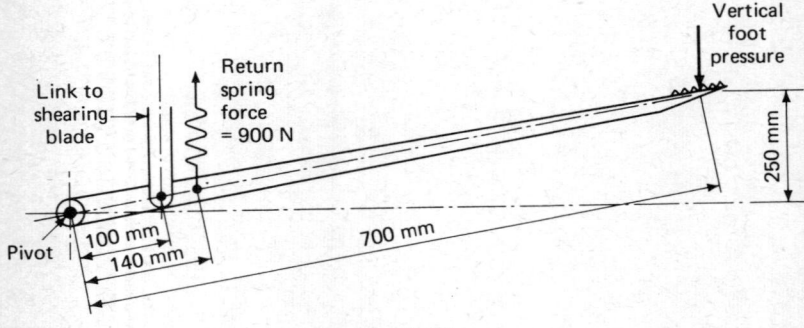

Fig. 5.57

Ans: 1191 N.

14. For the valve shown in Fig. 5.58, calculate the minimum force F required to keep the valve closed against the pressure of 500 kN/m², given that the spring force is 100 N and the valve diameter is 40.7 mm.

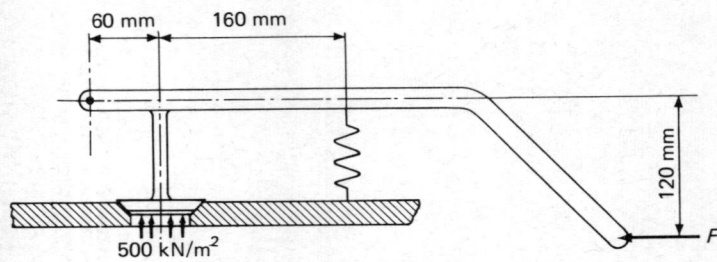

Fig. 5.58

Ans: 144.2 N.

FORCES IN EQUILIBRIUM 125

15. (a) Define the meaning of the terms 'torque' and 'couple'.
    (b) In tapping a hole, by means of a tap-wrench, a hand force of 50 N was applied at each end of the wrench. If the tap-wrench is 300 mm long and has 3 flutes calculate:
    (i) the couple applied to the tap, and
    (ii) the cutting force exerted on each flute when tapping a hole 16 mm diameter.
    Ans: (b) (i) 15 Nm, (ii) 625 N.

16. A total torque of 70 Nm is required to bring a flywheel to rest within a certain period of time. If there is a constant frictional torque of 15 Nm, calculate the tangential braking force required if this is applied at a radius of 220 mm.
    Ans: 250 N.

17. In a turning operation the tangential cutting force is 2400 N when the work diameter is 50 mm. If a torque of 12 Nm is required to overcome friction, calculate:
    (a) the torque required at the driving pulley, and
    (b) the effective driving force if the pulley is 240 mm diameter.
    Ans: (a) 72 Nm. (b) 600 N.

18. In a milling machine operation the effective tangential driving force at the pulley was 800 N. Given that the pulley diameter is 250 mm and a torque of 8 Nm is required to overcome friction, determine:
    (a) the torque available for cutting, and
    (b) the tangential cutting force that can be exerted by a cutter 115 mm diameter.
    Ans: (a) 92 Nm. (b) 1600 N.

19. A steel rod, 150 mm long and 40.7 mm diameter, is turned to 23.4 mm diameter for 50 mm of its length and 32.8 mm diameter for the middle 50 mm of its length the rest of the rod remaining at 40.7 mm diameter. Calculate the position of the centre of gravity measured from the unturned end.
    Ans: 57.98 mm.

20. A metal spindle, 21.5 mm diameter and 160 mm long, has a flat-bottomed hole 14.8 mm diameter bored centrally along its axis to a depth of 100 mm from one of its ends. Determine the position of the centre of gravity measured from the bored end.
Ans: 92.64 mm.

21. Determine the position of the centre of area for each of the laminae shown in Fig. 5.59, (a) to (c). Where applicable, make use of formulae for the position of centroids given in Figs. 5.39 and 5.41.

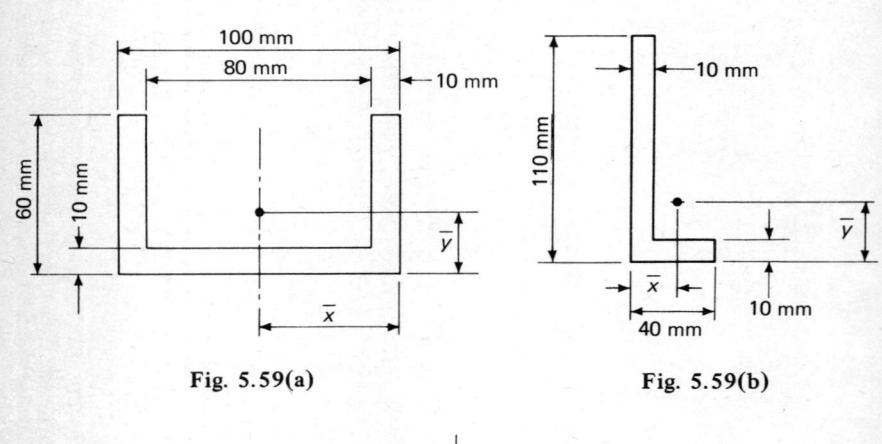

Fig. 5.59(a)   Fig. 5.59(b)

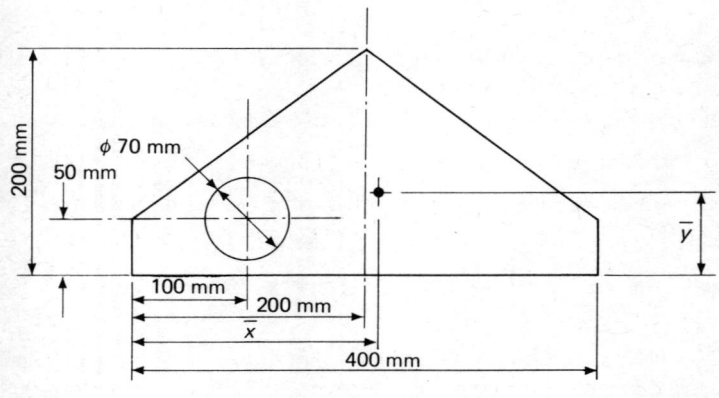

Fig. 5.59(c)

Ans: (a) $\bar{x} = 50$ mm   (b) $\bar{x} = 9.286$ mm   (c) $\bar{x} = 208.3$ mm
       $\bar{y} = 20$ mm $\bar{y} = 44.3$ mm $\bar{y} = 71.66$ mm

Section B (MT2)

22. A wedge has an included angle of 6°. Determine the normal force exerted by a side of the wedge when a load of 560 N is applied in the same direction as the bisector of the angle of 6°.
    Ans: 5351 N.

23. The tapered shank of a twist drill has an included taper angle of 3°. Determine the normal force exerted by the side of the tapered shank when the drill is forced into position with an axial force of 400 N.
    Ans: 7642 N.

24. The toggle mechanism shown in Fig. 5.60 exerts a vertical upward force as shown. Determine the force in each link and the vertical upward force exerted.

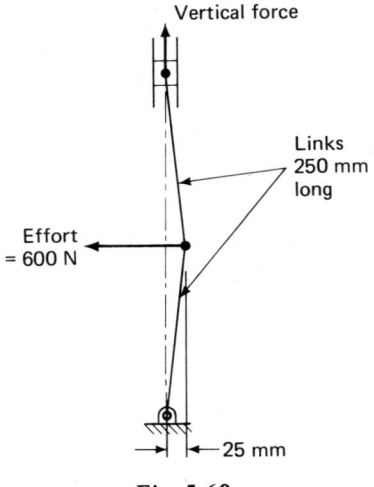

Fig. 5.60

Ans: 3000 N, 2986 N.

25. A toggle mechanism for making fuel briquettes is shown in Fig. 5.61. If the plunger A is 100 mm diameter, determine the effort E required if the plunger has to exert a pressure of 8000 kN/m^2.

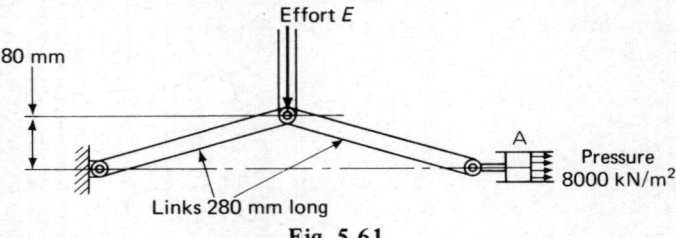

Fig. 5.61

Ans: 37.46 kN.

26. The upward reaction at the hinge of a framework is 2.5 kN and inclined at 53° 8′ to the horizontal. Calculate the vertical and horizontal components of this force.
Ans: R_v = 2 kN, R_H = 1.5 kN.

27. A component is clamped in position in a right-angled corner by force of 280 N inclined at 60° to the horizontal. Calculate the horizontal and vertical thrust exerted by this clamping force.
Ans: R_v = 242.5 N, R_H = 140 N.

28. Figure 5.62 shows a trapdoor of mass 100 kg held in an open position at 30° to the horizontal by means of a rope. Determine the force F and the magnitude and direction of the reaction at the hinge. Assume that g = 10 m/s^2.

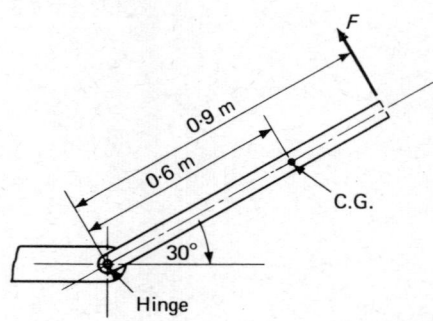

Fig. 5.62

C.G.L.I. (modified).
Ans: F = 577.3 N, R_H = 577.3 N at 60° to the horizontal.

FORCES IN EQUILIBRIUM 129

29. The cranked lever shown in Fig. 5.63 is in equilibrium. Determine the force F and the magnitude and direction of the reaction at the pivot P:

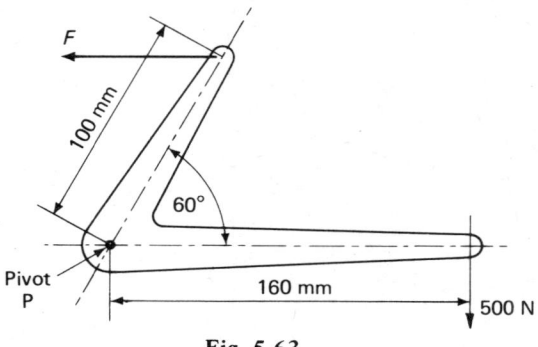

Fig. 5.63

Ans: $F = 923.9$ N, $R_P = 1050$ N $28° \; 25'$ to the horizontal.

30. In a crank and connecting-rod mechanism, at a particular instant, the crank lies at 90° to the line of the stroke as shown in Fig. 5.64. The crank radius is 60 mm and the connecting rod is 156 mm in length. A torque of 450 Nm is provided by the crankshaft. Neglecting frictional effects, determine:

(a) the force F in the connecting rod,
(b) the resistance P at the crosshead, and
(c) the reaction R between the crosshead and the guides.

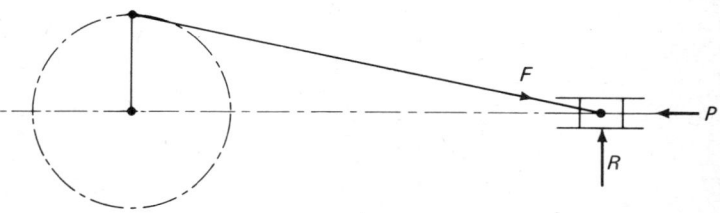

Fig. 5.64

C.G.L.I. (modified).
Ans: (a) 8.125 kN. (b) 7.5 kN. (c) 3.125 kN.

130   MECHANICAL ENGINEERING SCIENCE

31. If in the crank and connecting rod set up shown in Fig. 5.64 the crank radius is 75 mm, the connecting rod is 125 mm long, and the force P is 1800 N, determine:

   (a) the crosshead guide reaction R,

   (b) the force F in the connecting rod, and

   (c) the turning moment on the crankshaft.

   C.G.L.I. (modified).

   Ans: (a) 1350 N. (b) 2250 N. (c) 135 Nm.

32. Figure 5.65 shows the elements of a small pelleting press for metal powders. Find the intensity of pressure acting on the pellet of diameter 14 mm when the force P is 500 N and both toggle arms lie at 5° to the vertical.
   (All frictional effects can be neglected.)

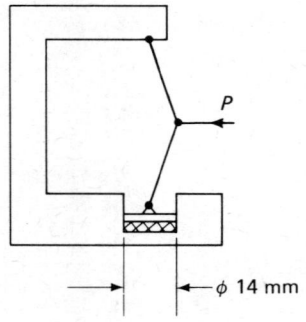

Fig. 5.65

C.G.L.I. (modified).
Ans: 18.56 MN/m².

FORCES IN EQUILIBRIUM

33. Figure 5.66 shows a line diagram of a toggle clamp mechanism. Determine the resisting spring force F and the vertical reaction R for the given clamp position when the hand force P is 140 N.

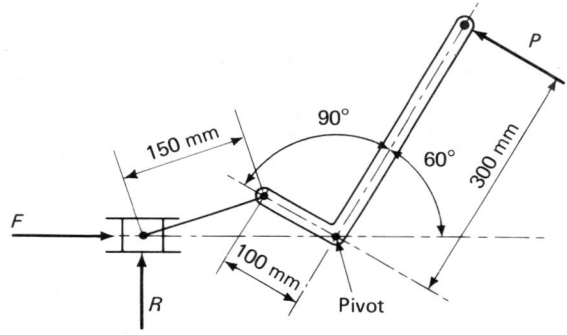

Fig. 5.66

Ans: $F = 521$ N, $R = 184.2$ N.

34. For the pivotted clamp shown in Fig. 5.67 calculate the vertical clamping reaction R and the magnitude and direction of the pivot reaction when the bolt force F is 800 N.

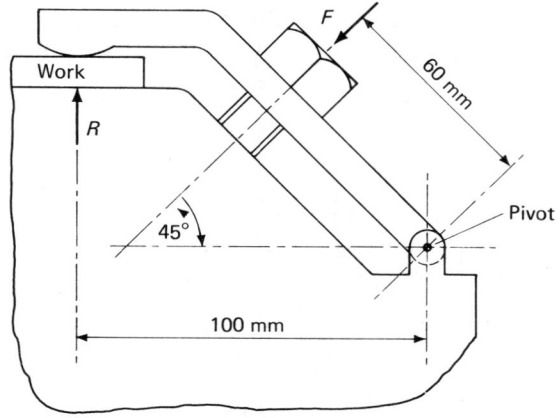

Fig. 5.67

Ans: $R = 480$ N, $R_P = 572$ N at $8° \ 36'$ to the horizontal.

6. Elementary strength of materials

6.1 Stresses and strains

A material is put in a state of stress and strain when it is subjected to an externally applied force. As stated in chapter 5 force is that which produces (or tends to produce) motion from rest, or change of motion, or change of shape, the SI unit of force being the newton (N). The types of force with which we shall be concerned in this chapter are: tensile (pulling), compressive (squeezing or crushing), shearing, and the force of gravity. Note that the weight of an object is the force exerted upon it by gravity and as previously explained may be calculated from the mass (m) kg multiplied by the gravitational acceleration (g) m/s^2.

Strain In this chapter we are concerned with the effect of force which produces a change of shape. A material is said to be strained when its shape is changed by the application of an externally applied force.

Stress This is the internal resistance set up in a material when its shape is changed by the application of an externally applied force.

Intensity of direct stress A direct stress is produced by the application of a tensile or compressive force and is the amount of this force applied over each unit of cross-sectional area taken in a plane at right angles to the line of action of the force:

$$\text{Intensity of direct stress} = \frac{\text{compressive or tensile force}}{\text{cross-sectional area}}$$

If
f = intensity of stress
F = load or force in newtons (N)
A = cross-sectional area in square millimetres (mm^2)

ELEMENTARY STRENGTH OF MATERIALS

Then $\qquad$ intensity of stress $f = \dfrac{F \text{ (N)}}{A \text{ (mm}^2)}$

Note, that since
$$1 \text{ m}^2 = 10^6 \text{ mm}^2$$
$$1 \text{ N/mm}^2 = 10^6 \text{ N/m}^2$$
$$= 1 \text{ MN/m}^2$$

and this will be a customary unit for intensity of stress.

Intensity of direct strain A direct strain is produced by the application of a tensile or compressive force and is given by the change of length per unit length or change of length divided by the original length.

If
$$e = \text{intensity of strain}$$
$$x = \text{change of length (mm)}$$
$$L = \text{original length (mm)}$$

$$\text{intensity of strain } e = \dfrac{x \text{ (mm)}}{L \text{ (mm)}}$$

The units of x and L must be the same, therefore, intensity of strain has no units, it is simply a ratio. The diagrams shown in Fig. 6.1 and 6.2 show the direction of force in relation to the cross-sectional area and the direction of the change of length in relation to the original length for direct stresses and strains.

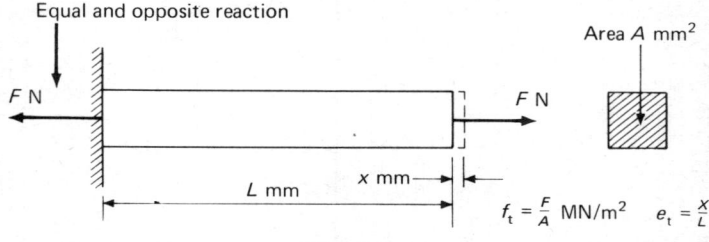

Fig. 6.1

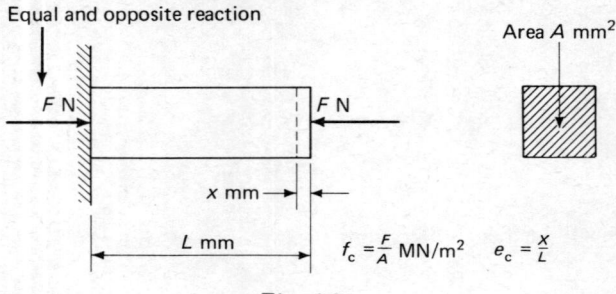

Fig. 6.2

Shearing stress and strain This is induced by a force which tends to make the planes of the material slip over each other as shown in Fig. 6.3. Shearing stresses and strains also arise in cutting operations. In this case the resisting area is always situated in a plane parallel to the line of action of the force and the change of shape or displacement is always measured at right angles to the direction of the original length.

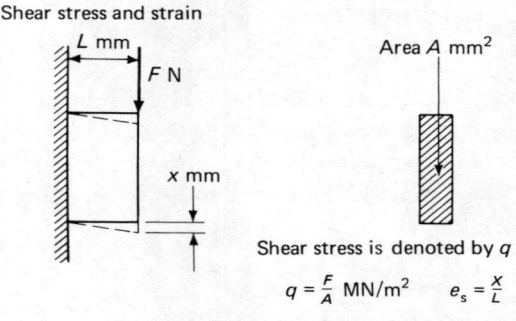

Fig. 6.3

If $\quad q$ = shear stress intensity
A = cross-sectional area (mm^2)
F = shearing load (N)

$$q = \frac{F}{A} \text{ MN/m}^2$$

if
ϕ = shearing strain
x = change of length (mm)
L = original length (mm)

intensity of strain $\phi = \dfrac{x}{L}$ (no units)

Figures 6.4 and 6.5 show a rivet being subjected to shearing load. In Fig. 6.5 the rivet is in double shear, that is, the shearing load F is being shared by two positions at which the rivet might fail in shear; in this case, since the shearing load is resisted by twice the cross-sectional area A of the rivet the shearing stress $q = \dfrac{F}{2A}$.

Single shear

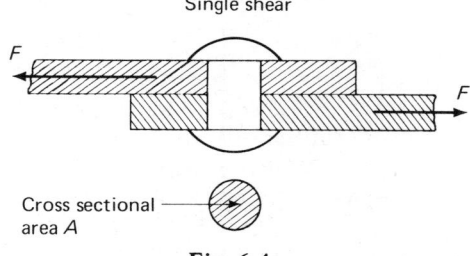

Fig. 6.4

Double shear

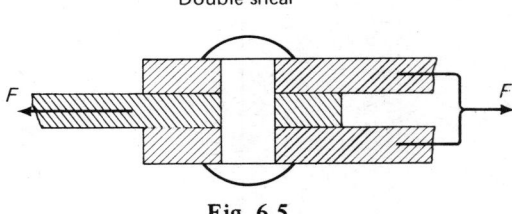

Fig. 6.5

Example 1

A specimen of free-machining brass was subjected to a tensile test, and when the applied load reached 2240 N the extension was 0.1 mm over a length of 50 mm. Given that the cross-sectional area of the specimen was 16 mm², calculate:

(a) the intensity of stress at the given load, and

(b) the intensity of strain for the given conditions of load and extension.

(a) $$\text{intensity of stress} = \frac{\text{applied load}}{\text{cross-sectional area}}$$

$$= \frac{2240}{16} \text{ MN/m}^2 \text{ (N/mm}^2\text{)}$$

$$= 140 \text{ MN/m}^2$$

(b) $$\text{intensity of strain} = \frac{\text{extension}}{\text{original length}}$$

$$= \frac{0.1}{50}$$

$$= 0.002$$

Example 2

Calculate the minimum diameter of a tie-rod required to withstand an axial tensile force of 9 kN, if the intensity of stress is limited to 60 MN/m². Give the answer correct to the nearest whole number.

Since the diameter of such a tie-rod would give a very small figure when measured in metres we will calculate the dimention in millimetres.

Now $\qquad$ 9 kN = 9000 N
and $\qquad$ 60 MN/m² = 60 N/mm²

Since $$f_t = \frac{F}{A}$$

$$A = \frac{F}{f_t}$$

that is, $$\text{area} = \frac{\text{force}}{\text{stress}}$$

$$= \frac{9000}{60} \text{ mm}^2$$

$$= 150 \text{ mm}^2$$

but $$\text{area} = \frac{\pi d^2}{4}$$

ELEMENTARY STRENGTH OF MATERIALS

∴ $$150 = \frac{\pi d^2}{4}$$

∴ $$d^2 = \frac{600}{\pi}$$

∴ $$d = \sqrt{\left(\frac{600}{\pi}\right)}$$

$$= 13.82 \text{ mm}$$

$$= 14 \text{ mm (to the nearest millimetre)}$$

Example 3

Determine the maximum axial thrust that can be applied to a tubular distance piece, 24 mm external diameter and 21 mm internal diameter, if the compressive stress is not to exceed 120 MN/m².

$$120 \text{ MN/m}^2 = 120 \text{ N/mm}^2$$

$$\text{cross-sectional area} = \frac{\pi}{4}(24^2 - 21^2)$$

$$= 452.4 - 346.4 \text{ mm}^2$$

$$= 106 \text{ mm}^2$$

since $$\text{intensity of stress} = \frac{\text{force}}{\text{cross-sectional area}}$$

maximum thrust = intensity of stress × cross-sectional area

$$= 120 \times 106 \text{ N}$$

$$= 12\,720 \text{ N}$$

$$= 12.72 \text{ kN}$$

Example 4

A press tool is required to punch out discs 42 mm diameter from steel sheet 2 mm thick. If the maximum shearing stress of the material is

320 MN/m², calculate the minimum force required to punch out a disc and the compressive stress set up in the punch.
Take $\pi = \dfrac{22}{7}$.

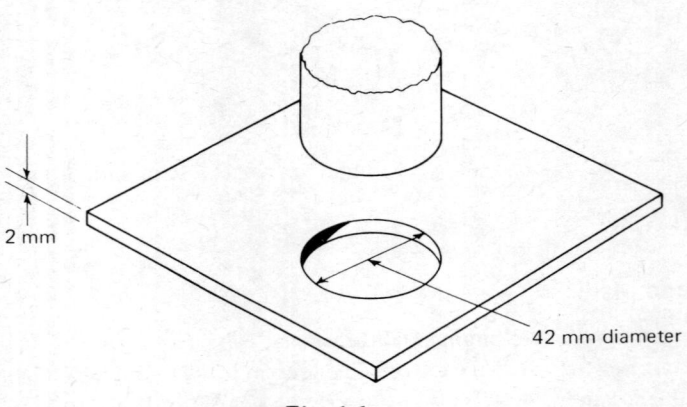

Fig. 6.6

(a) This is an example of shear stress. Figure 6.6 shows that the punch will have to shear past the area round the edge of the hole. The stress in this case is the maximum stress the steel will take before the punch will cut through the steel sheet.

$$\text{area to be sheared} = \pi \times \text{diameter} \times \text{thickness}$$

$$= \frac{22}{7} \times 42 \times 2 \text{ mm}^2$$

$$= 264 \text{ mm}^2$$

$$\text{maximum shear stress } (q) = \frac{\text{maximum force } (F)}{\text{area } (A)}$$

∴
$$F = qA$$
$$= 320 \times 264 \text{ N}$$
$$= 84\,480 \text{ N}$$
$$= 84.48 \text{ kN}$$

ELEMENTARY STRENGTH OF MATERIALS

(b) Cross-sectional area of the punch

$$= \frac{\pi \times 42^2}{4} \text{ mm}^2$$

$$= \frac{22 \times 42 \times 42}{7 \times 4} \text{ mm}^2$$

$$= 66 \times 21 \text{ mm}^2$$

$$\text{compressive stress in the punch} = \frac{\text{shearing load on the punch}}{\text{cross-sectional area of the punch}}$$

$$= \frac{84\,480}{66 \times 21} \text{ MN/m}^2$$

$$= 60.95 \text{ MN/m}^2$$

Example 5 (MT2)

A cylindrical pressure vessel of internal diameter 200 mm is subjected to a maximum internal pressure of 1200 kN/m². The circular cover is to be held in place by bolts having a minimum cross-sectional area at the core of 86 mm². If the maximum stress on the bolts is not to exceed 48 MN/m², determine the minimum number of bolts required.

In this case force is exerted on the bolts by the pressure trying to push off the cover, but note that pressure is not a force but force per unit area.

Therefore, $$\text{pressure} = \frac{\text{force}}{\text{area}}$$

∴ $$\text{force} = \text{pressure} \times \text{area}$$

Now the area over which the pressure is exerted

$$= \pi \times 100^2 \text{ mm}^2$$

$$= 10^4 \pi \text{ mm}^2$$

$$= 10^{-2} \pi \text{ m}^2$$

Since $1 \text{ m}^2 = 10^6 \text{ mm}^2$

∴ $$\text{force} = 1200 \times 10^{-2} \pi \text{ kN}$$

$$= 1200 \times 0.031\,42 \text{ kN}$$

$$= 1200 \times 31.42 \text{ N}$$

now
$$48 \text{ MN/m}^2 = 48 \text{ N/mm}^2$$
$$= \text{permitted stress}$$

Now the total area needed to resist this stress
$$= \frac{\text{force}}{\text{stress}}$$

since
$$\text{stress} = \frac{\text{force}}{\text{area}}$$

∴
$$\text{total area required} = \frac{1200 \times 31.42}{48} \text{ mm}^2$$
$$= 25 \times 31.42 \text{ mm}^2$$

The minimum cross-sectional area of each bolt
$$= 86 \text{ mm}^2$$

therefore, the number of bolts required
$$= \frac{25 \times 31.42}{86}$$
$$= \frac{785.5}{86}$$
$$= 9.135$$

therefore the minimum number of bolts needed is 10.

Example 6 (MT2)

A single-cylinder oil engine has a piston diameter of 144 mm. The piston is fixed to the connecting rod by means of a pin 24 mm in diameter which is in double shear. If the maximum pressure in the cylinder is 4200 kN/m^2, determine the maximum stress set up in the pin.

Cross-sectional area of the cylinder
$$= \pi \times 72^2 \text{ mm}^2$$
$$= 16\,290 \text{ mm}^2$$
$$= 0.016\,29 \text{ m}^2,$$

ELEMENTARY STRENGTH OF MATERIALS 141

as in the previous example,

$$\text{force} = \text{pressure} \times \text{area}$$
$$= 4200 \times 0.016\ 29\ \text{kN}$$
$$= 4200 \times 16.29\ \text{N}$$

the cross-sectional area of the pin

$$= \pi \times 12^2\ \text{mm}^2$$
$$= 452.4\ \text{mm}^2$$

The pin is in double shear; therefore, twice the cross-sectional area of the pin will be resisting the load;

∴ area resisting the force = $904.8\ \text{mm}^2$

$$\text{shear stress in the pin} = \frac{\text{force}}{\text{area resisting the load}}$$
$$= \frac{4200 \times 16.29}{904.8}\ \text{MN/m}^2\ (\text{N/mm}^2)$$
$$= 75.6\ \text{MN/m}^2$$

6.2 Hooke's law and the elastic limit

A material is said to possess elasticity if it will return to its original shape when it is no longer subjected to an applied force. If the force is too great the material will become permanently deformed and will lose its elasticity. The point at which the limiting load is reached is called the elastic limit.

Hooke's law states that the applied force is directly proportional to the change of shape within the elastic limit.

Since the original length and the original cross-sectional area are both constant, the same relationship can be applied between stress and strain. The point past which the applied force is no longer directly proportional to the change of length (or the stress is no longer directly proportional to the strain) is called the limit of proportionality. Since the elastic limit is difficult to determine exactly and does not necessarily coincide with the limit of proportionality, Hooke's law may be restated as: the stress is directly proportional to the strain it produces within the limit of proportionality. Up to this point the ratio

$$\frac{\text{stress}}{\text{strain}} = \text{a constant.}$$

142 MECHANICAL ENGINEERING SCIENCE

This constant is known as Young's modulus of elasticity and is dealt with in Part II of the Mechanical Engineering Technicians' course.

$$\text{The ratio} \quad \frac{\text{applied force}}{\text{change of length}}$$

is known as the stiffness of the material, that is, the force required to bring about a unit change of length (N/m).

6.3 Tensile and compressive tests

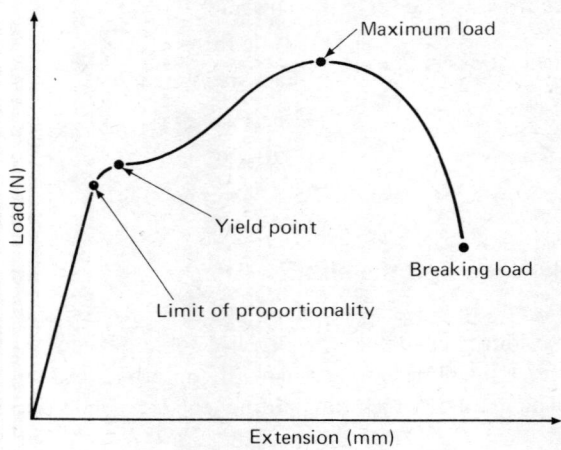

Fig. 6.7

If gradually-increasing tensile loads are applied to a ductile material, such as, a steel with a low carbon content, the graph of load against extension would be similar to that shown in Fig. 6.7. The first portion of the graph up to the limit of proportionality is a straight line passing through the true origin, showing that the load is directly proportional to the extension. With further increases of load direct proportionality ceases and a point is reached where extension continues without increases of load, this point is known as the yield point:

$$\text{yield stress} = \frac{\text{yield load}}{\text{original cross-sectional area}}$$

ELEMENTARY STRENGTH OF MATERIALS 143

After the yield point has been passed the load and extension again increase together until the maximum load is reached, after which the load decreases with continued extension until the specimen finally fractures. The maximum load reached during the test is used to obtain the ultimate tensile stress (or tensile strength) of the material:

$$\text{tensile strength} = \frac{\text{maximum load}}{\text{original cross-sectional area}}$$

For compressive tests the specimens must be short compared with the cross-sectional area in order to ensure that failure is due to pure compression and not due to buckling. Compressive tests are usually reserved for brittle materials such as concrete.

6.4 Factor of safety and working stresses

The main object of a tensile or compressive test to destruction is to obtain the strength or ultimate stress of the material (nominal breaking stress in the case of very brittle materials). In use as part of a structure, however, the material must not be stressed beyond its elastic limit, therefore, the strength of the material is divided by a number called the 'factor of safety' in order to obtain a safe working stress:

$$\text{safe working stress} = \frac{\text{ultimate stress (strength)}}{\text{factor of safety}}$$

$$\therefore \quad \text{factor of safety} = \frac{\text{ultimate stress}}{\text{working stress}}$$

The factor of safety is usually a whole number, the value of which depends on the conditions under which the material is to be used; the value being made higher if conditions such as: corrosion, wind loads, moving and indeterminate loads, frequent stress reversals, etc., are likely. In any case, the factor of safety must never be low enough to allow the working stress to exceed the limit of proportionality stress.

6.5 Percentage elongation and reduction of area

These values are sometimes required in order to assess the ductile property of a material, which is the ability of a material to be drawn into a wire. The values can be obtained from pre-set gauges, however,

if $\qquad L_1$ = original gauge length

and $\quad L_2$ = final distance between the gauge points

then $\quad$ % elongation $= \dfrac{100(L_2 - L_1)}{L_1}$ %

if $\quad A_1$ = original cross-sectional area

and $\quad A_2$ = final area at fracture

then $\quad$ % reduction of area $= \dfrac{100(A_1 - A_2)}{A_1}$ %

Example 7 (MT2)

A specimen of low carbon steel (En 3B) was subjected to a tensile test to destruction and the following results and details were noted:

Maximum load	34.04 kN
Yield load	31.39 kN
Limit of proportionality load	22.08 kN
Gauge length	50 mm
Final distance between gauge points	58 mm
Original cross-sectional area	64 mm^2
Diameter at fracture	6 mm

Calculate:
(a) the tensile strength,
(b) the yield stress,
(c) the limit of proportionality stress, and
(d) the percentage elongation and reduction of area.

(a) $\quad$ Tensile strength $= \dfrac{\text{maximum load}}{\text{original area}}$

$= \dfrac{34.04}{64}$ kN/mm^2

$= \dfrac{34\,040}{64}$ MN/m^2 (N/mm^2)

$= 531.9$ MN/m^2

(b) $\quad$ Yield stress $= \dfrac{\text{yield load}}{\text{original area}}$

$$= \dfrac{31.39}{64} \text{ kN/mm}^2$$

$$= \dfrac{31\,390}{64} \text{ MN/m}^2$$

$$= 490.4 \text{ MN/m}^2$$

(c) Limit of proportionality stress

$$= \dfrac{\text{limit of proportionality load}}{\text{original area}}$$

$$= \dfrac{22.08}{64} \text{ kN/mm}^2$$

$$= \dfrac{22\,080}{64} \text{ MN/m}^2$$

$$= 345 \text{ MN/m}^2$$

(d) $\quad$ Percentage elongation $= \dfrac{100(58-50)}{50} \%$

$$= 16\%$$

$$\text{final area} = \dfrac{\pi \times 6^2}{4} \text{ mm}^2$$

$$= 28.27 \text{ mm}^2$$

$$\% \text{ reduction of area} = \dfrac{100(64-28.27)}{64} \%$$

$$= \dfrac{3573}{64} \%$$

$$= 55.84\%$$

Example 8 (MT2)

A tie-rod of circular cross-section is made from En 3B steel and is to carry a maximum load of 50 kN. Using the appropriate information from the previous example, determine a suitable diameter (as a whole number) for the tie-rod if a factor of safety of 3 is to be employed.

From the previous example the tensile strength

$$= 531.9 \text{ MN/m}^2$$

∴ $$\text{safe working stress} = \frac{\text{tensile strength}}{\text{factor of safety}}$$

$$= \frac{531.9}{3} \text{ MN/m}^2$$

$$= 177.3 \text{ MN/m}^2$$

$$\text{the required area} = \frac{\text{working load}}{\text{working stress}}$$

now $$177.3 \text{ MN/m}^2 = 177.3 \text{ N/mm}^2$$

and $$50 \text{ kN} = 50\,000 \text{ N}$$

then $$\text{the required area} = \frac{50\,000}{177.3} \text{ mm}^2$$

$$= 281.9 \text{ mm}^2$$

$$= \frac{\pi d^2}{4}$$

∴ $$d = \sqrt{\left(\frac{4 \times 281.9}{\pi}\right)}$$

$$= 18.95 \text{ mm}$$

To the nearest whole number this gives a tie-rod 19 mm diameter (nearest obtainable diameter is probably 20 mm).

Example 9 (MT2)

A hollow cast-iron column has an outside diameter of 250 mm and an inside diameter of 210 mm. If the compressive strength of the cast iron is 960 MN/m², determine the maximum load that can be supported by the column, using a factor of safety of 12.

ELEMENTARY STRENGTH OF MATERIALS 147

$$\text{working stress} = \frac{\text{compressive strength}}{\text{factor of safety}}$$

$$= \frac{960}{12} \text{ MN/m}^2$$

$$= 80 \text{ MN/m}^2 \text{ (N/mm}^2\text{)}$$

$$\text{cross-sectional area} = \frac{\pi}{4}(250^2 - 210^2) \text{ mm}^2$$

$$= 14\,450 \text{ mm}^2$$

$$\text{working load} = \text{working stress} \times \text{area}$$

$$= 80 \times 14\,450 \text{ N}$$

$$= 80 \times 14.45 \text{ kN}$$

$$= 1156 \text{ kN}$$

6.6 Proof stress

Many metals and alloys in general use do not show a clear yield point when subjected to a tensile test to destruction. In order to have a clearer idea of the limit of elasticity of such a material it is necessary to determine the greatest load that can be applied before producing a large permanent extension. The stress produced by such a load is called the proof stress, and is defined as the stress at which a small non-proportional

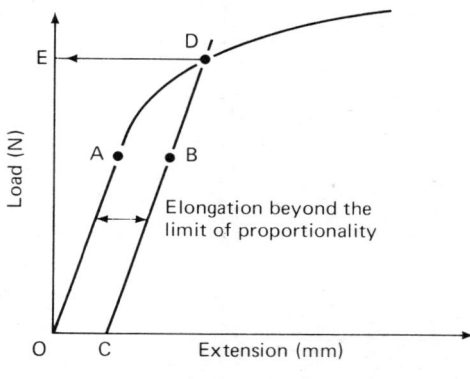

Fig. 6.8

extension has taken place. The proof stress is determined at small extensions beyond the limit of proportionality specified as 0.1, 0.2, and 0.5% of the gauge length.

The method of obtaining the proof stress is shown in Fig. 6.8. The required percentage of the gauge length is marked on the extension axis at C. A line BC is drawn parallel to OA and extended until it cuts the load extension curve at D. The proof load is then noted from the point E on the load axis. Thus:

$$\text{proof stress} = \frac{\text{proof load}}{\text{original cross-sectional area}}$$

Example 10 (MT2)

During a tensile test on a specimen of En 6 steel the following readings were noted:

Load kN	5.25	10.52	15.58	20.92	26.25	30.94
Extension mm	0.02	0.04	0.06	0.08	0.10	0.12
Load kN	34.71	36.82	38.03	38.93	40.00	
Extension mm	0.14	0.16	0.18	0.20	0.22	

Plot the load-extension graph and determine the 0.1% proof stress given that the cross-sectional area is 64 mm^2 and the gauge length is 50 mm.

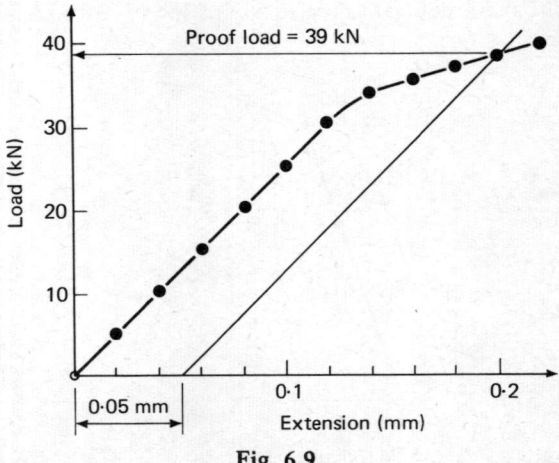

Fig. 6.9

ELEMENTARY STRENGTH OF MATERIALS

0.1% of 50 mm = 0.05 mm

This distance is marked on the graph shown in Fig. 6.9. From this graph the proof load is 39 kN.

$$0.1\% \text{ proof stress} = \frac{39\,000}{64} \text{ MN/m}^2$$

$$= 609.4 \text{ MN/m}^2$$

The 0.1% proof stress is 609.4 MN/m².

Problems (MT2)

1. A steel tie-rod has a square cross-section of 16 mm side. Calculate the tensile stress set up in the rod when it is subjected to an axial pull of 50 kN.
   Ans: 195.4 MN/m².

2. A distance piece, which is gripped between two cutters on the arbor of a milling machine, has an outside diameter of 42 mm and an inside diameter of 30 mm. If the clamping force is 2160 N, calculate the compressive stress in the distance piece.
   Ans: 3.184 MN/m².

3. Determine the size and type of stress set up in the milling machine arbor for the conditions given in the previous question.
   Assume that the arbor diameter is the same as the inside diameter of the distance piece.
   Ans: 3.056 MN/m².

4. A press tool is required to pierce slots in steel plate 4 mm thick. The slots, which have semicircular ends 10.5 mm radius, are 21 mm wide and 80 mm overall length. If the shearing strength of the steel plate is 325 MN/m² calculate:
   (a) the force required to punch out a slot, and
   (b) the compressive stress set up in the punch.
   Take $\pi = \frac{22}{7}$.
   Ans: (a) 239.2 kN. (b) 150.9 MN/m².

150   MECHANICAL ENGINEERING SCIENCE

5. A press tool is required to punch out circular blanks 24 mm in diameter from nickel sheet 1 mm thick. If the maximum force that can be exerted on the punch is 88.8 kN and the shearing strength of the nickel is 370 MN/m^2, calculate the maximum number of complete discs that can be produced in ten punching operations.
   Ans: 30.

6. A steel frame is to be constructed from steel tubes which are of the square cross-section shown in Fig. 6.10. If the maximum axial pull exerted on any of the tubes is 32.4 kN and the stress is not to exceed 100 MN/m^2, calculate a suitable wall thickness (t) for the tube.
   Ans: 3 mm.

7. A tie-rod of circular cross-section is made from steel with a tensile strength of 540 MN/m^2. If the rod is to be subjected to a maximum axial pull of 36 kN calculate:

   (a) the minimum permissible diameter of the rod correct to the nearest whole number (in mm) using a factor of safety of 6, and

   (b) the intensity of strain set up in such a rod under the given loading conditions if it extends by 1.35 mm over 3 m.

   Ans: (a) 23 mm (22.56 mm). (b) 4.5 × 10^{-4}.

8. In the clamping device shown in Fig. 6.11 the force required to clamp the workpiece in position is 3200 N and the shear stress in the dowel pins is not to exceed 32 MN/m^2. The two hinged bolts share the clamping force equally and the dowel pins are in double shear. Determine a suitable diameter (in mm) for the dowel pins correct to the nearest whole number above the calculated value.
   Ans: 6 mm (5.642).

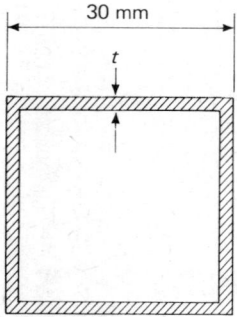

Fig. 6.10

ELEMENTARY STRENGTH OF MATERIALS 151

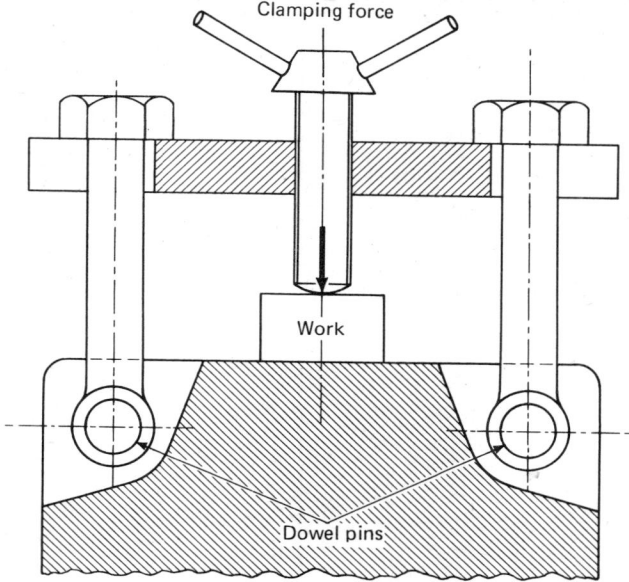

Fig. 6.11

9. A cylinder has a bore diameter of 175 mm, and the maximum cylinder pressure is 1350 kN/m². A cover plate is bolted on one end of the cylinder.

   (a) Calculate the force tending to push the cover plate off the cylinder.

   (b) Assuming that the minimum diameter of the bolts at the root of the thread is 10.5 mm and the safe working stress is 55 MN/m², calculate the minimum number of bolts required to hold the cover plate in position.

   Take $\pi = \frac{22}{7}$.
   C.G.L.I. (modified).
   Ans: (a) 32.48 kN. (b) 7.

10. (a) A tie-rod of circular cross-section has a diameter of 50 mm and the tensile strength of the material is 450 MN/m². Using a factor of safety of 6, calculate the safe working load.

    (b) In order to save weight the tie-rod is replaced by a tubular member of the same outside diameter and with a tensile strength of

720 MN/m². Using the same factor of safety, calculate the inside diameter of the tube so that it can carry the same working load.

Ans: (a) 147.3 kN. (b) 30.62 mm.

11. Two parts of a machine structure are to be bolted together in the manner shown in Fig. 6.12. The distance piece is cylindrical and has inside and outside diameters of 15 mm and 25 mm respectively. The bolt has a minimum diameter of 11.5 mm at the root of the thread and its nominal diameter is 14 mm. If the maximum tensile stress in the bolt is 40 MN/m² when the assembly is bolted together, determine:

(a) the compressive stress in the distance piece, and

(b) the shear stress in the bolt-head, if its height is 10 mm.

Ans: (a) 13.22 MN/m². (b) 9.443 MN/m².

(Note that the tensile load on the bolt must equal the compressive load on the distance piece.)

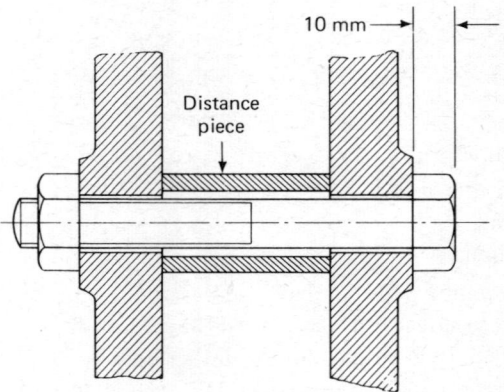

Fig. 6.12

12. Work is clamped to a machine table by a set-screw as shown in Fig. 6.13, and the total clamping force is shared equally by the two fixed bolts of 10-mm nominal diameter. If the total clamping force applied by the set-screw is 2000 N, calculate the tensile stress set up in the unthreaded portion of the fixed bolts and given that this stress is to be at least three times as great as the shear stress in the head of each fixed bolt, determine a suitable height h for the bolt-head.

Ans: 12.74 MN/m², 7.5 mm.

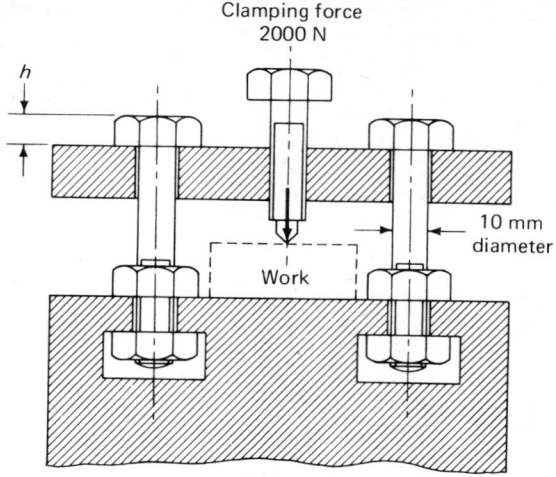

Fig. 6.13

13. In a blank and pierce tool set-up, four square holes of 13-mm side are to be punched simultaneously through steel strip 2 mm thick. If the shearing strength of the steel is 320 MN/m², determine:

    (a) the force required to punch the holes through the strip, and

    (b) the compressive stress set up in each punch.

    Ans: (a) 133.2 kN. (b) 196.8 MN/m².

14. A cropping machine is required to shear metal bars of circular and square cross-section. If the greatest shearing force available at the blade is 76.8 kN and the shearing strength of the metal being cut is 300 MN/m², calculate:

    (a) the maximum diameter of circular bar, and

    (b) the greatest size of square cross-section that can be cut separately. Give the answers correct to the nearest whole number.

    Ans: (a) 18 mm diameter. (b) 16 mm x 16 mm.

15. A storage rack in a workshop store is supported by six steel bars of equal angle cross-section, 20 mm x 20 mm x 2 mm. If the compressive strength of the steel is 600 MN/m², calculate the maximum load that the storage rack can carry using a factor of safety of 3. Assume that the bars share the load equally.
    Ans: 91.2 kN.

16. The cross-section of the fabricated mild steel support members for a machine are shown in Fig. 6.14. The overall dimensions of both members are 480 mm × 430 mm; the corners have an outside radius of 15 mm, and the wall thickness is 2 mm throughout. The maximum load to be supported is 30 kN and includes the weight of the machine and applied forces. Assuming that the two support members share the load equally calculate the maximum compressive stress set up in the members.
Take $\pi = \frac{22}{7}$.
Ans: 4.195 MN/m².

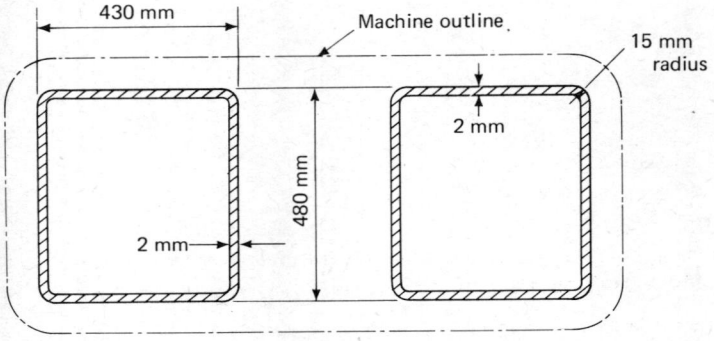

Fig. 6.14

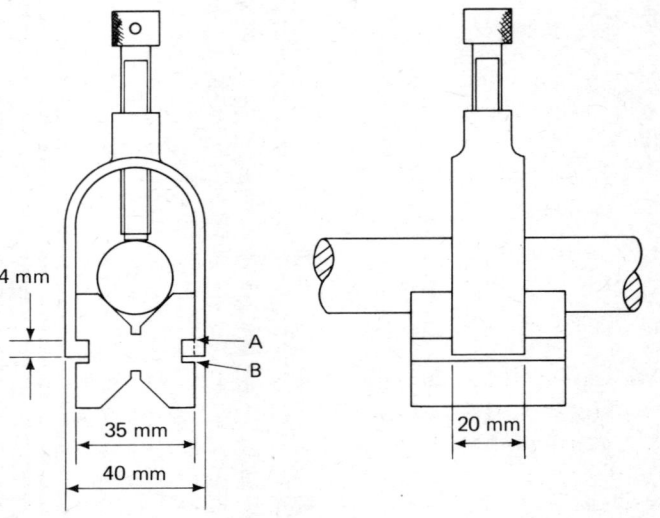

Fig. 6.15

17. For the vee block and clamp set up shown in Fig. 6.15, calculate for the given dimensions:
    (a) the tensile stress in the vertical sides of the clamp, and
    (b) the shear stress across the plane AB when the clamping force is 500 N.

    Ans: (a) 5 MN/m². (b) 3.125 MN/m².

18. A cylindrical pressure vessel has an internal diameter of 280 mm. One end of the cylinder is fitted with a cover plate, which is held in position with 8 ISO metric bolts, each with a minimum cross-sectional area of 125 mm². If the tensile strength of the bolt material is 693 MN/m², calculate the maximum permissible internal pressure using a factor of safety of 10.
    Take $\pi = \frac{22}{7}$.
    Ans: 1125 kN/m².

19. A specimen of 60/40 brass was subjected to a tensile test to destruction and the following results and details were noted:

Maximum load	7480 N
Limit of proportionality load	5000 N
Original diameter	4.5 mm
Diameter of fracture	3.9 mm
Gauge length	20 mm
Final distance over gauge length	24 mm

    Calculate:
    (a) the tensile strength,
    (b) the limit of proportionality stress,
    (c) the percentage elongation, and
    (d) the percentage reduction of area.

    Ans: (a) 470.4 MN/m². (b) 314.5 MN/m². (c) 20%. (d) 24.84%.

20. The following data were obtained during a tensile test on an aluminium alloy bar:

Load kN	4.48	8.97	13.45	17.00	19.50
Extension mm	0.02	0.04	0.06	0.08	0.10
Load kN	21.50	23.40	25.00	26.50	27.70
Extension mm	0.12	0.14	0.16	0.18	0.20
Load kN	29.00	30.10	30.90	31.70	
Extension mm	0.22	0.24	0.26	0.28	

Plot the load-extension graph and determine the 0.2% proof stress given that the cross-sectional area is 160 mm^2 and the gauge length is 50 mm.
Ans: 186.2 MN/m^2.

21. During a tensile test to destruction on a specimen En 8K carbon steel, the following results and details were noted:

Maximum load	36.6 kN
Limit of proportionality load	22.28 kN
Yield load	25 kN
Gauge length	50 mm
Final length over the gauge points	63 mm
Original cross-sectional area	64 mm^2
Diameter at fracture	6.4 mm

Calculate:

(a) the tensile strength,

(b) the limit of proportionality stress,

(c) the yield stress,

(d) the percentage elongation, and

(e) the percentage reduction of area.

Ans: (a) 571.8 MN/m^2. (b) 348.1 MN/m^2. (c) 390.6 MN/m^2. (d) 26%. (e) 49.73%.

22. A specimen of En 3B carbon steel was subjected to a tensile test to destruction and the following results were obtained:

Load kN	5.34	10.68	16.25	21.45	26.35
Extension mm	0.02	0.04	0.06	0.08	0.10
Load kN	29.46	31.08	31.70	32.20	32.40
Extension mm	0.12	0.14	0.16	0.18	0.20

Plot the load-extension graph and determine the 0.1% proof stress given that the original cross-sectional area is 64 mm^2 and the gauge length is 50 mm. Also use the graph to determine the stiffness of the material.

Ans: 496.8 MN/m^2, 270 kN/mm (MN/m).

7. Friction

7.1 The laws of dry friction

When two surfaces are made to slide over each other a resistance to motion is set up. This resistance is called friction and is caused by irregularities in the flatness of the two surfaces. A skilled craftsman may be able to produce a highly polished, smooth flat surface by machining, grinding, and polishing, but when such a surface is examined under a powerful microscope a series of high and low points become very apparent. If two such surfaces slide across each other the small surface imperfections will still give rise to friction. It is interesting to note that it is possible to 'wring' two surfaces of a high degree of flatness together by means of a combined sliding and twisting motion, that is, the two surfaces are held together without the application of any external force. This 'wringing' property is due to molecular attraction and is a very useful property where precision dimensions are required; such dimensions can be built up by 'wringing' together accurately finished hardened steel blocks known as slip gauges.

The amount of frictional resistance encountered between two sliding surfaces depends on a number of factors, which are:

(a) the kind of materials constituting the surfaces;

(b) the state of the surfaces, that is, whether they are rough or smooth, dry or lubricated;

(c) the force pressing the two surfaces together.

When sliding is started from rest the initial force needed to overcome static friction is a little greater than the force needed to just keep the surfaces sliding with a slow constant velocity.

We may now state the so-called laws of friction, but in doing so it must be realized that there is no set of laws which will apply exactly to friction under any sort of existing conditions. However, if it is assumed that the surfaces are dry at a normal temperature which remains con-

FRICTION

stant while sliding takes place and the speed of sliding is relatively low, a set of approximate laws can be stated as follows:

(1) The frictional resisting force F is directly proportional to the force W which presses the two surfaces together. From this law it follows that the ratio F/W will be constant.

(2) The frictional resistance F and hence the constant ratio F/W depends on the state of the surfaces in contact.

(3) The frictional resisting force depends on the materials constituting the surfaces in contact.

(4) The frictional resisting force does not depend on the area of contact between the sliding surfaces.

7.2 Coefficient of friction

As stated in law (1) above, the ratio F/W will be approximately constant for any two given surfaces and it is called the coefficient of friction for the two materials concerned. The Greek symbol μ is used to denote the coefficient of friction.

Consider a block of mass m kg at rest on a horizontal surface, as

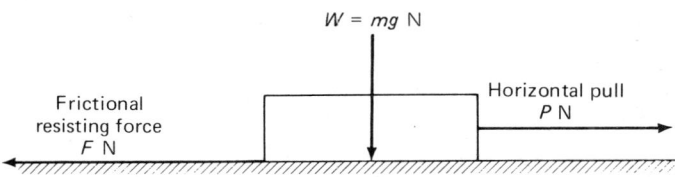

Fig. 7.1

shown in Fig. 7.1. The gravitational pull W on the block (or weight W) will be mg newtons, where $g = 9.81$ m/s². The force W newtons will be the force pressing the two surfaces together. If a horizontal pull P newtons is applied to try to overcome friction and slide the block along the surface, the force P will equal the frictional force F until the block starts to move. At the instant motion commences the force P will be a little greater than F in order to overcome static friction and to accelerate the block from rest. However, when the block is moving along the surface at a slow constant velocity the force P will once again be equal to the force of friction F, hence the pull or effort needed to cause sliding at a slow constant velocity is equal to the frictional resisting force F.

$$\text{The coefficient of friction } \mu = \frac{\text{frictional resisting force}}{\text{force pressing surfaces together}}$$

$$\mu = \frac{F}{W}$$

also

$$\mu = \frac{\left[\begin{array}{c}\text{pull required to produce constant} \\ \text{velocity}\end{array}\right]}{g \times \text{mass of the block}}$$

$$= \frac{P}{mg}$$

$$= \frac{P}{W}$$

$$\therefore \quad P = \mu W$$

Example 1 (MT2)

A small machine of mass 100 kg is to be hauled along a horizontal floor in a workshop. Taking the coefficient of friction between the machine and the floor to be 0.44, determine the effort required to keep the machine moving at a slow constant speed against friction when the effort is:

(a) applied horizontally,
(b) inclined upwards at 30° to the horizontal, and
(c) inclined downwards at 10° to the horizontal.

Take $g = 9.81 \text{ m/s}^2$.

(a) The gravitational pull acting on the machine (its weight)

$$W = mg$$
$$= 100 \times 9.81 \text{ N}$$
$$= 981 \text{ N}$$

now effort $P = \mu W$
$$= 0.44 \times 981 \text{ N}$$
$$= 431.7 \text{ N}$$

FRICTION

(b) In this case the force pressing the two surfaces together will be less than 981 N because of the upward component of the pull P. It will be necessary, therefore, to resolve P into its vertical and horizontal components (see Fig. 7.2).

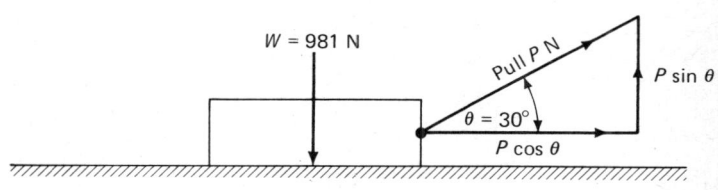

Fig. 7.2

As shown in chapter 5, paragraph 5.3,

the horizontal component of $P = P \cos \theta$

and

the vertical component of $P = P \sin \theta$.

Now the force pressing the two surfaces together

$$= W - P \sin \theta$$
$$= 981 - P \sin 30°$$
$$= 981 - 0.5P \text{ N}$$

The horizontal motion will be due to the horizontal component of P, namely, $P \cos \theta$

$$= P \cos 30°$$
$$= 0.866P \text{ N}$$

The coefficient of friction $\mu = \dfrac{\text{horizontal pull}}{\begin{bmatrix} \text{force pressing the two surfaces} \\ \text{together} \end{bmatrix}}$

∴ $\qquad 0.44 = \dfrac{0.866P}{981 - 0.5P}$

∴ $\qquad 0.44(981 - 0.5P) = 0.866P$

∴ $\qquad 0.44 \times 981 - 0.22P = 0.866P$

∴ $\qquad 0.44 \times 981 = 1.086P$

$$P = \frac{0.44 \times 981}{1.086} \text{ N}$$

$$= \frac{431.7}{1.086} \text{ N}$$

$$= 397.6 \text{ N}$$

(c) In this case the force pressing the two surfaces together

$$= W + P \sin \theta$$
$$= 981 + P \sin 10° \text{ (see Fig. 7.3)}$$

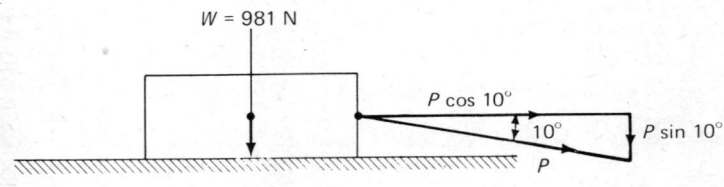

Fig. 7.3

in this case
$$\mu = \frac{P \cos 10°}{W + P \sin 10°}$$

$$\therefore \quad 0.44 = \frac{0.9848P}{981 + 0.1736P}$$

$$\therefore \quad 0.44(981 + 0.1736P) = 0.9848P$$
$$\therefore \quad 431.7 + 0.076\,38P = 0.9848P$$
$$\therefore \quad 431.7 = 0.908\,42P$$
$$\therefore \quad P = \frac{431.7}{0.9084}$$

$$= 475.2 \text{ N}$$

Example 2 (MT2)

In an experiment to determine the coefficient of friction between two sliding surfaces a metal slider with a flat leather base was hauled along a horizontal steel surface at constant velocity. The masses M kg of the

FRICTION

slider with its load and the masses *m* kg added to a suspended pan to provide the force to maintain motion were noted in the following table:

M kg	2	2.5	3	3.5	4	4.5	5
m kg	0.95	1.3	1.5	1.7	2	2.2	2.5

Plot a suitable graph of these results and then use the graph to determine the probable coefficient of friction for leather on steel. The experimental set up is shown in Fig. 7.4.

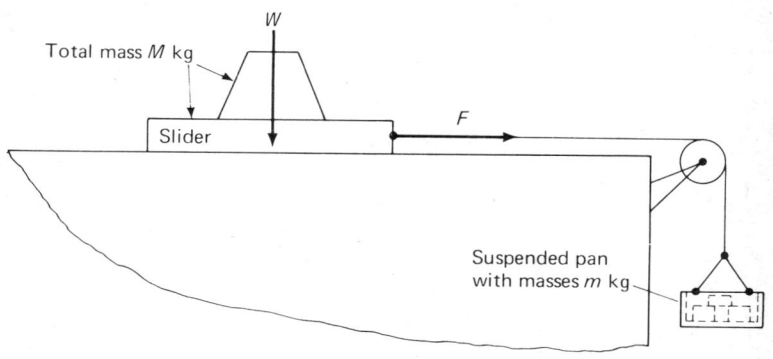

Fig. 7.4

Strictly speaking we are dealing with forces and the given masses should normally be converted to forces, however, in the equation $P = \mu W$ the factor 9.81 would be common to both sides, therefore, masses can be plotted without affecting the result. The graph should produce a straight line passing through the origin as shown in Fig. 7.5.

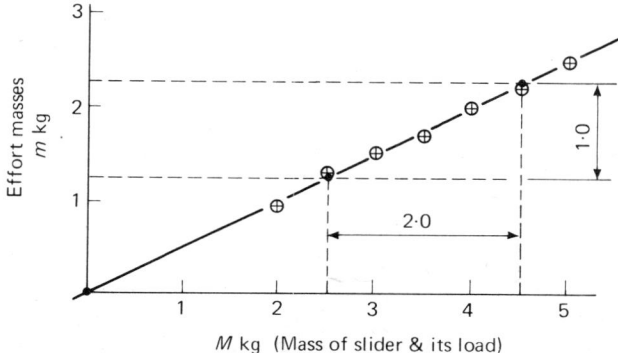

Fig. 7.5

The results are typical for a friction experiment and the points are not all exactly on a straight line, hence the straight line of closest fit is drawn as shown in Fig. 7.5. The gradient of this line is 0.5, therefore the average value for the coefficient of friction for leather on steel is 0.5 in this case.

7.3 Useful and wasteful friction in the workshop

Frictional resistance between surfaces is always present in varying degrees. There are occasions when we find the presence of friction helpful and essential and others when its inevitable existence is undesirable. Some examples of the usefulness of friction in the workshop are as follows:

(a) it prevents components and tools from moving when clamped in position for machining purposes,

(b) a belt-driven pulley will only transmit power while friction exists between the belt and the pulley,

(c) a magnetic chuck provides a magnetic force to press the surface of the work to that of the chuck, but only the existence of friction will prevent the work from slipping,

(d) friction between the jaws of a vice prevents work from slipping; the jaws are usually serrated to increase frictional resistance, note also that there are two pairs of surfaces thus doubling the frictional resistance which would have been encountered if there had been only one pair of surfaces,

(e) friction is necessary for the successful operation of clutches and brakes (see example 7 in this chapter for the principle of a simple clutch).

Example 3 (MT2)

A steel bar, rectangular in cross-section, is to have its width reduced in size by milling. During the machining operation the work is held in a machine vice fixed to the machine table with the line of its jaws at right angles to the arbor. During the operation the cutter applies a force of 440 N to the work.

Assuming that the coefficient of friction between the work and the machine vice jaws is 0.25 calculate the minimum tightening force that

FRICTION

must be applied to the vice jaws if the bar is not to slip through the vice jaws during the machining operation.

A simple sketch of the set up will be useful, and this is shown in Fig. 7.6.

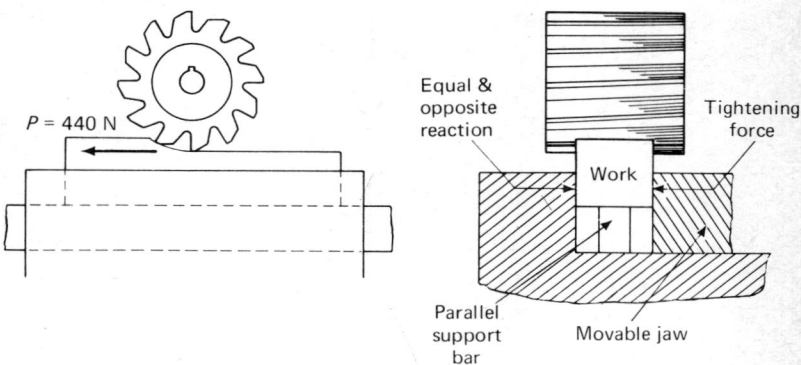

Fig. 7.6

From the diagram in Fig. 7.6 it is obvious that there are two pairs of surfaces providing frictional resistance, and this resistance must total at least 440 N.

Therefore, if $P = \mu W$

then $P = 220$ N for each pair of surfaces.

The same tightening or gripping force W will be applied to each pair of surfaces.

Since $\mu = 0.25$

then $220 = 0.25 W$

$W = 4 \times 220$ N

$= 880$ N,

that is, the tightening force must be at least 880 N, and should in practice be much greater than this for safety.

Example 4 (MT2)

A block of steel of mass 530 g is to have one of its surfaces ground on a surface grinder. The block is held on a magnetic chuck and the output torque at the grinding wheel is 8 Nm. If the coefficient of friction between the block and the magnetic chuck is 0.2, determine the least magnetic holding force required to prevent the block from slipping, given that the diameter of the grinding wheel is 320 mm.

What would be the effect of using a grinding wheel with a smaller diameter at the same output torque?

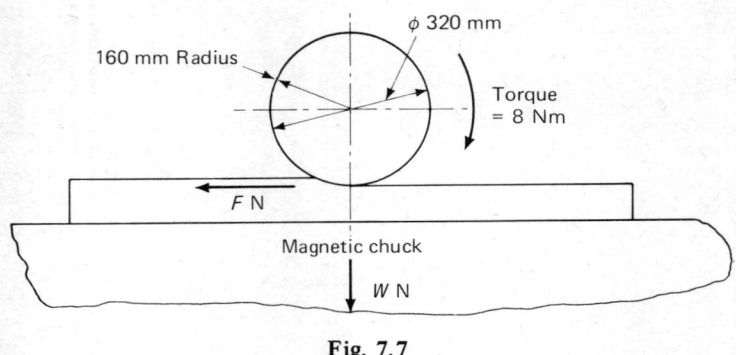

Fig. 7.7

Sketch the set up as shown in Fig. 7.7. From chapter 5, paragraph 5.7,

$$\text{torque} = \text{tangential force} \times \text{radius}$$
$$\text{the radius} = 160 \text{ mm}$$
$$= 0.16 \text{ m}$$
$$\therefore \qquad 8 = 0.16 F$$

where F is the tangential force

$$F = \frac{8}{0.16} \text{ N}$$
$$= 50 \text{ N}$$

Now W is the gravitational pull on the block plus the magnetic force;

$$\text{gravitational pull} = 0.53 \times 9.81 \text{ N}$$
$$= 5.2 \text{ N}$$
$$\therefore \qquad W = 5.2 + \text{magnetic force}$$

FRICTION

now $\quad\quad\quad\quad F = \mu W$

$\therefore\quad\quad\quad 50 = 0.2(5.2 + \text{magnetic force})$

$\therefore\quad\quad\quad 250 = 5.2 + \text{magnetic force}$

$\therefore\quad\quad \text{magnetic force} = 250 - 5.2$

$\quad\quad\quad\quad\quad\quad = 244.8 \text{ N}$

and this is the least magnetic force required to stop the work sliding along the table.

If a wheel of smaller diameter is used for the same torque, a greater tangential force will be exerted since torque = force × radius, therefore, the work would slip unless the magnetic force were to be increased. If the magnetic force is increased and the work does not slip the wheel would wear more quickly than one of a larger diameter because of the greater tangential force exerted.

Example 5 (MT2)

A double-purchase winch is fitted with a hand-brake as shown in Fig. 7.8. If the coefficient of friction between the brake block and the braking surface is 0.4, calculate the least hand force F N that must be applied to prevent a load of 520 N from running back with acceleration.

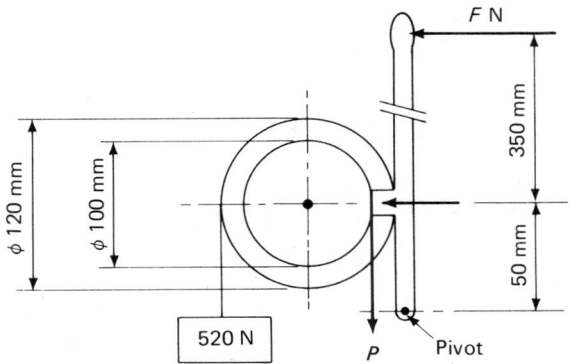

Fig. 7.8

The first step will be to obtain the force P required to just stop the load drum revolving. To do this the torque on the drum shaft must be obtained:

now
$$\text{torque} = \text{force} \times \text{radius}$$
$$= 520 \times 0.06 \text{ Nm}$$
$$= \text{torque due to force } P$$

$\therefore$
$$520 \times 0.12 = 0.1P$$
$$P = 520 \times 1.2 \text{ N}$$
$$= 624 \text{ N}$$

It is now necessary to determine the force W pressing the braking surfaces together.

Since
$$\text{coefficient of friction} = \frac{P}{W}$$
$$0.4 = \frac{624}{W}$$
$$W = \frac{624}{0.4}$$
$$= 1560 \text{ N}$$

To obtain the hand force F it will be necessary to take moments about the pivot:
$$\text{clockwise moment} = 400F \text{ Nmm}$$
$$= 0.4F \text{ Nm}$$
$$\text{anticlockwise moment} = 1560 \times 0.05 \text{ Nm}$$

$\therefore$
$$0.4F = 1560 \times 0.05$$

since anticlockwise moments = clockwise moments for equilibrium (chapter 5, paragraph 5.4)
$$F = \frac{1560 \times 0.05}{0.4}$$
$$= 195 \text{ N}$$

Example 6 (MT2)

A casting is to be clamped to a milling machine table by four clamps, one of which is shown in Fig. 7.9. The machining force is 800 N parallel to the surface of the machine table and at right angles to the clamps. If the coefficient of friction between all contacting surfaces is 0.15 determine the tightening force F for each bolt to prevent slipping, assuming that it is the same for each clamp, and that the clamps move with the work if it slips. Neglect the mass of the casting.

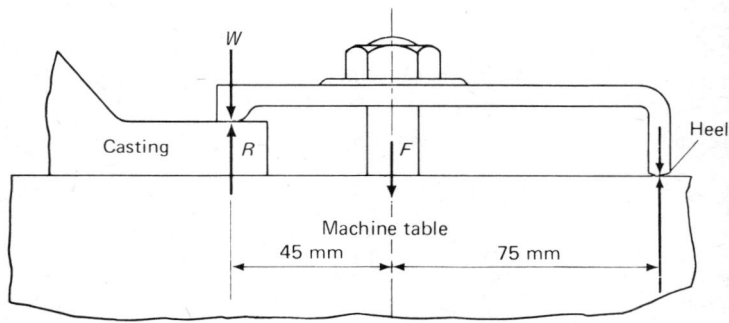

Fig. 7.9

Since the clamps will move with the casting if it slides along the table there will be one pair of surfaces providing frictional resistance at each clamp, therefore for four clamps there will be four pairs of such surfaces.

∴ 	machining force $P = 4 \mu W$

∴ 	$800 = 4 \times 0.15 \times W$

∴ 	$$W = \frac{200}{0.15} \text{ N}$$

To determine F take moments about the heel of the clamp

$$120W = 75F$$

∴ 	$$\frac{200 \times 120}{0.15} = 75F$$

∴ 	$$F = \frac{200 \times 120}{0.15 \times 75}$$

$$= 2133 \text{ N}$$

Example 7 (MT2)

A single-plate clutch exerts an axial pressure of 64 kN/m² over a friction surface area of 2000 mm². The axial thrust can be assumed to act at a radius of 84 mm and the coefficient of friction for the surfaces of contact is 0.3. Calculate the torque transmitted by the clutch when engaged.

$$\text{Take } \pi = \frac{22}{7}.$$

(Figure 7.10 shows a simple line diagram indicating the principle upon which such a clutch operates. The driven shaft will rotate when its disc contacts the friction surface with sufficient pressure.)

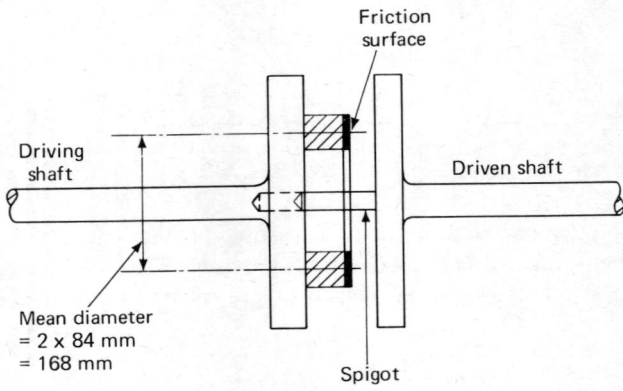

Fig. 7.10

To determine the axial force it will be necessary to remember that:

$$\text{force} = \text{pressure} \times \text{area}$$

now   the area = 2000 mm²

$$= 2 \times 10^{-3} \text{ m}$$

∴   axial thrust = $64 \times 2 \times 10^{-3}$ kN

$$= 128 \text{ N}$$

since $P = \mu W$

friction force $P = 0.3 \times 128$ N

$$= 38.4 \text{ N}$$

now   torque = force × radius
                            = 38.4 × 84 Nmm
                            = 38.4 × 0.084 Nm
                            = 3.225 Nm

Wasteful friction occurs in the workshop where it is necessary for one surface to slide over another in order to attain the necessary motion in a machine, as in the following examples:

(a) a milling machine table moving on its slides,
(b) the saddle of a lathe moving along the lathe bed,
(c) the ram of a shaping machine moving along its slides,
(d) any machine-shaft running in its bearings.

In all such cases the presence of friction is a disadvantage because some of the input energy required to give the necessary motion is wasted, which means that there will be less energy available for doing useful work at the machine tool. Friction is also the cause of wear on bearings and machine tools and is also responsible for generating heat with a consequent rise of temperature which could prove to be serious unless checked by the use of a coolant. It follows, therefore, that all possible steps should be taken to minimize the harmful effects of friction.

7.4 Methods of reducing friction

The reduction of frictional resistance between two sliding surfaces can be brought about by:

(a) selecting suitable materials for the surfaces which are to slide together, for example, in a plain bearing, a steel shaft should rotate in a white metal or suitable bronze bearing,
(b) using a suitable lubricant,
(c) making the sliding surfaces smooth by scraping, lapping, or honing,
(d) the use of ball or roller bearings,
(e) keeping the sliding surfaces free from dust, grit, and foreign matter.

The selection of the methods to be used will depend on the type and design of the machine or engine and the conditions under which it will operate. One of the objects of using a lubricant is to keep the sliding surfaces apart, as shown in the exaggerated sketch in Fig. 7.11. The layers of the lubricant itself slide over each other with little resistance. Suitable substances which act as lubricants include greases and oils, graphite, and molybdenum disulphide. Since friction also generates heat a lubricant can also act as a coolant, but its viscosity ('fluidity') must

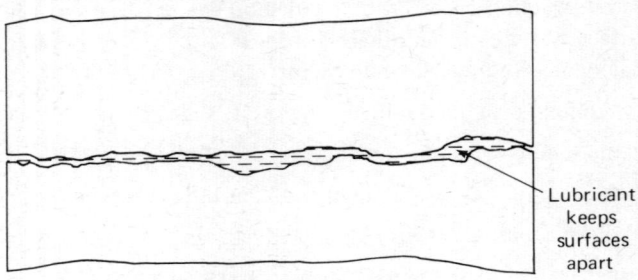

Fig. 7.11

suit the existing conditions; for example, if the viscosity of the oil is too low it will tend to run away too quickly thus allowing the surfaces to come into contact, thereby causing an increase of friction and temperature. The operating temperature under which a lubricant is used is also important because an increase of this temperature will tend to lower the viscosity and eventually allow contact of the sliding surfaces.

In the use of ball or roller bearings the moving surfaces are kept apart by freely-rotating balls or rollers. A simple experiment will show that the frictional resistance is reduced when rollers (or balls) are used, for example, in moving a machine from one part of a workshop to another, the job is made easier by inserting rollers (or lengths of cylindrical piping) between the base of the machine and the workshop floor.

Problems (MT2)

[Where applicable, assume that $g = 9.81$ m/s^2.]

1. The tailstock of a lathe has a mass of 42.2 kg. If the coefficient of friction between the base of the tailstock and the lathe bed is 0.15 calculate the force required to just move the tailstock along the lathe bed with constant velocity:
   (a) when the force is applied horizontally, and
   (b) when the force is applied in a downward direction at 30° to the horizontal.
   Ans: (a) 62.1 N. (b) 78.5 N.

FRICTION

2. A machine having a mass of 1300 kg is to be moved along a horizontal machine-shop floor. If the coefficient of friction between the base of the machine and the floor is 0.5, determine the force required to just move the machine with constant velocity when:
   (a) the force is applied horizontally,
   (b) the force is applied in an upward direction at 15° to the horizontal,
   (c) when the machine is mounted on rollers and the force is applied horizontally, given that the coefficient of friction in this case is 0.02.
   Ans: (a) 6.375 kN. (b) 5.82 kN. (c) 255 N.

3. A milling machine table has a mass of 210 kg and the job being milled together with its fixtures has a mass of 63 kg. The coefficient of friction between the machine table and its slides is 0.15. If the horizontal cutting force is 500 N, calculate the traversing force required to just keep the machine table moving with constant velocity during the machining operation.
   Ans: 901.8 N.

4. During an experiment to determine the coefficient of friction between two steel surfaces a slider with a flat steel base was hauled with constant velocity along a horizontal steel surface. A cord was attached to the slider and passed over a pulley, the remainder hanging vertically with a scale pan attached at the bottom end as shown in Fig. 7.12.

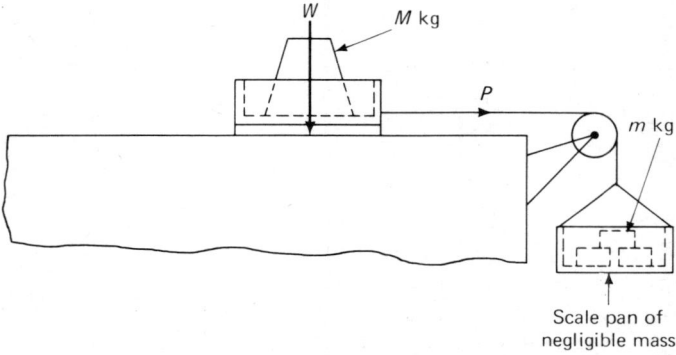

Fig. 7.12

MECHANICAL ENGINEERING SCIENCE

The following table gives the mass m kg to provide sufficient force in newtons to just haul the slider and its mass M kg with constant velocity.

m kg	0.44	0.56	0.65	0.78	0.88	1.00
M kg	0	0.5	1.0	1.5	2.0	2.5
m kg	1.10	1.22	1.30			
M kg	3.0	3.50	4.0			

The mass of the slider is 2 kg.

Plot a graph of m kg against (M + mass of slider) kg, draw the straight line of closest fit and estimate the probable value for the coefficient of friction between these two steel surfaces.
Ans: 0.22.

5. In a similar experiment to that carried out in the previous question, the slider was replaced by one with a base of brake-lining material, and the following results were obtained:

m kg	1.15	1.40	1.64	1.85	2.05	2.32
M kg	0.4	0.8	1.2	1.6	2.0	2.4
m kg	2.55	2.80				
M kg	2.8	3.2				

Plot a graph of m against M, draw the straight line of closest fit, and use the graph to estimate a probable value of the coefficient of friction for brake-lining material on steel. Also determine the mass of the slider.
Ans: 0.59, 1.543 kg.

6. A steel bar is turned to a diameter of 80 mm on a lathe using a three-jaw chuck. If, during the cutting operation, the lathe tool exerts a torque of 48 Nm on the bar and the coefficient of friction between the chuck jaws and the work is 0.25, calculate the least radial force that must be exerted by each jaw to prevent the bar slipping in the chuck.
Ans: 1600 N (1.6 kN).

7. A steel block of mass 3.7 kg is placed on a magnetic chuck for a surface-grinding operation. The coefficient of friction between the block and the magnetic chuck is 0.16. If the chuck exerts a maximum magnetic force of 400 N, calculate the maximum torque that can be exerted by a grinding wheel of 250 mm diameter.
Ans: 8.726 Nm.

FRICTION

8. A single-plate clutch exerts an axial pressure of 80 kN/m². The area of the friction surface has internal and external diameters of 70 mm and 140 mm respectively, the axial thrust can be assumed to act at the mean of these two radii. If the coefficient of friction is 0.3, calculate the torque transmitted by the clutch when engaged.
Take $\pi = \frac{22}{7}$.
Ans: 14.55 Nm.

9. A steel block of mass 3.25 kg is to have its thickness reduced on a shaping machine. The block is to be held in position between the jaws of a machine vice which has a mass of 10 kg. The coefficient of friction between the vice jaws is 0.25. The maximum thrust on the work and the vice, due to cutting, is 1.2 kN.

   (a) If the line of the vice jaws is parallel to the cutting stroke, determine the minimum tightening force required on the vice jaws to prevent the block from slipping.

   (b) The machine vice is held in position by two bolts, each with a minimum cross-sectional area of 125 mm². The coefficient of friction between the base of the vice and the machine table is 0.2. If each bolt is tightened by a force of 615 N in excess of the minimum required to prevent the vice from slipping on the machine table, calculate the tensile stress set up in each bolt.
   Ans: (a) 2.4 kN. (b) 28.4 MN/m².

10. A winch is fitted with a hand-brake in the form shown in Fig. 7.13. If the coefficient of friction between the brake block and the braking

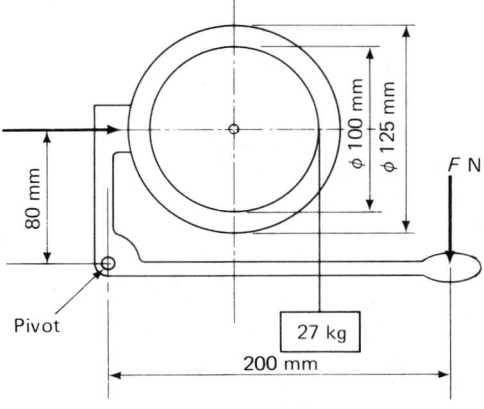

Fig. 7.13

surface is 0.5, calculate the least hand force F newtons required to prevent the mass of 27 kg from running back with acceleration.
Ans: 169.6 N.

11. The set-up for routing out a die on a vertical milling machine is shown in Fig. 7.14. The die is held in position by two clamps. The end mill used is 20 mm diameter and it exerts a torque of 1.26 Nm throughout the cutting operation. Assuming that the coefficient of friction between all surfaces of contact is 0.15, determine the minimum tightening force required on each clamp for the machining position shown. Neglect the mass of the die.
Ans: 700 N.

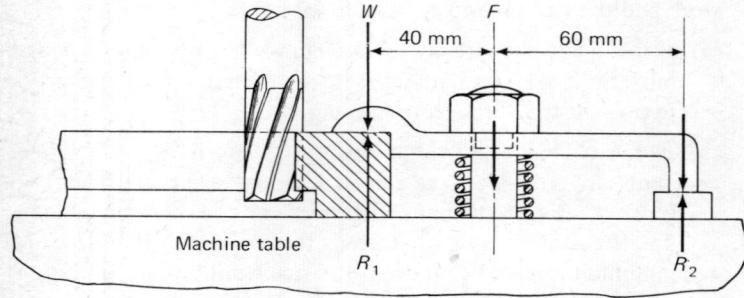

Fig. 7.14

12. A short cylindrical steel bar is to have a hole 24 mm diameter drilled through along its axis. The bar is to be held in a three-jaw chuck, the drill being fed into the work by the tailstock operating handle. The tailstock has a mass of 40 kg and the horizontal thrust due to the axial drilling force is 240 N. During the operation the bar transmits a torque of 2.4 Nm to the drill.

   (a) If the coefficient of friction for both pairs of clamping surfaces is 0.15, calculate the minimum force required to clamp the tailstock in position so that it will not slip during the drilling operation.

   (b) If the coefficient of friction between the work and the chuck jaws is 0.25, determine the minimum radial force that must be exerted by each jaw to prevent the work from slipping in the chuck.

Ans: (a) 407.6 N. (b) 320 N.
(Longitudinal slip occurs before circumferential slip.)

8. Work and power transmission

8.1 Work done by a constant force

When a force causes an object to move, the force is said to perform some work. No work is done if there is no motion. Thus, in the workshop, work is done in every machining operation since force and motion are both essential to such an operation, for example, work is done:

(a) by a milling cutter as it rotates and cuts metal from a component being traversed past the arbor,
(b) by a lathe tool cutting work revolving past its tip,
(c) by a drill revolving and boring a hole,
(d) by a craftsman filing a piece of metal held in a vice.

The amount of work done is equal to the product of the force and the distance moved in the direction of the force. In SI units force is measured in newtons (N) and distance in metres (m), therefore, work done in newton metres (Nm) is equal to the product of the force F newtons and distance d metres. The unit newton metre is called a joule (J) when used as a measure of work or energy, where energy is the ability to perform some work. Thus

$$\text{work done} = Fd \text{ joules}$$

If the force is inclined to the direction of motion as in the simple slider mechanism shown in Fig. 8.1 the formula for work done will have to be modified since the force F will have to be resolved into the component in line with the direction of motion.

Assuming that the force F is applied at a constant angle θ to the direction of motion

$$\text{work done on the slider} = dF \cos \theta \text{ joules}$$

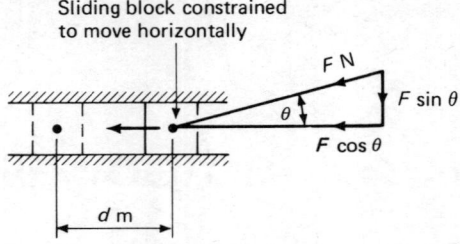

Fig. 8.1

Example 1 (MT1)

A drilling machine operator raises the machine table a distance of 400 mm. If the table has a mass of 70 kg calculate the work done in raising the table.

To lift the table the operator has to overcome the gravitational pull (weight) of the table, which is equal to 70×9.81 N:

$$\text{distance moved} = 400 \text{ mm}$$
$$= 0.4 \text{ m}$$
$$\text{work done} = \text{force} \times \text{distance moved}$$
$$= 70 \times 9.81 \times 0.4 \text{ (J)}$$
$$= 274.7 \text{ J}$$

Example 2 (MT1)

A slab mill exerts a constant tangential force of 900 N during a milling operation. If the length of work fed past the cutter is 225 mm, calculate the work done during the cutting operation:

$$\text{work done} = \text{force} \times \text{distance}$$
$$= 900 \times 0.225 \text{ J}$$
$$= 202.5 \text{ J}$$

Note, again, the conversion of millimetres to metres in order to obtain the basic unit of work.

Example 3 (MT1)

A fuel conveyor system at a power station consists of a number of trucks each of which has a mass of 4240 kg when fully loaded. The fuel is conveyed in the trucks up an inclined railway with a gradient of 1 in 2.5 measured along the slope. If there is a constant frictional resistance to motion of 250 N, calculate the work done in hauling a fully laden truck 20 m up the incline.

It will be helpful in this problem to draw a simple diagram of the situation as shown in Fig. 8.2. In this case work has to be done against gravity and frictional resistance.

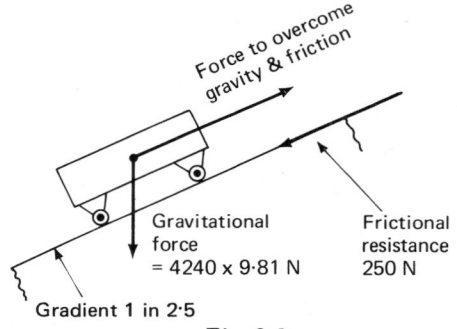

Fig. 8.2

The work done against friction will be equal to the constant frictional resisting force of 250 N multiplied by the distance moved of 20 m

$$= 250 \times 20 \text{ J}$$
$$= 5000 \text{ J}$$
$$= 5 \text{ kJ}$$

The gravitational force to be overcome

$$= 4240 \times 9.81 \text{ N}$$
$$= 41\ 600 \text{ N}$$
$$= 41.6 \text{ kN}$$

The gradient is 1 in 2.5, that is, the truck will be raised a vertical distance of 1 m while travelling a distance of 2.5 m along the slope, therefore, the vertical distance in 20 m along the slope

$$= \frac{20}{2.5} \text{ m}$$
$$= 8 \text{ m}$$

∴ work done against gravity = 41.6 × 8 kJ
= 332.8 kJ
∴ total work done = 332.8 + 5 kJ
= 337.8 kJ

Note that it needs less work to raise an object along an incline than it does to raise it vertically upward.

Example 4 (MT2)

A groove 200 mm long is to be cut by hand in a brass sheet using a scoring tool. If a constant force of 150 N is applied downwards along the cutting tip which is inclined at 10° to the vertical, as shown in Fig. 8.3, calculate the work done per stroke.

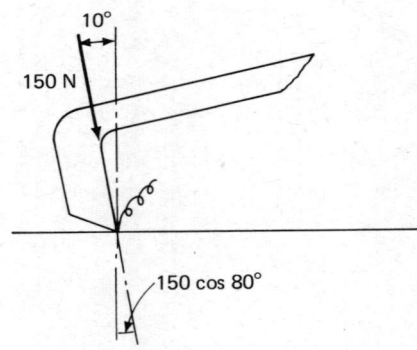

Fig. 8.3

Since the direction of the motion is horizontal we will require the horizontal component of the force

$$= 150 \cos 80° \text{ N}$$
$$= 150 \times 0.1736 \text{ N}$$
$$= 26.04 \text{ N}$$

∴ work done per stroke = 26.04 × 0.2 J
= 5.208 J

WORK AND POWER TRANSMISSION

8.2 Work done in overcoming friction

One of the ever present evils as far as friction is concerned is the fact that to operate any machine some energy, in varying degrees, always has to be 'wasted' in overcoming friction and this energy will, therefore, not be available for the purpose of doing 'useful' work.

Since the force needed to overcome friction P is equal to μW, the energy needed to overcome friction

$$= \mu W d$$

where
μ = coefficient of friction
W = the force pressing the surfaces together
d = distance moved against friction

Example 5 (MT2)

The ram of a shaping machine has a mass of 80 kg and for a particular job is set to have a cutting stroke of 125 mm. The coefficient of friction between the ram and its slide is 0.1. If the cutting force exerted throughout the stroke is 720 N, calculate:

(a) the work done in overcoming friction during one cutting stroke,
(b) the total work done during one cutting stroke.

(a) The force pressing the ram to the slide W

$$= 80 \times 9.81 \text{ N}$$
$$= 784.8 \text{ N}$$

the force required to overcome friction P

$$= \mu W$$
$$= 0.1 \times 784.8 \text{ N}$$
$$= 78.48 \text{ N}$$

therefore work done against friction

$$= 78.48 \times 0.125 \text{ J}$$
$$= 9.81 \text{ J}.$$

(b) Useful work done due to the cutting force in one stroke

$$= 720 \times 0.125 \text{ J}$$
$$= 90 \text{ J}$$

therefore the total work done during one cutting stroke

$$= 90 + 9.81 \text{ J}$$
$$= 99.81 \text{ J}.$$

Example 6 (MT2)

The table of a planing machine and the job it carries have a total mass of 1000 kg. The coefficient of friction between the table and its slides is 0.107, and the length of stroke is 2 m. Cutting takes place in one direction only and is intermittent, amounting to 1.6 m of the stroke. If the cutting force is 1.25 kN and five complete cutting and return strokes are made in one minute calculate the ratio

$$\frac{\text{work done against friction per minute}}{\text{total work done per minute}}$$

The force W pressing the table to the slide

$$= 1000 \times 9.81 \text{ N}$$
$$= 9.81 \text{ kN}$$

the force required to overcome friction

$$= \mu W$$
$$= 0.107 \times 9.81 \text{ kN}$$
$$= 1.05 \text{ kN}$$

distance moved in one minute allowing for cutting and return

$$= 2 \times 5 \times 2 \text{ m}$$
$$= 20 \text{ m}$$

therefore work done against friction $= 1.05 \times 20$ kJ/min
$$= 21 \text{ kJ/min}$$

cutting velocity $= 1.6 \times 5$ m/min
$$= 8 \text{ m/min}$$

work done in cutting $= 1.25 \times 8$ kJ/min
$$= 10 \text{ kJ/min}$$

total work done per minute = 21 + 10 kJ
$$= 31 \text{ kJ}$$
$$\frac{\text{work to friction per minute}}{\text{total work per minute}} = \frac{21}{31}$$

8.3 Work diagrams and work done by a variable force

By plotting a graph of applied force against the distance moved, the work done may be represented by the area covered by the graph, providing that the actual measurements of the horizontal and vertical axes are replaced by the units they represent. Such graphs are called work diagrams.

Suppose that a constant horizontal force of 50 N is applied to the tailstock of a lathe to move it a distance of 0.5 m, the resulting work diagram would be rectangular as shown in Fig. 8.4.

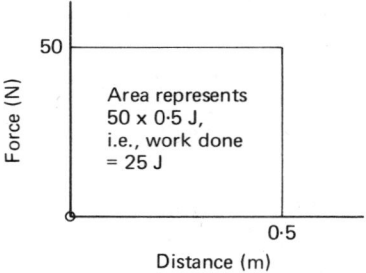

Fig. 8.4

Applied forces are not necessarily always constant, in fact in practice they are more likely to be variable. However, the area of the work diagram may be obtained by multiplying the mean height (representing the average value of the applied force) by the length of the base (representing the distance moved). In such cases the work done formula is modified to

work done = average force × distance moved.

If the work done and the distance moved are known the average force can be determined by dividing the work done by the distance moved.

Example 7 (MT2)

During a tensile test on a steel specimen a gradually applied force of 6.25 kN produced an extension of 25 μm and when the force was increased gradually to 25 kN the extension was 100 μm. Assuming that the extension is directly proportional to the applied load draw the work diagram and determine the work done on the specimen in changing the extension from 25 μm to 100 μm.

Since the extension is directly proportional to the applied force the graph will produce a straight line passing through the origin, as shown in Fig. 8.5.

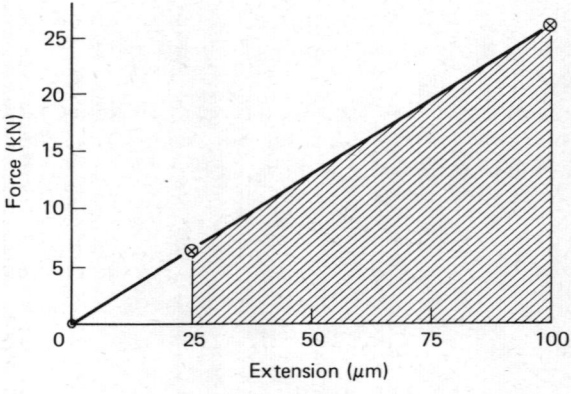

Fig. 8.5

In this case the work diagram is in the form of a trapezoid, the area of which is the product of the average of the parallel sides and the perpendicular distance between them. The shaded portion in Fig. 8.5 shows the area concerned.

Therefore, work done $= \left[\dfrac{6.25 + 25}{2}\right] \times (100 - 25)$

$= 15.625 \times 75$ kNμm (Nmm)

$= 15.625 \times 0.075$ J

$= 1.172$ J

If the force varies in an irregular manner or the graph formed is bounded partly by a curve, it will be necessary to use the mid-ordinate rule to determine the area covered. This entails dividing the base into a number of equal parts and erecting vertical ordinates from the mid-points of these divisions. The average height of these ordinates multiplied by the base length gives the approximate area.

Example 8 (MT2)

A slider in a linkage mechanism is subjected to a varying force when moved along its path of motion. The following table gives the force F newtons being exerted at various distances in its path of motion (S mm).

S mm	0	20	40	60	80	100
F newtons	750	730	690	610	450	130

Draw the work diagram to suitable scales and then determine the approximate amount of work done on the slider during this period of motion. The graph is shown in Fig. 8.6.

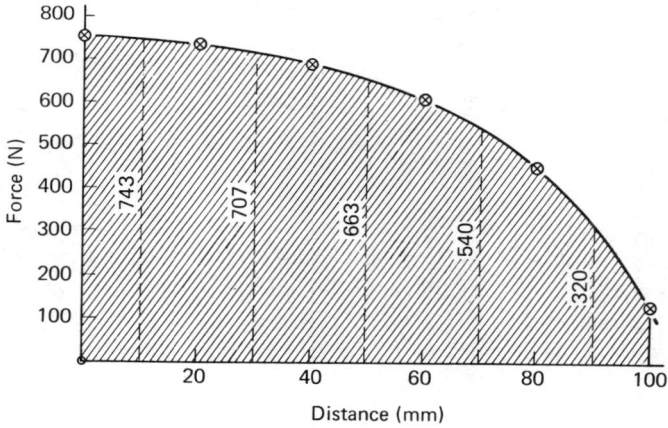

Fig. 8.6

From the graph the average mid-ordinate

$$= \frac{743 + 707 + 663 + 540 + 320}{5}$$

$$= \frac{2973}{5} \text{ N}$$

$$= 594.6 \text{ N}$$

work done = average mid-ordinate × base length

$$= 594.6 \times 0.1 \text{ J}$$

$$= 59.46 \text{ J}$$

8.4 Speed and velocity

So far, we have dealt with amounts of work done without considering the time taken, but obviously this factor must be taken into account. For example, to obtain a good surface finish an ideal surface machining speed is required depending on the type of machining, the cutting tool material and the metal being cut. The following are a few approximate ranges of cutting speeds used when turning with a high-speed steel tool:

Material	Surface speed mm/s
Cast iron	200 – 400
Mild steel (black)	350 – 500
Mild steel (bright)	400 – 1000
Brass	1000 – 2000
Bronze	200 – 400

From the units it is evident that speed is distance travelled per unit time:

$$\text{average speed} = \frac{\text{distance travelled}}{\text{time taken}} \text{ m/s}$$

Velocity is speed with direction taken into account, and is measured in the same units as speed (m/s), velocity is a vector quantity (see chapter 5, paragraph 5.1). Velocities are often quoted in magnitude only, without any reference to direction, this happens when the velocity is assumed or known to be in connection with motion in a straight line; this sort of velocity is known as linear velocity.

Angular velocity There are many instances in the workshop when work is done in rotation, such as: turning on a lathe where the work rotates, or milling where the cutter rotates. In order to determine the rate of doing work in such cases it is necessary to know the rate of rotation. This can be done either by counting the number of revolutions per unit time, that is, rotational frequency in revolutions per second or revolutions per minute. Alternatively, we may obtain the angular velocity in radians per second and this can be related directly to the peripheral velocity at any radius in metres per second. First we must define the angular measure known as the radian.

An angle of one radian is subtended by an arc equal in length to the radius of the arc. Considering one revolution the length of arc becomes

WORK AND POWER TRANSMISSION

the circumference of the circle, which is $2\pi \times$ radius. Since the angle subtended is directly proportional to the length of arc, the angle turned through in one revolution is 2π radians, that is:

$$1 \text{ rev} = 2\pi \text{ radians}$$
$$1 \text{ rev/s} = 2\pi \text{ rad/s}$$
$$1 \text{ rev/min} = 2\pi \text{ rad/min}$$

In practice, rotational frequency is generally measured in rev/min, however it is often convenient to convert this to an angular velocity in rad/s.

$$N \text{ rev/min} = 2\pi N \text{ rad/min}$$
$$= \frac{2\pi N}{60} \text{ rad/s}$$
$$= \frac{\pi N}{30} \text{ rad/s}$$

To convert rad/s to rev/min, given that the Greek symbol ω is used for angular velocity in rad/s,

$$\omega \text{ rad/s} = \frac{\omega}{2\pi} \text{ rev/s}$$
$$= \frac{60\omega}{2\pi} \text{ rev/min}$$
$$= \frac{30\omega}{\pi} \text{ rev/min}$$

To convert N rev/min to a surface cutting speed when turning work of diameter d mm:

the distance moved past the tool tip in one revolution $\}$ = circumference of work

$$= \pi d$$
$$\text{cutting speed} = \pi d N \text{ mm/min}$$
$$= \frac{\pi d N}{60} \text{ mm/s}$$

If the rotational frequency N rev/min is required for a particular surface cutting speed v mm/s then

$$N = \frac{60v}{\pi d} \text{ rev/min}$$

To obtain a direct relation between peripheral velocity v m/s and angular velocity ω rad/s let us assume that the spoke of a wheel revolves through an angle θ radians as shown in Fig. 8.7.

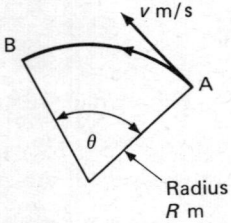

Fig. 8.7

Let the length of arc AB be S metres, then since S = radius of arc (R m)
when $\qquad \theta = 1$ rad
then $\qquad S = R\theta$
for any angle θ radians.
If the point moves from A to B in a time of t seconds then

$$\frac{S}{t} = R\frac{\theta}{t}$$

now $\qquad \dfrac{S}{t}$ = peripheral velocity v m/s

and $\qquad \dfrac{\theta}{t}$ = angular velocity ω rad/s

$$v = R\omega \text{ m/s}$$
or $\qquad v = 10^3 \, R\omega$ mm/s

Example 9 (MT1)

The machine spindle on a lathe rotates at the rate of 210 rev/min.
(a) What is the angular velocity of the spindle in rad/s?
(b) What surface cutting speed in mm/s will this produce when the diameter of the work being turned is 30 mm?
(c) What spindle speed (in rev/min) will be required to produce a cutting speed of 440 mm/s on work 20 mm diameter?

Take $\pi = \frac{22}{7}$.

(a) Since N rev/min $= \dfrac{\pi N}{30}$ rad/s

$$210 \text{ rev/min} = \dfrac{22 \times 210}{7 \times 30} \text{ rad/s}$$

$$= 22 \text{ rad/s}$$

(b) cutting speed $v = \dfrac{\pi d N}{60}$ mm/s

hence
$$v = \dfrac{22 \times 30 \times 210}{7 \times 60}$$

$$= 330 \text{ mm/s}$$

or
$$v = R\omega$$
$$= 15 \times 22$$
$$= 330 \text{ mm/s}$$

(c) spindle speed $N = \dfrac{60v}{\pi d}$ rev/min

$$= \dfrac{440 \times 7 \times 60}{22 \times 20} \text{ rev/min}$$

$$= 420 \text{ rev/min}$$

8.5 Power consumption in machining operations

Power is the rate of doing work. In any machining operation it is not only important to know the amount of work done, but also the rate at which the work is done. This is because it is necessary to apply tool cutting forces at specified speeds to keep tool wear and tear to a minimum and to obtain a good surface finish. In addition, it is important to have a source of energy which will be sufficient to overcome frictional resistances and to do the machining work at the required rate. Remember that energy is the ability to do work. In the case of machines in the workshop, the source of driving energy is generally an electric motor with a known power rating.

$$\text{power} = \dfrac{\text{work done}}{\text{time taken}} \text{ joules/second (J/s)}$$

also
$$\text{power} = \text{applied force} \times \text{velocity J/s}$$

The SI unit of power is the watt (W)

where
$$1 \text{ watt} = 1 \text{ joule/second}$$
$$(1W = 1 \text{ J/s})$$

Example 10 (MT1)

What power (in watts) is absorbed in cutting:

(a) during a turning operation in which the tangential cutting force is 600 N and the cutting speed is 420 mm/s.

(b) during a shaping operation in which the cutting force is 820 N and the cutting stroke, which takes six seconds, is 150 mm long?

(a) Remembering that 1 watt
$$= 1 \text{ J/s} = 1 \text{ Nm/s}$$

we must convert the cutting speed in mm/s to m/s
$$420 \text{ mm/s} = 0.42 \text{ m/s}$$

now
$$\text{power} = \text{force} \times \text{velocity}$$
$$= 600 \times 0.42 \text{ W}$$
$$= 252 \text{ W}$$

(b) In this case we use the alternative formula

$$\text{power} = \frac{\text{work done}}{\text{time taken}}$$

$$= \frac{\text{force} \times \text{distance}}{\text{time taken}}$$

$$= \frac{820 \times 0.15}{6} \text{ W} \quad (150 \text{ mm} = 0.15 \text{ m})$$

$$= 20.5 \text{ W}$$

Example 11 (MT1)

In a milling operation the horizontal force exerted by the cutter was 880 N. The diameter of the cutter was 112 mm and its rotational frequency was 80 rev/min. Determine:

(a) the surface cutting speed in mm/s,

(b) the power absorbed in cutting, and

(c) the power due to feed if this is at the rate of 0.125 mm per tooth and there are 24 teeth on the cutter. Assume that the average feed force is equal to the tangential cutting force.

Take $\pi = \frac{22}{7}$.

(a) From the previous paragraph the cutting speed

$$v = \frac{\pi d N}{60} \text{ mm/s}$$

$$= \frac{22 \times 112 \times 80}{7 \times 60} \text{ mm/s}$$

$$= 469.3 \text{ mm/s}$$

(b) power = force × velocity
= 880 × 469.3 Nmm/s

It is usual to express power in the basic unit of the watt, it is necessary, therefore, to convert the cutting velocity to m/s:

469.3 mm/s = 0.4693 m/s

power = 880 × 0.4693 W

= 413 W

(c) Feed = 0.125 mm per tooth

= 0.125 × 24 mm per rev

since the cutter makes 80 rev/min

feed velocity = 0.125 × 24 × 80 mm/min

= 240 mm/min

= 0.004 m/s

feed power = force × feed velocity

= 880 × 0.004 W

= 3.52 W

Example 12 (MT1)

In a grinding operation the surface grinding speed is 25.5 m/s and the tangential grinding force is 40 N. The work is fed past the grinding wheel at 120 mm/s. The coolant is pumped vertically upwards a distance of

1.5 m and is applied to the grinding zone at the rate of 40 l/min. Determine:

(a) the power absorbed in grinding,
(b) the power due to the feed, assuming that the feed force is equal to the tangential grinding force, and
(c) the power needed to pump the coolant up to the grinding zone. (One litre of coolant has a mass of 0.8 kg.)

(a)   Grinding power = grinding force x velocity

$$= 40 \times 25.5 \text{ W}$$
$$= 1020 \text{ W}$$
$$= 1.02 \text{ kW}$$

(b)   Feed velocity = 120 mm/s
$$= 0.12 \text{ m/s}$$
feed power = 40 x 0.12 W
$$= 4.8 \text{ W}$$

(c)   Rate of flow = 40 l/min
$$= 32 \text{ kg/min}$$

To raise the coolant at this rate the weight (gravitational pull) of the coolant must be overcome hence

$$32 \text{ kg/min} = 32 \times 9.81 \text{ N/min}$$

work done per minute in raising the coolant 1.5 m

$$= 32 \times 9.81 \times 1.5 \text{ J/min}$$
$$= \frac{48 \times 9.81}{60} \text{ J/s (W)}$$
$$= 7.848 \text{ W}$$

8.6 Output to input efficiency calculations

In any machine, which is after all a device used for the purpose of doing some useful work, there must be a source of energy made available in order to drive the machine. This source of driving energy is called the

WORK AND POWER TRANSMISSION

input, the actual useful work done being called the output. Since some of the driving energy (input) will always be lost in the transmission of power from input to output chiefly because of friction, the output will always be less than the input. It follows, therefore, that

$$\text{energy wasted} = \text{energy input} - \text{work output}$$

$$\therefore \quad \text{output} = \text{input} - \text{power wasted}$$

The performance of a machine, therefore, can be expressed by its efficiency where

$$\text{efficiency} = \frac{\text{useful work output}}{\text{energy input}} \times 100\%$$

or

$$\text{efficiency} = \frac{\text{power output}}{\text{power input}} \times 100\%$$

Efficiency is simply a ratio and will have no units itself, but the input and output must both be in the same units. Note that the efficiency will always be less than 100%.

Example 13 (MT1)

In a particular shaping operation the stroke was set to give a mean cutting speed of 360 mm/s and the cutting force was 1.6 kN. If the electric motor provides 0.8 kW during the operation, determine the efficiency of the shaper during the cutting stroke.

The input power = 0.8 kW

To determine the output power it is necessary to convert the cutting speed to m/s so that the output power can be calculated in kilowatts:

$$\text{cutting speed} = 0.36 \text{ m/s}$$

$$\text{output power} = 1.6 \times 0.36 \text{ kW}$$

$$= 0.576 \text{ kW}$$

$$\text{efficiency} = \frac{\text{output}}{\text{input}}$$

$$= \frac{0.576}{0.8} \times 100\%$$

$$= 72\%$$

The efficiency of this machine will not always be at this value, since it will depend on the cutting force and the cutting velocity. Actually, the efficiency of any machine will not be constant, for example, if the machine is idling the efficiency is zero.

Example 14 (MT1)

A milling machine is driven by an electric motor which provided 4 kW during a particular machining operation. The cutter used had a diameter of 100 mm and its rotational frequency was 105 rev/min. If the efficiency of the power transmission was 75% determine the tangential cutting force exerted by the cutter.

Take $\pi = \frac{22}{7}$.

First determine the output power from

$$\text{efficiency} = \frac{\text{output power}}{\text{input power}}$$

$$0.75 = \frac{\text{output power}}{4}$$

output power = 4 × 0.75

= 3 kW

= cutting force × cutting velocity

now   cutting velocity = $\frac{\pi d N}{60}$ mm/s

$$= \frac{22 \times 100 \times 105}{7 \times 60} \text{ mm/s}$$

= 550 mm/s

= 0.55 m/s

3 kW = 0.55 × cutting force

cutting force = $\frac{3}{0.55}$ kN

= 5.455 kN

Example 15 (MT2)

A bar of steel is being turned to a diameter of 77 mm using a tungsten-carbide tipped tool. The cutting force is 770 N, the feed is 0.25 mm per revolution and the depth of cut is 1.25 mm. The electric motor provides a power of 2.25 kW continuously throughout the cutting operation. If the efficiency under these conditions is 70%, determine:

(a) the cutting velocity in mm/s,

(b) the speed of the machine spindle in rev/min,

WORK AND POWER TRANSMISSION

(c) the cutting pressure exerted by the tool tip, and
(d) the volume of metal removed per minute.

Take $\pi = \frac{22}{7}$.

(a) Since the details required depend on the output power, the first step will be to obtain this power from

$$\text{efficiency} = \frac{\text{output power}}{\text{input power}}$$

$$0.7 = \frac{\text{output power}}{2.25}$$

$\therefore$ output power = 0.7 × 2.25 kW
= cutting force × cutting velocity
= 0.77 × cutting velocity kW

since 770 N is 0.77 kN this will give the cutting velocity in m/s:

$$0.7 \times 2.25 = 0.77 \times \text{cutting velocity}$$

$\therefore$ $$\text{cutting velocity} = \frac{0.7 \times 2.25}{0.77} \text{ m/s}$$

$$= 2045 \text{ mm/s}$$

(b) Now cutting velocity = $\frac{\pi d N}{60}$ mm/s

where N = rev/min
and d = diameter in mm

$\therefore$ $$2045 = \frac{22 \times 77 \times N}{7 \times 60}$$

$\therefore$ $$N = \frac{2045 \times 60 \times 7}{22 \times 77} \text{ rev/min}$$

$$= 507 \text{ rev/min}$$

(c) The cutting pressure = $\dfrac{\text{cutting force}}{\text{area of cut}}$

area of cut = feed/rev × depth of cut
= 0.25 × 1.25 mm^2

$\therefore$ cutting pressure = $\dfrac{770}{0.25 \times 1.25}$ N/mm^2 (MN/m^2)

= 2464 MN/m^2

= 2.464 GN/m^2

(d) Volume removed/rev = πd × area of cut
= $\tfrac{22}{7}$ × 77 × 0.25 × 1.25 mm^3

Volume removed/min = 242 × $\tfrac{5}{16}$ × 507 mm^3/min
= 38 350 mm^3/min

Example 16 (MT1)

A small geared crane is driven by an electric motor which provides a driving power of 200 W when raising a load which has a mass of 60 kg. If the efficiency is 80%, how long will it take to raise the load a distance of 7.5 m?

The first step will be to obtain the output power.

From efficiency = $\dfrac{\text{output}}{\text{input}}$

$0.8 = \dfrac{\text{output}}{200}$

$\therefore$ output = 200 × 0.8 W
= 160 W

The force required to overcome the gravitational pull on the load
= 60 × 9.81 N
= 588.6 N

The work done in raising the load a distance of 7.5 m
= 588.6 × 7.5 J
= 4415 J

WORK AND POWER TRANSMISSION

Output work is provided at the rate of 160 J every second,

$$\therefore \quad \text{time taken} = \frac{4415}{160} \text{ seconds}$$
$$= 27.6 \text{ s}$$

8.7 Loss of power due to friction

It was shown in paragraph 8.2 that the energy needed to overcome friction was given by the formula:

$$\text{work required} = \mu W d$$

where
- W = force pressing the two surfaces together
- μ = coefficient of friction

and
- d = distance moved against friction

It follows, therefore, that the power loss in overcoming friction

$$= \mu W v$$

where v = the velocity of sliding

Example 17 (MT2)

The table of a horizontal milling machine has a mass of 350 kg. The job mounted on the table together with its fixtures has a mass of 17 kg. The coefficient of friction between the table and its slides is 0.1. If the feed is 250 mm/min determine the power lost due to traversing the table against friction at the required feed.

$$v = 250 \text{ mm/min}$$
$$= \frac{0.25}{60} \text{ m/s}$$
$$\mu = 0.1$$
$$W = \text{force pressing the surfaces together}$$

this is equal to the gravitational pull (weight) on the table and the job with its fixtures

$$= (350 + 17) \times 9.81 \text{ N}$$
$$= 367 \times 9.81 \text{ N}$$
$$= 3600 \text{ N}$$

now the power lost in overcoming friction

$$= \mu W v$$
$$= 0.1 \times 3600 \times \frac{0.25}{60} \text{ W}$$
$$= 1.5 \text{ W}$$

8.8 Work done and power transmitted by constant and variable torque

Consider a bar of radius R metres being turned on a lathe and subject to a tangential force F newtons as shown in Fig. 8.8.

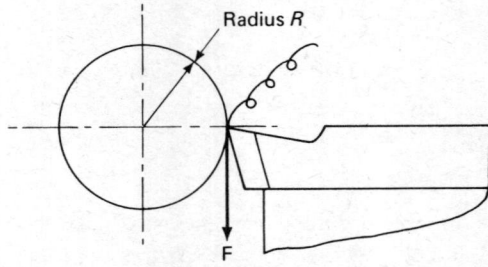

Fig. 8.8

The example shown in Fig. 8.8 is one of many in the workshop where the work is done in rotation, that is to say the distance moved either by the work past the tool tip or by a revolving cutting tool, is in a circumferential path.

work done = force F × distance

WORK AND POWER TRANSMISSION

but the distance moved in one revolution of the work is equal to the circumference

$$= 2\pi R \text{ metres}$$

$\therefore$ work done per rev $= 2\pi RF$ joules

In chapter 5, paragraph 5.7 it was stated that the product 'force × radius' is called 'torque' or 'turning moment'.

$\therefore \quad RF = $ torque T in Nm

$\therefore \quad$ work done per rev $= 2\pi T$ joules

If the work makes N revolutions, then

$$\text{work done} = 2\pi NRF$$
$$= 2\pi NT$$

We know from paragraph 8.4 that one revolution is equivalent to an angle turned through of 2π radians, therefore, in N revolutions the angle turned through is $2\pi N$ radians. The symbol θ may be used to denote any angle in radians, hence

if $\quad\quad\quad$ work done $= 2\pi NT$

and $\quad\quad\quad \theta = 2\pi N$ rad

then $\quad\quad\quad$ work done $= T\theta$

that is:
work done in joules is equal to torque in newton metres multiplied by the angle turned through in radians.

If the rotational frequency of the work is N revolutions per minute

$$\text{the power} = 2\pi NT \text{ joules/min}$$

$$= \frac{2\pi NT}{60} \text{ watts (J/s)}$$

$$= \frac{\pi NT}{30}$$

but $\quad\quad\quad \dfrac{\pi N}{30} = \omega$ rad/s

$$\text{power} = T\omega$$

that is:
power in watts is equal to torque in newton metres multiplied by the angular velocity in radians per second.

Example 18 (MT2)

A winch is driven by an electric motor which can provide a continuous power of 1.5 kW at a speed of 1260 rev/min. The overall speed reduction ratio from the motor shaft to the load drum is 18 to 1 and the overall efficiency of the power transmission is 70%. Determine, for maximum power conditions:

(a) the torque exerted by the motor shaft,

(b) the speed of the load drum in rev/min and rad/s, and

(c) the torque available at the load drum.

Take $\pi = \frac{22}{7}$.

(a) $$\text{Power} = T\omega$$

therefore to obtain the torque it will be necessary to convert rev/min to rad/s:

$$1260 \text{ rev/min} = 1260 \times \frac{\pi}{30} \text{ rad/s}$$

$$= \frac{1260 \times 22}{7 \times 30} \text{ rad/s}$$

$$= 132 \text{ rad/s}$$

$$1.5 \text{ kW} = 1500 \text{ W}$$

$$1500 = 132 T$$

$$T = \frac{1500}{132} \text{ Nm}$$

$$= 11.36 \text{ Nm}$$

(b) As the speed reduction is 18 to 1 the speed at the load drum
$$= \tfrac{1}{18} \times 1260 \text{ rev/min}$$
$$= 70 \text{ rev/min}$$

angular velocity in rad/s

$$= \frac{132}{18} \text{ rad/s}$$

$$= 7\tfrac{1}{3} \text{ rad/s}$$

WORK AND POWER TRANSMISSION 201

(c) To obtain the torque at the load drum it is necessary to determine the power output from

$$\text{efficiency} = \frac{\text{output}}{\text{input}}$$

$$0.7 = \frac{\text{output}}{1.5}$$

∴ output power = 0.7 × 1.5 kW

= 1.05 kW

= 1050 W

= $T\omega$

∴ $1050 = 7\frac{1}{3} T$

$$\text{torque } T = \frac{3 \times 1050}{22} \text{ Nm}$$

= 143.2 Nm

Example 19 (MT2)

During a grinding operation the grinding wheel exerts a tangential force of 45 N on the work at a surface speed of 33 000 mm/s. If the diameter of the grinding wheel is 200 mm and the efficiency of the machine is 77% for the given conditions, determine:

(a) the torque and power output at the grinding wheel,

(b) the torque and power input from the motor if the speed of the motor driving shaft is 1428 rev/min.

Take $\pi = \frac{22}{7}$.

(a) Since the tangential force on the cutter and its radius are known the torque T is easily obtainable from

$$T = \text{force} \times \text{radius}$$

= 45 × 100 Nmm

= 4.5 Nm

the power output can be obtained from

$$\text{power} = T\omega$$

therefore it will be necessary to obtain the angular velocity ω rad/s from

$$v = R\omega \text{ (paragraph 8.4)}$$

$$\therefore \quad 33\,000 = 100\omega$$

$$\omega = 330 \text{ rad/s}$$

$$\therefore \quad \text{power output} = 4.5 \times 330 \text{ W}$$

$$= 1485 \text{ W}$$

$$= 1.485 \text{ kW}$$

(b)
$$\text{Efficiency} = \frac{\text{output}}{\text{input}}$$

$$\therefore \quad 0.77 = \frac{1.485}{\text{input}}$$

$$\therefore \quad \text{input power} = \frac{1.485}{0.77} \text{ kW}$$

$$= 1.93 \text{ kW}$$

Angular velocity of the motor shaft

$$= 1428 \times \frac{\pi}{30} \text{ rad/s}$$

$$= \frac{1428 \times 22}{30 \times 7} \text{ rad/s}$$

$$= 149.6 \text{ rad/s}$$

$$\text{input power} = 1930 \text{ W}$$

$$= T\omega$$

$$\text{input torque } T = \frac{1930}{149.6} \text{ Nm}$$

$$= 12.9 \text{ Nm}$$

Belt drives Power may be transmitted from one shaft to another by means of a belt drive, the belt passing over pulleys which are keyed to the shafts. The effectiveness of this type of drive depends on the friction existing between the underside of the belt and the pulley-rim surface. The drive can also be made more effective by increasing the angle of lap. When at rest the tension in both sides of the belt will be equal, but when the power is being transmitted the tension in one side of the belt must exceed that on the other side (see Figs. 8.9 and 8.10).

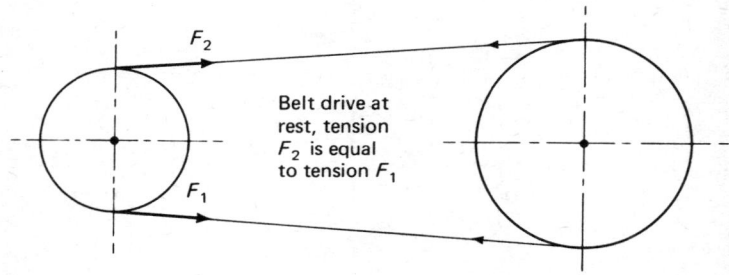

Fig. 8.9

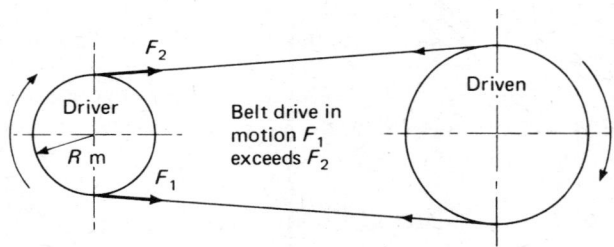

Fig. 8.10

The tight side-tension F_1 exceeds the slack side-tension F_2 when the drive is in motion. This gives a resultant tangential force on the driving pulley of $(F_1 - F_2)$ newtons.

$$\text{driving torque} = (F_1 - F_2)R$$

since

$$\text{power} = T\omega$$

then the power transmitted by the belt drive

$$= (F_1 - F_2)R\omega$$

where $\quad \omega =$ the angular velocity (rad/s)

Figure 8.11 shows a crossed-belt drive. In this case the calculations are unaffected, but the increased angle of lap increases the effectiveness of the drive. It will also be observed that the directions of rotation of the driver and driven pulleys are reversed in this case.

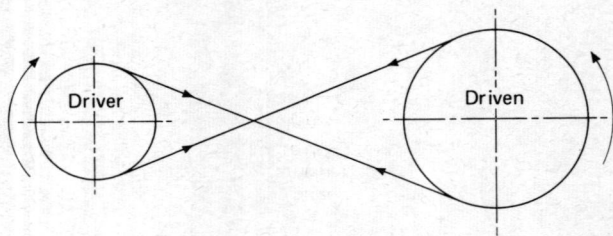

Fig. 8.11

Example 20 (MT2)

An electric motor provides 4 kW to a belt-driven pulley, 150 mm diameter; the rotational frequency of the pulley is 1250 rev/min. Determine the tight and slack side-tensions in the belt if they are in the ratio 3 to 1.

In this problem it will be necessary to determine the torque at the belt pulley and then the resultant force on the pulley by dividing the torque by the radius of the pulley.

$$\text{Power} = T\omega$$

$$\omega = \frac{\pi}{30} \times 1250 \text{ rad/s}$$

$$= \frac{125\pi}{3} \text{ rad/s}$$

$$4 \text{ kW} = 4000 \text{ W}$$

∴ $$4000 = \frac{125\pi}{3} \times T$$

∴ $$\text{torque } T = \frac{3 \times 4000}{125 \times \pi} \text{ Nm}$$

$$= 30.56 \text{ Nm}$$

The resultant force on the pulley

$$= \frac{\text{torque}}{\text{radius}} \text{ newtons}$$

$$= \frac{30.56}{0.075} \text{ N} \quad (75 \text{ mm} = 0.075 \text{ m})$$

$$= 407.5 \text{ N}$$

now $\qquad \dfrac{F_1}{F_2} = 3$

∴ $\qquad F_1 = 3F_2$

and $\qquad F_1 - F_2 = 407.5 \text{ N}$

∴ $\qquad 3F_2 - F_2 = 407.5 \text{ N}$

∴ $\qquad 2F_2 = 407.5$

∴ $\qquad F_2 = 203.75 \text{ N}$

and $\qquad F_1 = 611.25 \text{ N}$

Torque-angle diagrams The work done by a torque can be represented by the area covered by the graph of torque against angle turned through in radians. This is the same way in which work done by a force was represented by the work diagrams shown in paragraph 8.3.

Suppose that a constant torque of 50 Nm is applied in a turning operation on a lathe. The work done per revolution of the machine spindle would be represented by the rectangular area shown in Fig. 8.12.

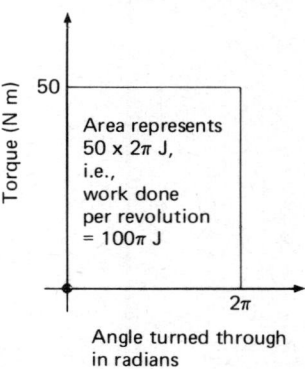

Fig. 8.12

As with forces, torques are not always constant in practice. Typical examples are: the torque on a piston-driven engine crankshaft, due to the varying pressures in the engine cylinder and varying inertia forces, also the resisting torque on a power-press crankshaft due to variations in inertia and shearing forces and the intermittent nature of the work. Once again, however, the area of the torque-angle graph represents the work done and when the torque is variable the area of the diagram may be obtained by multiplying the average height of the diagram by the base length. In this case, the work done = average torque × angle turned through in radians.

Example 21 (MT2)

The variation of the driving torque acting on a flywheel while making its first 400 revolutions starting from rest was as follows: uniform increase from 80 Nm to 120 Nm for the first 100 revolutions, uniform decrease to 60 Nm for the next 160 revolutions and uniform decrease to 40 Nm for the remaining 140 revolutions. If this starting period of 400 revolutions takes 2 minutes draw the torque-angle diagram and determine:

(a) the work done during the 400 revolutions, and

(b) the power absorbed in driving the flywheel during this period.

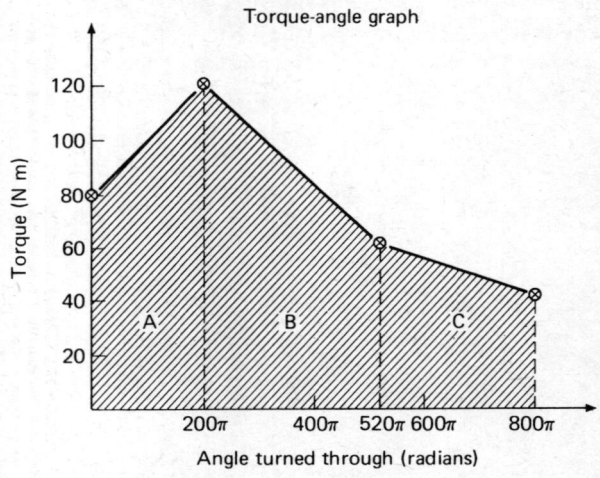

Fig. 8.13

WORK AND POWER TRANSMISSION

Since the torque changes are uniform the graph is bounded by straight lines. Figure 8.13 shows the torque-angle graph drawn to scale. Notice that the revolutions have been converted to angles turned through in radians:

since
$$1 \text{ rev} = 2\pi \text{ radians}$$
$$100 \text{ rev} = 200\pi \text{ radians}$$
$$260 \text{ rev} = 520\pi \text{ radians}$$
$$400 \text{ rev} = 800\pi \text{ radians}$$

(a) The shaded area of the torque-angle graph represents the work done in joules. The area may be divided for convenience into three trapezoids A, B, and C. Remembering that the area of a trapezoid is equal to the average of the parallel sides multiplied by the perpendicular distance between them.

Work done represented by area A
$$= \left[\frac{120 + 80}{2}\right] \times 200\pi \text{ J}$$
$$= 20\,000\pi \text{ J}$$
$$= 20\pi \text{ kJ}$$

Work done represented by area B
$$= \left[\frac{120 + 60}{2}\right] \times 320\pi \text{ J}$$
$$= 28\,800\pi \text{ J}$$
$$= 28.8\pi \text{ kJ}$$

Work done represented by area C
$$= \left[\frac{60 + 40}{2}\right] \times 280\pi \text{ J}$$
$$= 14\,000\pi \text{ J}$$
$$= 14\pi \text{ kJ}$$

Work done represented by the whole area
$$= 20\pi + 28.8\pi + 14\pi \text{ kJ}$$
$$= 62.8\pi \text{ kJ}$$
$$= 197.3 \text{ kJ}$$

(b) To obtain the power the time taken must be converted to seconds so that the units of power will be kJ/s, that is, kW;

thus
$$\text{power} = \frac{\text{work done}}{\text{time taken}}$$
$$= \frac{197.3}{2 \times 60} \text{ kW}$$
$$= 1.644 \text{ kW}$$

8.9 Frictional torque and journal friction

A journal is that part of a shaft or axle which is enclosed within a bearing. This is an obvious source of power loss due to friction.

Consider a shaft of radius R metres rotating at N rev/min in a bearing. The gravitational pull W newtons due to the load on the bearing can be considered as the force pressing the two bearing surfaces together as shown in Fig. 8.14.

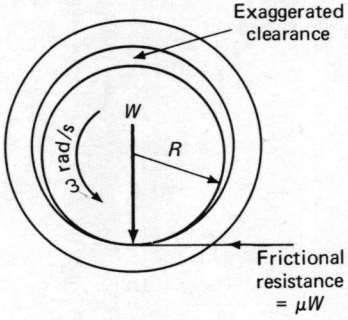

Fig. 8.14

We have seen previously in chapter 7 that frictional resistance $P = \mu W$ where μ is the coefficient of friction. In this case, the frictional resistance can be considered acting tangentially to the shaft.

frictional torque = frictional resistance × radius

that is
$$T = \mu W R$$

WORK AND POWER TRANSMISSION

As previously shown, the work done by a torque T is given by $T\theta$ joules, where θ is the angle turned through in radians. Also power transmitted by a torque is given by $T\omega$ watts where ω is the angular velocity in rad/s. Therefore,

work done in rotation against friction

$$= \mu WR\theta$$

and the power lost in overcoming frictional torque

$$= \mu WR\omega$$

Example 22 (MT2)

A flywheel together with its shaft is mounted in bearings, and makes 400 revolutions in coming to rest against friction. The total mass of the flywheel and its shaft is 16 kg and the coefficient of friction between the bearing surfaces is 0.08. If the shaft diameter is 30 mm calculate:

(a) the frictional torque resisting motion, and

(b) the work done against friction in coming to rest.

(a) The force pressing the bearing surfaces together will be the weight (gravitational pull) W of the flywheel and shaft.

$$W = 16 \times 9.81 \text{ N}$$
$$= 157 \text{ N}$$

The frictional resisting force $= \mu W$
$$= 0.08 \times 157 \text{ N}$$
$$= 12.56 \text{ N}$$

∴ frictional torque $= 12.56 \times 15$ Nmm
$$= 188.4 \text{ Nmm}$$
$$= 0.1884 \text{ Nm}$$

(b) Work done $= T\theta$
$$= 0.1884 \times 400 \times 2\pi \text{ J}$$
$$= 473.6 \text{ J}$$

Example 23 (MT2)

A journal bearing is lubricated by means of a drip-feed lubricator. The load on the bearing is 4 kN and the coefficient of friction between the bearing surfaces is 0.008. The shaft is 80 mm in diameter and its rotational speed is 630 rev/min. If the temperature rise of the lubricating oil is not to exceed 4°C, determine:

(a) the power loss due to friction, and

(b) the rate of flow for the lubricant in litres per hour (l/h) in order to keep the temperature rise within the specified limit, assuming that the lubricant carries away 80% of the heat generated.
Take the specific heat of the lubricant to be 2.1 kJ/kg K and one litre (l) of the lubricant to have a mass of 0.9 kg.

(a) Frictional resistance = μW

$$= 0.008 \times 4 \text{ kN}$$

$$= 32 \text{ N}$$

frictional torque = 32×40 Nmm

$$= 1280 \text{ Nmm}$$

$$= 1.28 \text{ Nm}$$

power loss to friction = $T\omega$

$$= 1.28 \times \frac{\pi}{30} \times 630 \text{ W}$$

$$= 1.28 \times 66 \text{ W}$$

$$= 84.47 \text{ W}$$

(b) The heat carried away by the lubricant

$$= 0.8 \times 84.47 \text{ J/s}$$

$$= 67.58 \text{ J/s}$$

and this will be equal to the mass m of lubricant flowing per second × the specific heat c × the temperature rise t;

∴ $mct = 67.58$ J/s

WORK AND POWER TRANSMISSION 211

Now the specific heat of 2.1 kJ/kg K must be converted to J/kg K because the heat generated is in J/s.

$$2.1 \text{ kJ/kg K} = 2100 \text{ J/kg K}$$

$$\therefore \quad 67.58 = 2100 \times 4 \times m$$

$$m = \frac{67.58}{8400} \text{ kg/s}$$

$$= \frac{67.58 \times 3600}{8400} \text{ kg/h}$$

$$= \frac{67.58 \times 3600}{0.9 \times 8400} \text{ l/h}$$

$$= 32.18 \text{ l/h}$$

Problems

Section A MT1

($g = 9.81$ m/s² when required, unless otherwise stated.)

1. A chain-block and tackle lifting device is used to raise a large component of mass 60 kg vertically upwards from a lathe, in order to transfer it to another machine. Calculate the work done in raising the component a vertical distance of 1.4 m.
   Ans: 824 J.

2. The cutting force exerted by the tool in a shaping operation is 440 N and the machine makes 28 cutting strokes per minute. If it takes 2.5 min to machine a particular surface and the length of the cutting stroke is 125 mm, calculate the work done in cutting.
   Ans: 3.85 kJ.

3. In a milling operation the horizontal-feed force is 840 N and the rate of feed is 0.25 mm per tooth. The cutter has 16 teeth and its rotational speed is 100 rev/min. If one cutting operation takes 1.6 min to complete, calculate the work done due to the feed during this operation.
   Ans: 537.6 J.

4. In a punching operation an average force of 20 kN is required to punch a hole through metal plate 6 mm thick. Calculate the power absorbed in punching alone if the machine punches out 20 holes per minute.
   Ans: 40 W.

212 MECHANICAL ENGINEERING SCIENCE

5. Part of a conveyor system at a foundry raises castings, each of mass 5 kg, up an incline of 1 in 4.5 measured along the slope. If there is a constant frictional resisting force of 0.5 N per kilogramme mass of casting, calculate the work done in raising 20 castings along 6 m of the incline.
   Ans: 1.608 kJ.

6. In a shaping operation the tool is set at an angle of 50° to the horizontal and the cutting force along the centre line of the tool is 400 N, as shown in Fig. 8.15. If 30 cutting strokes of length 50 mm are made every minute calculate the work done per minute due to:
   (a) horizontal feed, and
   (b) vertical feed.
   Ans: (a) 385.7 J. (b) 459.6 J.

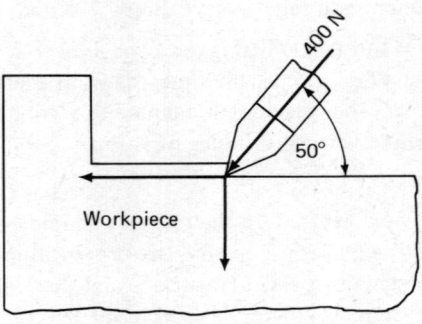

Fig. 8.15

7. A grinding wheel of 350 mm diameter is given a rotational speed of 1890 rev/min.
   (a) Calculate: (i) the angular velocity in rad/s, and (ii) the surface grinding speed in mm/s.
   (b) Calculate: (i) the rotational speed in rev/min, and (ii) the angular velocity in rad/s to give a surface-grinding speed of 51 700 mm/s.
   Ans: (a) (i) 198 rad/s   (ii) 34 650 mm/s.
           (b) (i) 2820 rev/min   (ii) 295.4 rad/s.

WORK AND POWER TRANSMISSION   213

8. A lathe is driven by a motor which provides 2200 W continuously when cutting aluminium alloy at a surface speed of 4000 mm/s. If the tangential cutting force is 440 N, calculate the power wasted in overcoming frictional and other resistances.
Ans: 440 W.

9. A bar of steel is being turned to a diameter of 70 mm using a tungsten-carbide tipped tool and a rotational speed of 700 rev/min. The tangential cutting force is 1.2 kN and the axial feed force is 960 N. The feed is 0.25 mm/rev and the depth of cut is 2 mm. Calculate:

(a) the ratio $\dfrac{\text{power due to axial feed}}{\text{power due to tangential cutting}}$,

(b) the volume of metal removed per minute.

Take $\pi = \tfrac{22}{7}$.
Ans: (a) 1:1100. (b) 77 000 mm³/min.

10. The power provided by a coolant pump on a grinding machine was 7.5 W during a particular operation and the coolant was raised through a vertical height of 1.2 m. Neglecting losses, calculate the rate at which the coolant was supplied to the grinding zone in litres per minute.
Assume that $g = 10$ m/s² and that one litre of coolant has a mass of 0.9 kg.
Ans: 41.67 l/min.

11. A travelling crane at a large factory is fitted with a lifting crab. When raising a load of 100 kN vertically upwards at a speed of 30 m/min the hoisting motor provides a power of 60 kW. When moving the load of 100 kN with a horizontal speed of 60 m/min the motor which provides power for horizontal travel provides a power of 5 kW in overcoming a constant rail resistance of 3 kN. Calculate:

(a) the efficiency of the lifting gear, and

(b) the efficiency of the gear for horizontal motion.

Ans: (a) 83.3%. (b) 60%.

12. A radial drilling machine is fitted with a motor for the purpose of raising the drilling spindle unit and its motor. The drilling spindle unit has a mass of 800 kg and the lifting motor is able to provide

600 W continuously during a lifting operation. If the efficiency of the lifting speed reduction gear is 70% calculate the speed at which the drilling spindle unit can be raised.
Assume that $g = 10$ m/s^2.
Ans: 52.5 mm/s.

13. During a drilling operation using a twin-fluted drill the cutting force at each flute is 320 N and the cutting speed is 1000 mm/s. If the electric motor provides 750 W during the operation calculate the efficiency of the power transmission under these conditions.
Ans: 85.33%.

14. The spindle of a surface-grinding machine was set to give a rotational speed of 4000 rev/min when using a wheel 252 mm in diameter. The tangential grinding force was 32 N and the efficiency of power transmission under these conditions was 80%. Calculate:

    (a) the surface grinding speed in mm/s, and

    (b) the power provided by the driving motor.

    Ans: (a) 52 800 mm/s. (b) 2.112 kW.

15. During a particular operation on a planing machine the cutting force exerted was 800 N at a cutting speed of 200 mm/s. The power provided by the electric motor during this particular operation was 400 W.

    (a) Calculate the efficiency during the cutting operation.

    (b) If the motor provides 2 kW in another cutting operation determine the cutting force which will be exerted on the assumption that the cutting speed and the efficiency remain unchanged.
    Ans: (a) 40%. (b) 4 kN.

Section B (MT2)

16. The saddle of a lathe has a mass of 120 kg and the coefficient of friction between the saddle and its slide is 0.096. The effect of the cutting force provides an additional downward force of 500 N on the saddle slideway. Calculate:

    (a) the traversing force that must be applied to the saddle in order to overcome slideway friction and an axial feed cutting force of 425 N,

(b) the work done in traversing the saddle when taking such a cut 160 mm long.
Assume that $g = 10$ m/s².
Ans: (a) 588.2 N. (b) 94.11 J.

17. A milling machine table of mass 200 kg carries a job to be milled, which together with its fixtures has a mass of 14 kg. The coefficient of friction between the machine table and its slides is 0.1 and the work is fed past the cutter at 10 mm/s. Calculate:

    (a) the feed force required to overcome frictional and cutting resistance if the cutting force was 790 N, and

    (b) the power due to the feed.

    Ans: (a) 1000 N. (b) 10 W.

18. A steel block is to have two of its sides made parallel to each other by machining on a shaper. Due to lack of parallelism when taking the first cut, the cutting force increases uniformly from 820 N to 1.15 kN. If the length of cut is 100 mm draw the work diagram for one cutting stroke and determine the work done during this stroke.
    Ans: 98.5 J.

19. A broach has a stroke of 750 mm. The resistance offered by the workpiece is variable for the first 600 mm of the stroke, rising uniformly from 4450 N to 8900 N. The resistance is constant at 8900 N for the last 150 mm of the stroke. The broach cuts at a constant speed of 110 mm/s and a complete cycle of operations (i.e., cutting and returning) takes 10 s. Neglecting resistance on the return stroke, calculate:

    (a) the work done in a cutting stroke,

    (b) the average rate of working in watts, and

    (c) the maximum rate of working in watts.

    C.G.L.I. (modified).
    Ans: (a) 5.34 kJ. (b) 534 W. (c) 979 W.

20. A buffer stop incorporates a compression spring of unloaded length 230 mm, and the spring shortens by 1 mm for every 14 N of applied load. When assembled in the buffer stop the spring has a length of 203.5 mm. At the instant a moving part contacts the buffer, the part possesses 67.2 J of energy. What is the length of the spring at

the instant the moving part has been brought to rest? A graphical solution will be accepted.

C.G.L.I. (modified).

Ans: 128.5 mm (i.e., the amount of additional compression = 75 mm)

21. A lathe is driven by an electric motor with a rated maximum output of 2.2 kW at 1440 rev/min. When working on maximum power the efficiency of transmission is 80%, and the maximum and minimum machine spindle speeds attainable are 3000 rev/min and 35 rev/min respectively. Determine the torque at maximum power

    (a) at the motor shaft, and
    (b) at the machine spindle (i) at maximum speed and (ii) at minimum speed.

    Take $\pi = \frac{22}{7}$.

    Ans: (a) 14.58 Nm. (b) (i) 5.6 Nm. (ii) 480 Nm.

22. A milling machine is driven by an electric motor with a rated output of 2.86 kW at a speed of 1425 rev/min. The belt pulley on the motor shaft has a diameter of 160 mm. The milling cutter has a diameter of 133 mm and for a particular job is driven through a power transmission with an overall efficiency of 76% and a speed reduction ratio of 19 to 2. Calculate, for maximum power conditions:

    (a) the effective pull of the belt drive, allowing 5% belt slip, and

    (b) the tangential force exerted by the milling cutter.

    Take $\pi = \frac{22}{7}$.

    Ans: (a) 227.5 N. (b) 2.08 kN.

23. The tight and slack-side tensions of a belt drive are 520 N and 180 N respectively and the diameter of the driving pulley is 0.5 m. If the rotational speed of the pulley is 420 rev/min, calculate the power provided by the drive.

    Ans: 3.74 kW.

24. An electric motor provides 6.6 kW to a belt-driven pulley, 125 mm in diameter. The rotational speed of the pulley is 1050 rev/min. Calculate the tight and slack-side tensions of the belt if these are in the ratio 7 to 2.

    Take $\pi = \frac{22}{7}$.

    Ans: 1344 N, 384 N.

25. The torque T newton metres exerted by a camshaft when driving a spring-loaded push-rod through a cam and follower mechanism varies during each revolution as follows: constant at 15 Nm for the first $\frac{1}{24}$ th revolution, uniform increase from 15 Nm to 30 Nm for the next $\frac{5}{24}$ th revolution, uniform decrease from 30 Nm to 15 Nm for the remaining $\frac{3}{4}$ revolution. Draw the torque-angle diagram and then determine:

(a) the work done per revolution, and

(b) the average power transmitted by the camshaft if its rotational speed is 300 rev/min.

Ans: (a) 139.4 J. (b) 697.1 W.

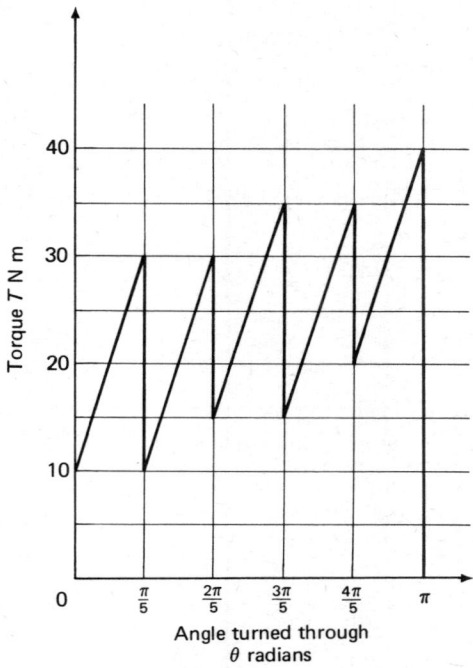

Fig. 8.16

26. Figure 8.16 shows the variation in arbor torque for the first half of each cutter revolution in a particular milling operation. The second

half of each cutter revolution produces the same variations of arbor torque in reverse order. Calculate:

(a) the work done per revolution in cutting,

(b) the mean torque, and

(c) the mean power absorbed in cutting at 126 rev/min.

Ans: (a) 150.8 J. (b) 24 Nm. (c) 316.8 W.

27. The load carried by a particular journal bearing was 7.5 kN and the coefficient of friction between the bearing surfaces was 0.01. The shaft diameter was 60 mm and its rotational speed was 700 rev/min. Lubricant was supplied at a rate sufficient to keep its temperature rise to a limit of 5°C. Determine:

(a) the power absorbed in overcoming friction, and

(b) the rate of flow of the lubricant in litres per minute.

Assume that the specific heat of the lubricant is 2 kJ/kg K, and that one litre of the lubricant has a mass of 0.88 kg.

Take $\pi = \frac{22}{7}$.

Ans: (a) 165 W. (b) 1.125 l/min.

28. During an experiment to find the value of the coefficient of friction at a journal bearing, the following results were obtained:

Power absorbed	94 W
Rotational speed	420 rev/min
Load on bearing	12 kN
Shaft diameter	44.5 mm

Determine:

(a) the frictional torque resisting motion, and

(b) the coefficient of friction for these particular circumstances.

Take $\pi = \frac{22}{7}$.

C.G.L.I. (modified).

Ans: (a) 2.136 Nm. (b) 8×10^{-3}.

WORK AND POWER TRANSMISSION

29. A component of mass 1.6 kg is to be clamped to the top of a drilling machine table for the purpose of boring a hole 20 mm in diameter in the component. The drilling torque is 7 Nm and the axial feed force is 800 N.

   (a) If the coefficient of friction between the table and the component is 0.25 determine the minimum total clamping force required to prevent the work from slipping.

   (b) Calculate the power due to the torque if the rotational speed is 60 rev/min.

   (c) Calculate the power due to the feed if the feed per revolution is 0.05 mm.

   Assume that $g = 10$ m/s^2 and $\pi = \frac{22}{7}$.

   Ans: (a) 1.984 kN. (b) 44 W. (c) 0.04 W.

30. When a drilling operation is being performed, part of the power consumption is due to torque, the remainder due to feed.
    The following results were obtained in a drilling test:

Torque	5.1 Nm
Speed	140 rev/min
Feeding force	2700 N
Feed rate	0.33 mm/rev

    Calculate:

    (a) the power due to torque,

    (b) the power due to feed, and

    (c) the ratio $\dfrac{\text{power due to torque}}{\text{power due to feed}}$.

    Take $\pi = \frac{22}{7}$.

    C.G.L.I. (modified).
    Ans: (a) 74.8 W. (b) 2.079 W. (c) 35.97.

9. Simple machines

9.1 Mechanical advantage, velocity ratio, and efficiency

From the previous chapter it is evident that a machine is a device for the purpose of doing work. This is accomplished by applying a force at one point in order to overcome a force or resistance at another position. The force or resistance to be overcome, such as a cutting force or load to be lifted, is generally called the load, the other force often much smaller than the load is called the effort. Even the simplest lifting device can be called a machine. When using a hand-operated lifting device the operator would, naturally, wish to raise a large load with the least possible effort.

The ratio $\dfrac{\text{load}}{\text{effort}}$

is called the 'mechanical advantage' often abbreviated to M.A. Note that this is simply a ratio and will have no units. Thus

$$\text{M.A.} = \dfrac{\text{load}}{\text{effort}}$$

and for any machine this is a variable factor. When the machine is operated with no load some effort is needed to overcome friction and the mechanical advantage is zero. As the load is increased the mechanical advantage increases but not in direct proportion. With further increases of load the rate at which the mechanical advantage increases becomes less pronounced and it will be shown later in this chapter that every machine has a limit to its mechanical advantage.

The use of a small effort to lift a relatively large load sometimes has its advantage offset when it becomes necessary to apply the effort through a large distance when moving the load a relatively small distance. The 'velocity ratio' of a machine gives a comparison of these two distances.

SIMPLE MACHINES

The ratio $\dfrac{\text{distance moved by the effort}}{\text{distance moved by the load in the same time}}$

is called the velocity ratio and this is often abbreviated to V.R. The velocity ratio of a machine depends on the dimensions and arrangement of the machine and will remain constant for any load. The velocity ratio of a machine can only be altered by changing a gear train or other means of speed reduction, since velocity ratio can also be given by

$$\text{V.R.} = \frac{\text{speed of effort}}{\text{speed of load}}$$

Again it should be noted that this is another factor which is simply a ratio and there are no resulting units.

We can now express the efficiency of a machine in terms of its mechanical advantage and velocity ratio. As shown previously

$$\text{efficiency} = \frac{\text{output work}}{\text{input work}}$$

the output being associated with the load and input with the effort. Thus

$$\text{efficiency} = \frac{\text{load} \times \text{distance moved by the load}}{\text{effort} \times \text{distance moved by the effort}}$$

but $\dfrac{\text{load}}{\text{effort}} = \text{M.A.}$

and $\dfrac{\text{distance moved by the load}}{\text{distance moved by the effort}}$

$$= \frac{1}{\text{V.R.}}$$

$\therefore$ $\quad \text{efficiency} = \text{M.A.} \times \dfrac{1}{\text{V.R.}}$

$$= \frac{\text{M.A.}}{\text{V.R.}} \times 100\%$$

For any machine this must give less than 100%.

Since the velocity ratio remains constant no matter how the load varies, the efficiency will only change when the mechanical advantage changes, that is, it will depend on the loading conditions. Thus the efficiency will not be constant and will change according to the load. As with mechanical advantage, every machine will have a limit to its efficiency.

Example 1 (MT2)

A screw jack has a velocity ratio of 176. Calculate the mechanical advantage and efficiency when an effort of 12 N is required to lift a mass of 26.4 kg.
Assume that $g = 10$ m/s^2.

$$\text{The load} = 26.4 \times 10 \text{ N}$$
$$= 264 \text{ N}$$
$$\text{M.A.} = \frac{\text{load}}{\text{effort}}$$
$$= \frac{264}{12}$$
$$= 22$$

Note that there are no units to this answer, but care must be taken to ensure that both the load and the effort are in the same units.

$$\text{Efficiency} = \frac{\text{M.A.}}{\text{V.R.}}$$
$$= \frac{22}{176} \times 100\%$$
$$= 12.5\%$$

The efficiency is very low, but this does not mean that the machine should be scrapped. In fact, such machines are arranged with a high velocity ratio to enable heavy loads to be lifted with a reasonably small effort, and to keep the efficiency below 50% so that the machine will not run backwards when the effort is removed (see overhauling in paragraph 9.3). Machines with a lower velocity ratio and possibly a higher efficiency would not be able to deal with such heavy loads. The velocity ratio of a machine is, therefore, a very important factor. The determination of the velocity ratio of a selection of lifting devices will now be considered.

The screw jack Consider one revolution of the effort in Fig. 9.1:
the distance moved by the effort
$$= 2\pi R$$

SIMPLE MACHINES

The distance moved by the load in the same time will depend on the pitch and the number of starts to the screw-thread. The pitch of a thread is the distance between two adjacent crests of thread, for a square thread this amounts to one thread plus one space as shown in Fig. 9.1.

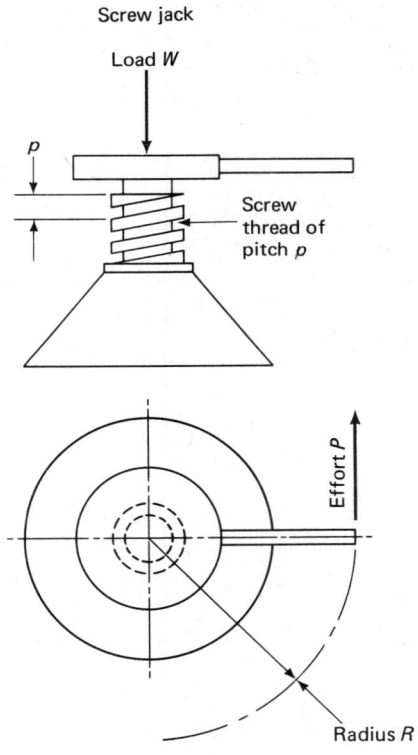

Fig. 9.1

Now the product pitch × number of starts is called the lead and this will be the distance moved by the load for one revolution of the effort.

For a single-start thread, lead = pitch p

For a double-start thread, lead = 2 × pitch (see Fig. 9.17)

For n starts
$$\text{lead} = n \times \text{pitch}$$
$$= np$$
$$\text{V.R.} = \frac{2\pi R}{\text{lead}}$$

for n-start thread
$$\text{V.R.} = \frac{2\pi R}{np}$$

The differential wheel and axle

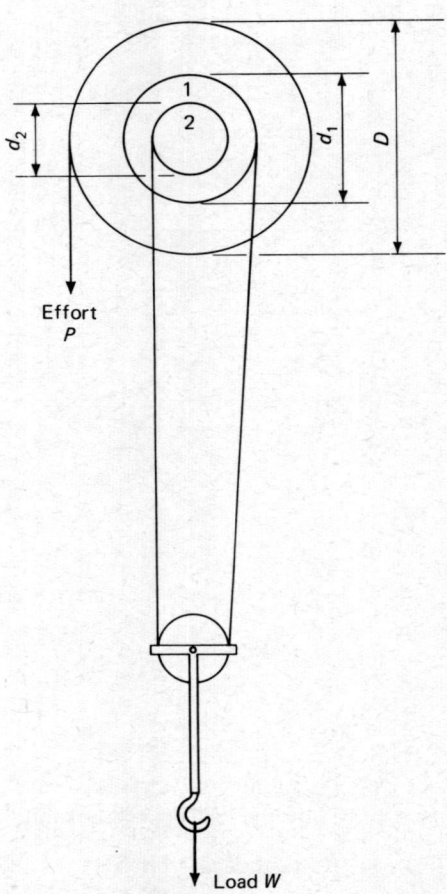

Fig. 9.2

Consider one revolution of the effort:
the distance moved by the effort rope
$$= \pi D$$

The load rope winds up on the axle (1) and unwinds from axle (2), therefore the distance moved by the load rope
$$= \pi d_1 - \pi d_2$$

but this is shared by two sides of rope as shown in Fig. 9.2, therefore, the distance moved by the load
$$= \frac{\pi d_1 - \pi d_2}{2}$$

$$\text{V.R.} = \frac{2\pi D}{\pi d_1 - \pi d_2}$$

$$= \frac{2D}{d_1 - d_2}$$

The differential chain block and tackle This device is similar in principle to the differential wheel and axle. In this case, the effort wheel is not completely separated from the load. A chain is used instead of a rope and the links of the chain fit into recesses on the circumference of the two pulleys. (See Fig. 9.3)

Consider one revolution of the pulleys; N links of the effort chain will unwind, therefore the distance moved by the effort = N links.

The load chain winds up N links but unwinds n links, therefore the distance moved by the load chain is $N - n$ links, but this is shared by two sides of the chain, therefore the distance moved by the load

$$= \tfrac{1}{2}(N - n)$$

$$\text{V.R.} = \frac{N}{\tfrac{1}{2}(N - n)}$$

$$= \frac{2N}{N - n}$$

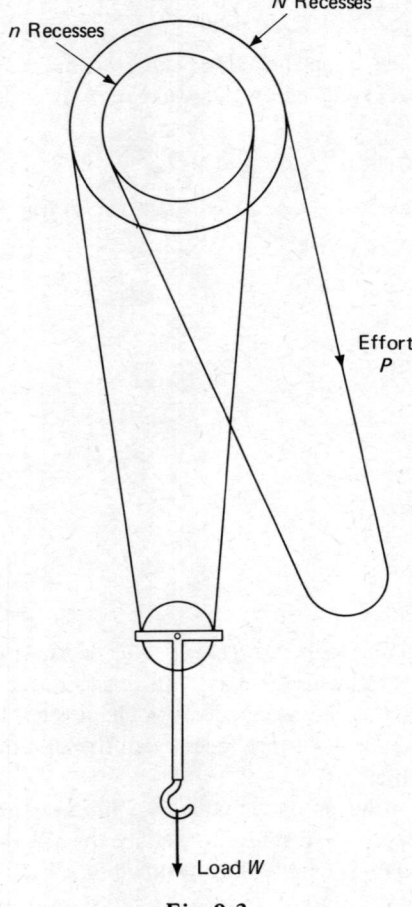

Fig. 9.3

Pulley tackle In this type of lifting device (Fig. 9.4) the velocity ratio is independant of the pulley dimensions, but does depend on the number of pulleys.

Suppose the load on this lifting device is to be raised by 1 m, then each part of the rope supporting the load must shorten by 1 m. Since there are 6 parts of the rope supporting the load in this case, the amount of rope unwound at the effort will be 6 m. The velocity ratio is, therefore, 6, and this is equal to the number of pulleys in the tackle.

∴   V.R. = number of pulleys

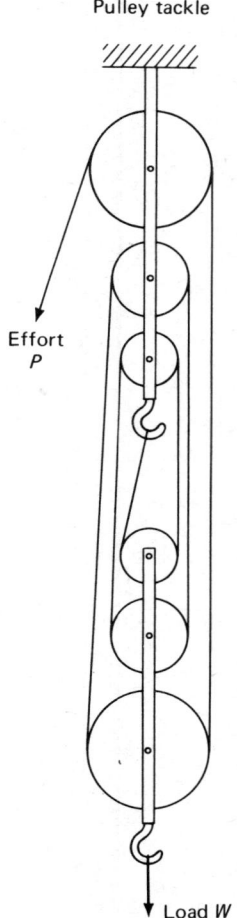

Fig. 9.4

Hydraulic jack In this type of lifting device (Fig. 9.5) the effort is usually applied by means of a simple lever mechanism.

The volume displaced by the effort $= \dfrac{\pi d^2 x}{4}$ and this is equal to the volume moved through by the load piston

$$= \dfrac{\pi D^2 y}{4}$$

$\therefore \qquad \dfrac{\pi d^2 x}{4} = \dfrac{\pi D^2 y}{4}$

$\therefore \qquad d^2 x = D^2 y$

$$\text{V.R.} = \dfrac{x}{y}$$

$$= \dfrac{D^2}{d^2}$$

$$= \dfrac{\text{square of load diameter}}{\text{square of effort diameter}}$$

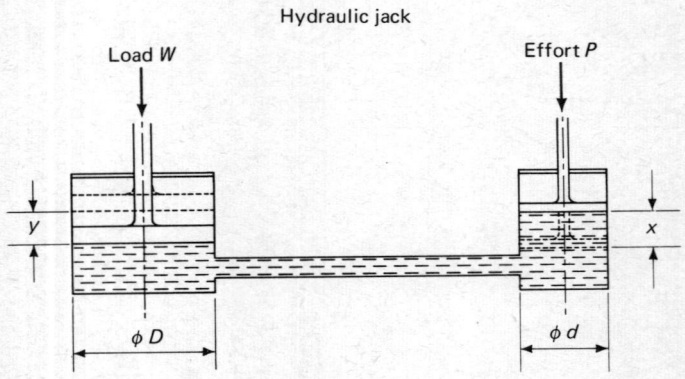

Fig. 9.5

Worm and wheel

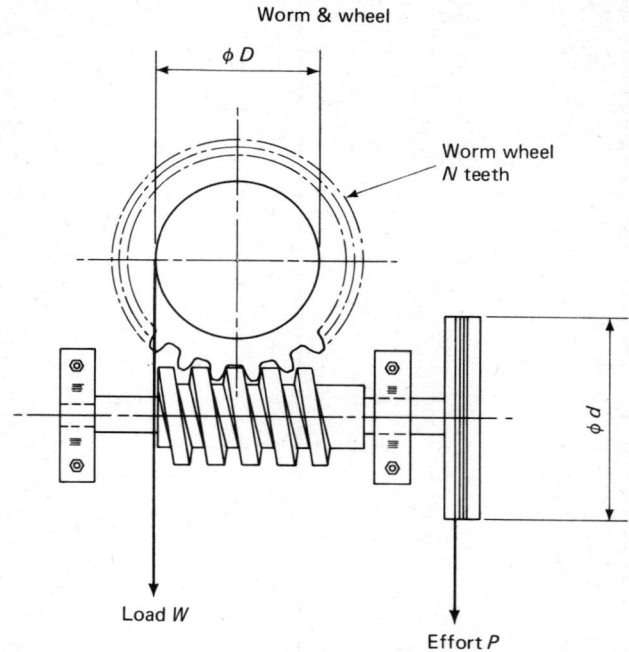

Fig. 9.6

A worm is similar to a screw-thread and may be single- or multi-start. If the worm has a single-start, one revolution of the worm advances one tooth on the worm wheel.

Thus for one revolution of the effort wheel the worm wheel makes $\frac{1}{N}$ revolutions where N is the number of teeth on the worm wheel.

The distance moved by the effort in one revolution

$$= \pi d$$

and the distance moved by the load at the same time

$$= \frac{\pi D}{N}$$

230   MECHANICAL ENGINEERING SCIENCE

$$\therefore \quad \text{V.R.} = \frac{\pi dN}{\pi D}$$

$$= \frac{dN}{D}$$

For a multi-start worm of n starts, one revolution of the effort advances n teeth on the worm wheel, therefore the distance moved by the load

$$= \frac{\pi Dn}{N}$$

$$\text{V.R.} = \frac{\pi dN}{\pi Dn}$$

$$= \frac{dN}{Dn}$$

Thus the velocity ratio is reduced when a multi-start worm is used.

Example 2 (MT2)

A screw jack has a double-start square thread of 5-mm pitch. The effort is applied at a radius of 350 mm. An effort of 20 N is required to raise a load of 1.1 kN.

(a) Determine the velocity ratio.

(b) Determine the mechanical advantage and efficiency for the given loading conditions.

Take $\pi = \frac{22}{7}$.

(a) Consider one revolution of the effort. The distance moved by the effort

$$= 2 \times \pi \times 350 \text{ mm}$$

$$= \frac{2 \times 22 \times 350}{7} \text{ mm}$$

$$= 2200 \text{ mm}$$

the distance moved by the load = number of starts × pitch

$$= 2 \times 5 \text{ mm}$$

$$= 10 \text{ mm}$$

$$\text{V.R.} = \frac{2200}{10}$$

$$= 220$$

(b)
$$\text{M.A.} = \frac{\text{load}}{\text{effort}}$$
$$= \frac{1100}{20}$$
$$= 55$$
$$\text{efficiency} = \frac{\text{M.A.}}{\text{V.R.}} \times 100\%$$
$$= \frac{55}{220} \times 100\%$$
$$= 25\%$$

Example 3 (MT2)

A differential chain block and tackle is known to have an efficiency of 45% when raising a load of 630 N. The large pulley has 8 recesses and the smaller pulley has 7 recesses. Calculate:

(a) the velocity ratio,

(b) the mechanical advantage, and

(c) the effort needed to raise the load.

(a) For one revolution of the pulley axle the effort unwinds 8 links, the load winds up 8 links but unwinds 7 links, therefore the distance moved by the effort
$$= 8 \text{ links}$$
and the distance moved by the load
$$= \tfrac{1}{2}(8 - 7) \text{ links}$$
∴
$$\text{V.R.} = \frac{8}{\tfrac{1}{2}}$$
$$= 16$$

(b)
$$\text{efficiency} = \frac{\text{M.A.}}{\text{V.R.}} \times 100\%$$
∴
$$0.45 = \frac{\text{M.A.}}{16}$$
∴
$$\text{M.A.} = 7.2$$

(c)
$$\text{M.A.} = \frac{\text{load}}{\text{effort}}$$

$$7.2 = \frac{630}{\text{effort}}$$

$$\text{effort} = \frac{630}{7.2}$$

$$= 87.5 \text{ N}$$

Example 4 (MT2)

A worm and wheel lifting device has a single-start worm driving a wheel with 50 teeth. The effort wheel has a diameter of 120 mm and the load drum diameter is 200 mm. If an effort of 15 N is required to raise a load of 171 N, determine:

(a) the velocity ratio,

(b) the mechanical advantage, and

(c) the efficiency.

(a) For one revolution of the effort the load drum makes $\frac{1}{50}$ th of a revolution.

The distance moved by the effort in one revolution
$$= 120 \pi \text{ mm}$$

The distance moved by the load for one revolution of the effort
$$= \frac{1}{50} \times 200 \times \pi \text{ mm}$$

$$= 4\pi \text{ mm}$$

$$\therefore \quad \text{V.R.} = \frac{120\pi}{4\pi}$$

$$= 30$$

(b)
$$\text{M.A.} = \frac{\text{load}}{\text{effort}}$$

$$= \frac{171}{15}$$

$$= 11.4$$

(c) $$\text{efficiency} = \frac{\text{M.A.}}{\text{V.R.}} \times 100\%$$

$$= \frac{11.4}{30} \times 100\%$$

$$= 38\%$$

Example 5 (MT2)

If a hydraulic jack of the type shown in Fig. 9.5 has effort and load piston diameters of 20 mm and 50 mm respectively, determine the velocity ratio. Also, calculate the efficiency when raising a load of 8.1 kN with an effort of 1.44 kN.

As previously shown

$$\text{V.R.} = \frac{(\text{load piston diameter})^2}{(\text{effort piston diameter})^2}$$

∴ $$\text{V.R.} = \frac{50^2}{20^2}$$

$$= \frac{2500}{400}$$

$$= 6.25$$

$$\text{M.A.} = \frac{\text{load}}{\text{effort}}$$

$$= \frac{8.1}{1.44}$$

$$= 5.625$$

$$\text{efficiency} = \frac{\text{M.A.}}{\text{V.R.}} \times 100\%$$

$$= \frac{5.625}{6.25} \times 100\%$$

$$= 90\%$$

Example 6 (MT2)

The upper and lower sheaves of a rope pulley tackle have four pulleys each, and the tackle is used to raise a load of 1000 N. If it is known that the efficiency is 80% at this load calculate the effort required to raise the load.

$$\text{V.R.} = \text{number of pulleys}$$
$$= 8$$

$$\text{efficiency} = \frac{\text{M.A.}}{\text{V.R.}} \times 100\%$$

$\therefore$
$$0.8 = \frac{\text{M.A.}}{8}$$

$\therefore$
$$\text{M.A.} = 6.4$$

$$\text{M.A.} = \frac{\text{load}}{\text{effort}}$$

$\therefore$
$$6.4 = \frac{1000}{\text{effort}}$$

$\therefore$
$$\text{effort} = \frac{1000}{6.4} \text{ N}$$
$$= 156.25 \text{ N}$$

9.2 The law of a machine

When purchasing a lifting machine a correct choice of type should be made having due regard for the magnitude and nature of the loads which are to be lifted. Obviously we should make certain that the machine can lift the requisite loads. This can be done provided that the law of the machine is known. Such a law will give the relation between the effort and the load and is obtained experimentally by noting the efforts needed to raise a variety of corresponding loads. If a graph of effort P is plotted against load W an approximate straight line should be obtained, the equation of such a line will be of the form $P = aW + b$ where a and b are constants. The constant *a* will be the gradient of the straight line and *b* will be the effort required to operate the machine against friction and the weight of the moving parts when there is no load being raised (see Fig. 9.7).

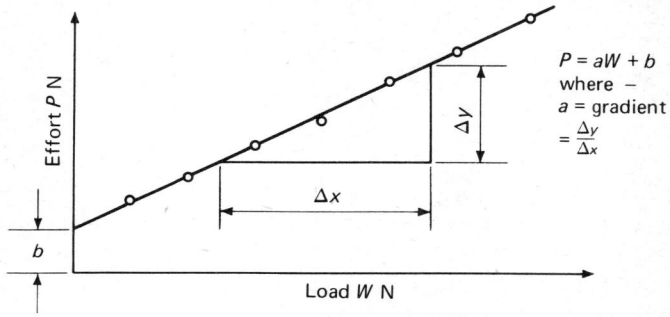

Fig. 9.7

9.3 Limiting efficiency and overhauling

Every machine will have a limit to its efficiency of working. This particular efficiency could be approximately estimated by plotting a graph of efficiency against load as shown in Fig. 9.8. However, a much shorter method can be employed, using a simple formula.

Now it is known that $\text{M.A.} = \dfrac{\text{load}}{\text{effort}}$

$$= \frac{W}{P}$$

The law of a machine can be expressed as $P = aW + b$ therefore, substituting for P

$$\text{M.A.} = \frac{W}{aW + b}$$

Now if the load W is increased indefinitely the term b will eventually become insignificant when compared with the term aW. From this reasoning we can say that the mechanical advantage will never exceed $\dfrac{1}{a}$, i.e., $\left(\dfrac{W}{aW}\right)$.

thus $\quad\quad\quad$ limiting M.A. $= \dfrac{1}{a}$

Since the velocity ratio is constant and efficiency

$$= \frac{\text{M.A.}}{\text{V.R.}} \times 100\%$$

$$\text{the limiting efficiency} = \frac{\text{limiting M.A.}}{\text{V.R.}} \times 100\%$$

$$= \frac{100}{a \times \text{V.R.}} \%$$

In fact, the efficiency of any machine will never quite reach this value.

Figure 9.8 shows a typical efficiency-load graph. It will be noticed that the efficiency increases rapidly from zero as the load increases from zero, but this rate of increase is not constant and is in fact reducing until the efficiency curve is almost horizontal.

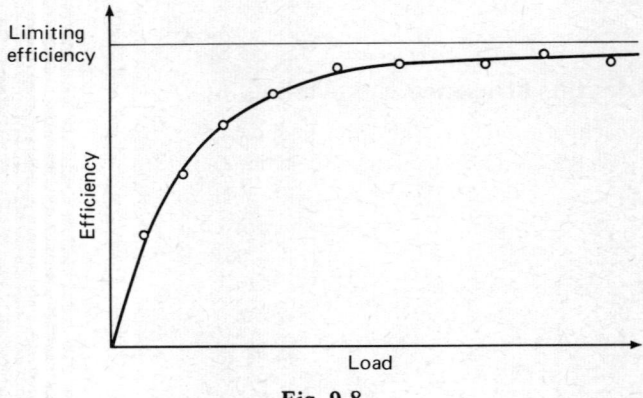

Fig. 9.8

It is possible for some machines to run backwards when the effort is removed. This is called overhauling and will only happen if the work done by the load is greater than the work needed to overcome friction, that is, the output must be greater than the difference between the input and the output, therefore, since

$$\text{efficiency} = \frac{\text{output}}{\text{input}}$$

the condition for overhauling is that that the output must be greater than half the input; in other words, the efficiency must be more than 50%. Thus a machine will only run backwards when the effort is removed if the machine efficiency is greater than 50% for the existing loading conditions. Some machines in which overhauling could take place are fitted with a safety device such as a brake, or ratchet and pawl, to prevent the load running back. In fact, it is essential for some types of machine not to overhaul, for example, a toolmakers jack, which is really a small screw jack, would be useless in its purpose if it were to run back after the toolmaker had set his work in the required position.

Example 7 (MT2)

During a test on a small geared crane the loads W newtons and the corresponding efforts P newtons required were noted in the following table:

Effort P	24	33	41	53	60
Load W	160	240	320	400	480

Plot the graph of effort P against load W and determine the law of the machine in the form $P = aW + b$. Also, determine the limiting efficiency of the crane given that the velocity ratio is 10.

The points are plotted and the straight line of closest fit is drawn, as shown in Fig. 9.9.

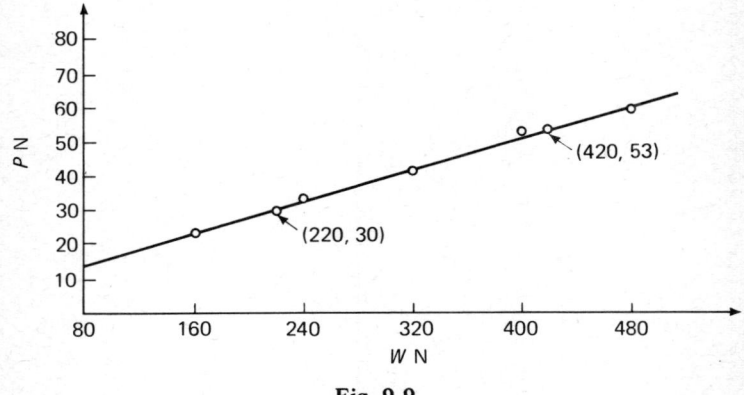

Fig. 9.9

Selecting two convenient points on the straight line
when $\qquad W = 420, P = 53$
and when $\qquad W = 220, P = 30$
the expected law is $\qquad P = aW + b$

substituting for P and W

$$53 = 420a + b \quad (1)$$
$$30 = 220a + b \quad (2)$$

Subtracting eq. (2) from eq. (1)

$$23 = 200a$$

$$\therefore a = 0.115$$

Substituting for a in eq. (2)

$$30 = 220 \times 0.115 + b$$

$$\therefore 30 = 25.3 + b$$

$$\therefore b = 4.7$$

$$\therefore P = 0.115W + 4.7$$

now

$$\text{limiting M.A.} = \frac{1}{a}$$

$$= \frac{1}{0.115}$$

$$\text{limiting efficiency} = \frac{100}{a \times \text{V.R.}} \%$$

$$= \frac{100}{0.115 \times 10} \%$$

$$= 86.96\%$$

9.4 Pulley drives and gear wheel ratios

The power needed to drive a machine in the workshop is normally transmitted from an electric motor by means of belt drives. Necessary speed changes at the machine spindle can be made by using pulleys of different diameters and sometimes by the inclusion of a suitable train of gears. Consider the simple belt drive shown in Fig. 9.10.

SIMPLE MACHINES

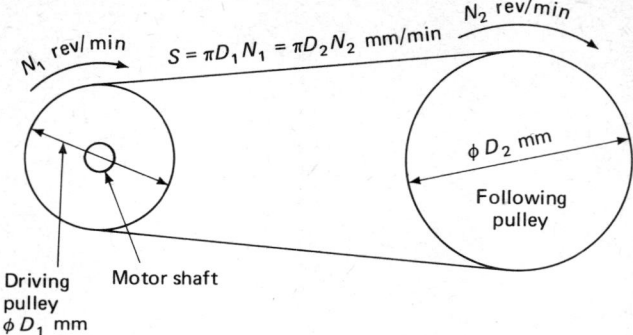

Fig. 9.10

Since the belt speed S mm/s is the same at any part of the belt then the linear speed of the driving pulley is equal to the linear speed of the following pulley:

$\therefore$ $$\pi D_1 N_1 = \pi D_2 N_2$$
$\therefore$ $$D_1 N_1 = D_2 N_2$$
or $$\frac{N_1}{N_2} = \frac{D_2}{D_1}$$

that is, the rotational speed of the pulleys are inversely proportional to their diameters.

Example 8 (MT2)

If a drive similar to that shown in Fig. 9.10 has a driving pulley diameter of 150 mm and a following pulley diameter of 750 mm, determine the rotational speed of the following pulley if the motor shaft rotates at 875 rev/min; also calculate the belt speed in mm/s. Take $\pi = \frac{22}{7}$.

Since
$$\frac{N_1}{N_2} = \frac{D_2}{D_1}$$
$$\frac{875}{N_2} = \frac{750}{150}$$
$$= 5$$
$$N_2 = 175 \text{ rev/min}$$

The belt speed S mm/s is given by $\dfrac{\pi D_1 N_1}{60}$ or $\dfrac{\pi D_2 N_2}{60}$

$$= \dfrac{22 \times 150 \times 875}{7 \times 60}$$

$$= 6875 \text{ mm/s}$$

Example 9 (MT2)

In the belt drive shown in Fig. 9.11 the 225-mm and 300-mm diameter pulleys rotate together at the same speed on the intermediate shaft. From the information given determine:

(a) the rotational speed of the intermediate shaft,

(b) the speed of the open belt in mm/s,

(c) the speed of the crossed belt in mm/s, and

(d) the rotational speed and direction of rotation of the follower.

Take $\pi = \tfrac{22}{7}$.

(a) Since the 225-mm and 300-mm pulleys rotate together on the intermediate shaft, all at the same rotational speed,

$$\dfrac{1400}{N_2} = \dfrac{300}{150}$$

where N_2 is the rotational speed of the intermediate shaft,

$$\therefore \quad N_2 = \dfrac{1400}{2} \text{ rev/min}$$

$$= 700 \text{ rev/min}$$

(b) The speed of the open belt

$$= \dfrac{\pi D_1 N_1}{60}$$

$$= \dfrac{22 \times 150 \times 1400}{7 \times 60} \text{ mm/s}$$

$$= 11\,000 \text{ mm/s}$$

(c) The speed of the crossed belt

$$= \frac{\pi D_2 N_2}{60}$$

$$= \frac{22 \times 225 \times 700}{7 \times 60} \text{ mm/s}$$

$$= 8250 \text{ mm/s}$$

(d)
$$\frac{N_2}{N_3} = \frac{D_3}{D_2}$$

$$\frac{700}{N_3} = \frac{75}{225}$$

$$N_3 = 3 \times 700 \text{ rev/min}$$

$$= 2100 \text{ rev/min}$$

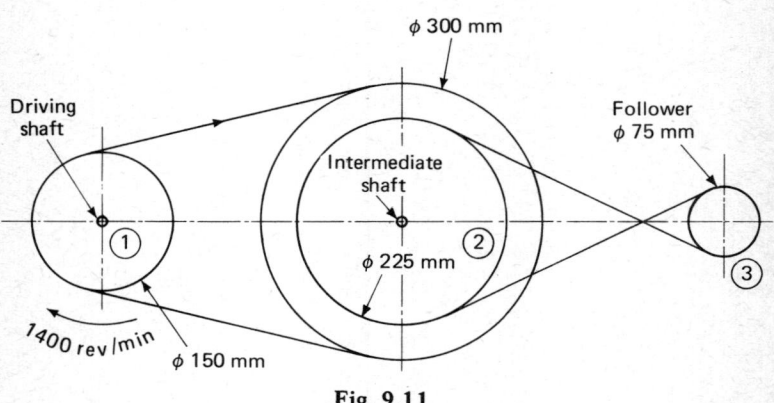

Fig. 9.11

Since an open belt connects the driving pulley to the intermediate shaft through the 300-mm diameter pulley, the intermediate shaft will rotate in the same direction as the driving pulley, that is, clockwise. A crossed belt connects the intermediate pulleys with the follower, therefore, the direction of rotation of the follower will be reversed, that is, anticlockwise. It should be noted that a crossed belt does not affect the speed ratio.

Cone pulleys A cone(stepped)-pulley drive is used to vary the rotational speed of an intermediate shaft or machine spindle, although the driving shaft speed remains constant. Figure 9.12 shows the belt in position to give the fastest rotational speed to the machine spindle. The sum of the corresponding step diameters should be constant unless one of the pulley shaft positions is adjustable. This is to allow for the fact that the belt length is fixed.

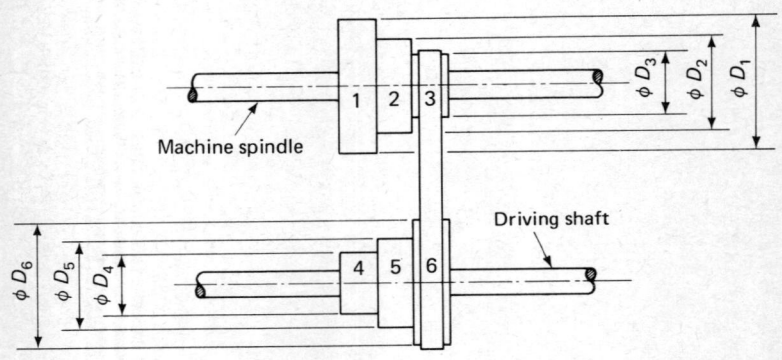

Fig. 9.12

The rotational speed ratios will be

$$\frac{N_1}{N_4} = \frac{D_4}{D_1}$$

$$\frac{N_2}{N_5} = \frac{D_5}{D_2}$$

$$\frac{N_3}{N_6} = \frac{D_6}{D_3}$$

Simple gear trains The speed ratios for gear trains can be determined in a similar manner to that employed for belt drives. For gear trains, however, it is more convenient to replace the wheel diameters by the numbers of teeth on the gears considered.

Figure 9.13 shows two gears in mesh with each other. It should be noted that the two gear wheels rotate in opposite directions.

SIMPLE MACHINES

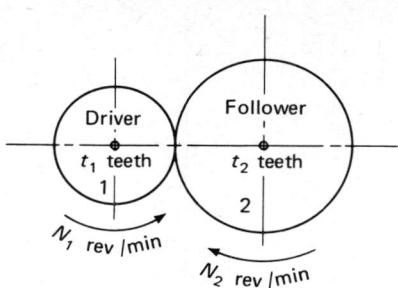

Fig. 9.13

The speed ratio can be determined in a similar manner to a belt drive, in this case the rotational speeds are inversely proportional to the numbers of teeth on the gears, thus:

$$\frac{N_2}{N_1} = \frac{t_1}{t_2}$$

Figure 9.14 shows another simple gear train, this time with an additional gear inserted between the driver and the follower. It can be shown that this intermediate gear does not affect the speed ratio between the driver and the follower. It should be noted, however, that the relation between the directions of rotation of driver and follower is affected by the insertion of intermediate gear wheels, or idlers as they are called.

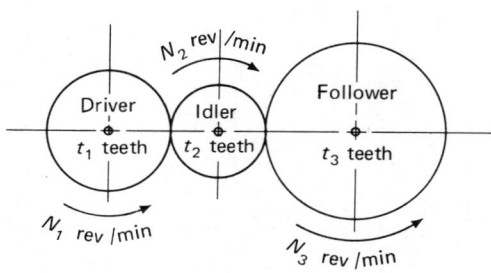

Fig. 9.14

244   MECHANICAL ENGINEERING SCIENCE

As before
$$\frac{N_2}{N_1} = \frac{t_1}{t_2}$$

$\therefore$
$$N_2 = \frac{N_1 t_1}{t_2} \qquad (1)$$

similarly
$$\frac{N_3}{N_2} = \frac{t_2}{t_3}$$

$\therefore$
$$N_3 = \frac{N_2 t_2}{t_3}$$

substituting for N_2 from eq. (1)

$$N_3 = \frac{N_1 t_1}{t_2} \times \frac{t_2}{t_3}$$

$\therefore$
$$N_3 = \frac{N_1 t_1}{t_3}$$

or
$$\frac{N_3}{N_1} = \frac{t_1}{t_3}$$

This shows that the speed ratio between driver and follower is unaffected by the idler. However, idlers are sometimes necessary to take up intervening space between the driver and follower when their shafts are too far apart, and/or to reverse the direction of rotation of the follower.

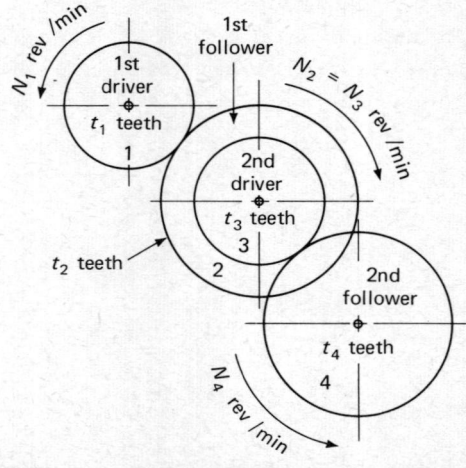

Fig. 9.15

SIMPLE MACHINES

Compound gear trains Figure 9.15 shows a compound gear train. In this case, a compound gear is keyed to the intermediate shaft. This compound gear may take the form of one single unit or two separate gears keyed to the same shaft, in either case the whole unit revolves together at the same rotational speed. Such a gear train is sometimes used to increase the overall speed ratio.

Working through the gear train, step-by-step,

$$\frac{N_2}{N_1} = \frac{t_1}{t_2}$$

$$N_2 = \frac{N_1 t_1}{t_2}$$

since $\qquad N_2 = N_3$

then $\qquad N_3 = \dfrac{N_1 t_1}{t_2}$ \hfill (1)

similarly $\qquad \dfrac{N_4}{N_3} = \dfrac{t_3}{t_4}$

$\therefore \qquad N_4 = \dfrac{N_3 t_3}{t_4}$

substituting for N_3 from eq. (1)

$$N_4 = \frac{N_1 t_1 t_3}{t_2 t_4}$$

$\therefore \qquad \dfrac{N_4}{N_1} = \dfrac{t_1 t_3}{t_2 t_4}$ \hfill (2)

Since the power input is at the first driver we may regard this as the effort side of the gear train

since $\qquad$ velocity ratio $= \dfrac{\text{speed of effort}}{\text{speed of load}}$

$\qquad$ V.R. of the gear train $= \dfrac{N_1}{N_4}$

from eq. (2) $\qquad \dfrac{N_1}{N_4} = \dfrac{t_2 t_4}{t_3 t_1}$

that is, $\qquad$ V.R. $= \dfrac{\text{product of the teeth on followers}}{\text{product of the teeth on drivers}}$

Example 10 (MT2)

Suppose the numbers of teeth for gear wheels 1, 2, 3, and 4 are 20, 50, 25, and 50 respectively for the gear train shown in Fig. 9.15, calculate:

(a) the velocity ratio, and

(b) the rotational speed of the intermediate shaft and second follower if the rotational speed of the first driver is 800 rev/min.

(a)
$$\text{Overall V.R.} = \frac{t_2 t_4}{t_1 t_3}$$
$$= \frac{50 \times 50}{20 \times 25}$$
$$= 5$$

(b)
$$N_2 = \frac{N_1 t_1}{t_2}$$
$$= 800 \times \frac{20}{50} \times \text{rev/min}$$
$$= 320 \text{ rev/min}$$

To obtain the rotational speed of the last follower:

$$\text{overall V.R.} = 5$$
$$= \frac{N_1}{N_4}$$

∴
$$\frac{800}{N_4} = 5$$

∴ $N_4 = 160$ rev/min

Example 11 (MT2)

Figure 9.16 shows a line diagram of the arrangement of a double-purchase winch for the purpose of lifting a load. Using the given dimensions and the numbers of teeth on the gears involved calculate:

(a) the overall velocity ratio, and

(b) the efficiency when a load of 300 N is being raised by an effort of 20 N;

SIMPLE MACHINES

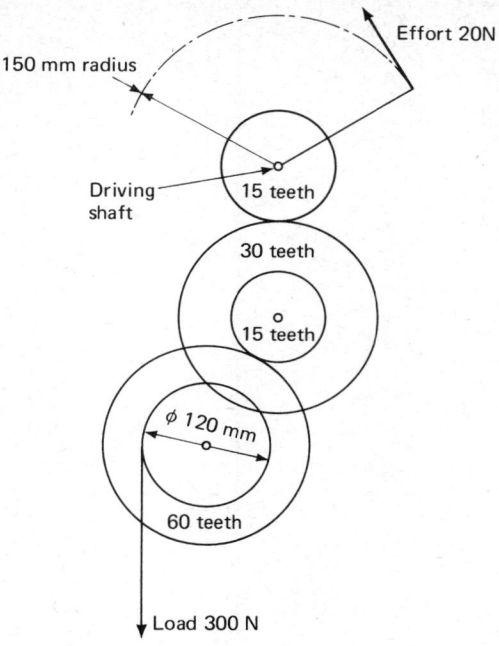

Fig. 9.16

(a) the velocity ratio of the gear train

$$= \frac{60 \times 30}{15 \times 15}$$

$$= 8$$

Consider one revolution of the effort.

The distance moved by the effort in one revolution

$$= 2 \times \pi \times 150 \text{ mm}$$

$$= 300\pi \text{ mm}$$

The first driver gear revolves with the effort, therefore, the load drum makes $\frac{1}{8}$th of a revolution, therefore, the distance moved by the load

$$= \tfrac{1}{8} \times \pi \times 120 \text{ mm}$$

$$= 15\pi \text{ mm}$$

$$\therefore \quad \text{overall V.R.} = \frac{300\pi}{15\pi}$$

$$= 20$$

(b) To obtain the efficiency the mechanical advantage must be determined:

$$\text{M.A.} = \frac{\text{load}}{\text{effort}}$$

$$= \frac{300}{20}$$

$$= 15$$

$$\text{Efficiency} = \frac{\text{M.A.}}{\text{V.R.}} \times 100\%$$

$$= \frac{15}{20} \times 100\%$$

$$= 75\%$$

9.5 Gear trains for screw-cutting and other workshop applications

It will be recalled that the pitch of a screw thread is the distance between two adjacent crests of thread. The lead of a screw-thread on the other hand is the axial distance moved by the screw during one complete turn.

$$\text{the lead} = \text{pitch} \times \text{number of starts}$$

For a single-start thread the lead is equal to the pitch. Figure 9.17 shows the outline of a double-start thread.

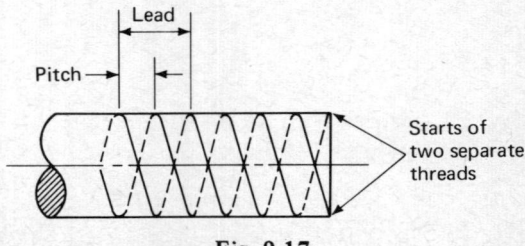

Fig. 9.17

SIMPLE MACHINES

When dealing with screw-cutting problems it is always the lead of the screw to be cut that is taken into account. As far as the leadscrew of a lathe is concerned this will invariably have a single-start thread. Most modern lathes are fitted with a self-contained gearbox making separate change wheels unnecessary. When using a lathe without a self-contained gearbox a set of change wheels is necessary and calculations will be required to determine a suitable gear train to cut a given screw-thread. The starting equation for this calculation will be as follows:

$$\frac{\text{product of teeth on drivers}}{\text{product of teeth on followers}} = \frac{\text{lead of screw to be cut}}{\text{lead of lathe leadscrew}}$$

Example 12 (MT2)

Calculate the change wheels for cutting a single-start screw-thread of 2-mm pitch on a lathe with a leadscrew pitch of 6 mm.
Assume that the gears available range from 20 teeth to 120 teeth, in steps of 5.

$$\frac{\text{product of teeth on driver(s)}}{\text{product of teeth on follower(s)}} = \frac{2}{6}$$

$$= \frac{20}{60}$$

A simple gear train comprising of a pinion with 20 teeth driving a follower with 60 teeth will suffice.

Example 13 (MT2)

Calculate the change wheels required for cutting a four-start square thread of 8-mm pitch on a lathe with a leadscrew pitch of 4 mm.
Assume that the gears available range from 20 teeth to 120 teeth in steps of 5.

$$\frac{\text{lead of screw to be cut}}{\text{lead of lathe leadscrew}} = \frac{4 \times 8}{4}$$

$$= 8$$

This ratio is too large for a simple gear train, therefore, the ratio must be broken down as follows:

$$8 = \frac{4 \times 2}{1}$$

$$= \frac{80 \times 2}{20}$$

$$= \frac{80 \times 50}{20 \times 25}$$

80 drives 25 and 50 drives 20

Circular pitch (C.P.) This is the distance between the centres of two adjacent gear teeth measured along the pitch circle.

Pitch diameter This is the diameter of the pitch circle (or mean diameter) of a gear wheel.

The module (M) This is the pitch diameter divided by the number of teeth on the gear wheel. If the pitch diameter is in millimetres the module is the number of millimetres of pitch diameter per tooth:

$\therefore$ pitch diameter = $M \times$ number of teeth

pitch circumference = number of teeth $\times$ C.P. (1)

= $\pi \times$ pitch diameter

= $\pi M \times$ number of teeth (2)

from eq. (1)   C.P. = $\dfrac{\text{pitch circumference}}{\text{number of teeth}}$

and from eq. (2)   C.P. = $\dfrac{\pi M \times \text{number of teeth}}{\text{number of teeth}}$

$\therefore$ C.P. = πM

Example 14 (MT2)

A gear wheel has 50 teeth and a module of 5 mm. Calculate the pitch diameter and the circular pitch.
Take $\pi = 3.142$

The module M = 5 mm

This means that there is one tooth for every 5 mm of the pitch diameter, therefore:

$$\text{pitch diameter} = M \times \text{number of teeth}$$
$$= 5 \times 50 \text{ mm}$$
$$= 250 \text{ mm}$$
$$\text{C.P.} = \pi M$$
$$= 5\pi \text{ mm}$$
$$= 5 \times 3.142 \text{ mm}$$
$$= 15.71 \text{ mm}$$

Rack and pinion A rack may be regarded as a portion of a gear wheel with an infinitely large pitch diameter, so that the pitch circumference becomes a straight line.

A pinion is the smaller of two mating gears. Thus any gear wheel which is in mesh with a rack is called the pinion.

A rack and pinion mechanism is a means of converting rotary motion to motion in a straight line (see Fig. 9.18).

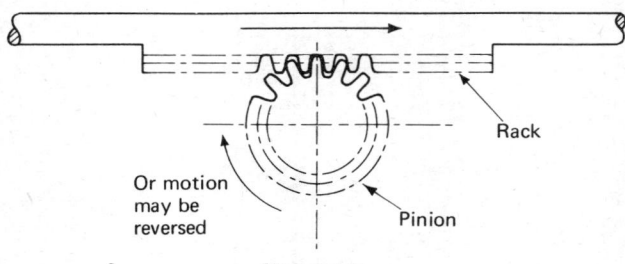

Fig. 9.18

Example 15 (MT2)

Figure 9.19 shows the outline of part of the pinion and sleeve mechanism on a drilling machine. The pinion has 40 teeth and a module of 1.75 mm.

(a) Calculate the pitch diameter and the circular pitch of the pinion.

(b) If an effort of 160 N is applied tagentially at a radius of 280 mm and the efficiency of the mechanism is 90%, determine the axial feed force on the drill, allowing for a return spring force of 20 N.

Take $\pi = \frac{22}{7}$.

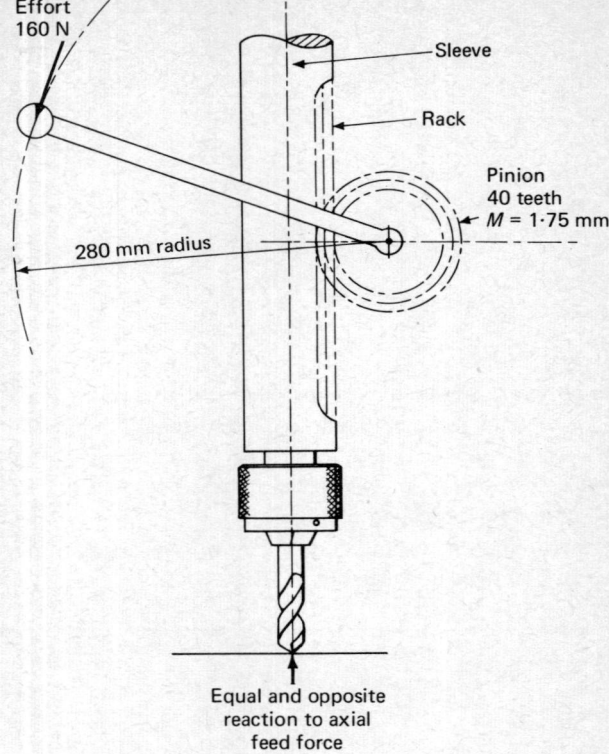

Fig. 9.19

(a) Pitch diameter = M × number of teeth
= 1.75 × 40 mm
= 70 mm

C.P. = πM

= $\dfrac{22}{7}$ × 1.75

= 5.5 mm

SIMPLE MACHINES

(b) The mechanism can be regarded as a simple machine for which the efficiency

$$= \frac{M.A.}{V.R.}$$

Consider one revolution of the effort.

The distance moved by the effort

$$= 2 \times \pi \times 280 \text{ mm}$$

$$= 2 \times \frac{22}{7} \times 280 \text{ mm}$$

$$= 1760 \text{ mm}$$

The distance moved by the drill

$$= \text{pitch circumference}$$

$$= \text{C.P.} \times \text{number of teeth}$$

$$= 5.5 \times 40 \text{ mm}$$

$$= 220 \text{ mm}$$

$$\therefore \quad V.R. = \frac{1760}{220}$$

$$= 8$$

Efficiency = 90%

$$= 0.9$$

$$= \frac{M.A.}{V.R.}$$

$$\therefore \quad 0.9 = \frac{M.A.}{8}$$

$$\therefore \quad M.A. = 7.2$$

$$= \frac{\text{load}}{\text{effort}}$$

$$7.2 = \frac{\text{load}}{160}$$

$$\therefore \quad \text{load} = 1152 \text{ N}$$

Allowing for a spring return force of 20 N, axial feed force

$$= 1132 \text{ N } (1.132 \text{ kN})$$

Gear drive power The power transmitted by a gear drive is equal to the tangential force F between the gear teeth multiplied by the linear speed of the pitch circle

$$= \pi DNF$$

where D = pitch diameter of the gear (metres) transmitting the power

and N = the rotational speed of the same gear in revolutions per minute:

$$\text{power in watts} = \frac{\pi DNF}{60}$$

Example 16 (MT2)

Figure 9.20 shows a simple line diagram of the gears contained in a two-speed gearbox. The driving shaft and gear A transmit 6 kW at 840 rev/min. Given that the transmission has an efficiency of 88% calculate the rotational speed and torque at the driven shaft:

(a) for the position shown, and

(b) when gear F is in mesh with gear C. The gears have the following numbers of teeth: A, 28; B, 42; C, 20; D, 45; E, 25; F, 50.

Take $\pi = \frac{22}{7}$.

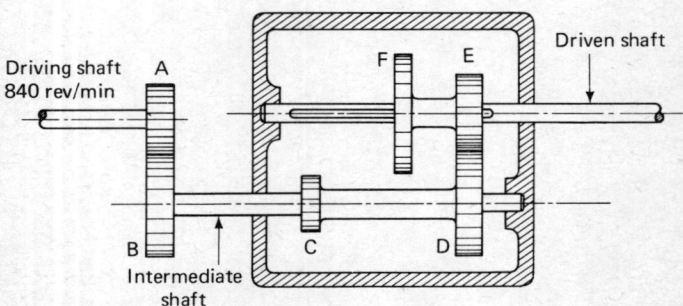

Fig. 9.20

SIMPLE MACHINES

(a) The rotational speed of B (N_B) is equal to the speed of the intermediate shaft.

Therefore,
$$\frac{N_B}{840} = \frac{28}{42}$$

$\therefore$
$$N_B = \frac{2}{3} \times 840$$
$$= 560 \text{ rev/min}$$
$$N_E = \text{speed of driven shaft}$$

$\therefore$
$$\frac{N_E}{560} = \frac{45}{25}$$

$$N_E = \frac{9}{5} \times 560$$
$$= 1008 \text{ rev/min}$$
$$= \text{speed of driven shaft}$$

$$\text{power output} = 0.88 \times 6 \text{ kW}$$
$$= 5.28 \text{ kW}$$
$$= 5280 \text{ W}$$
$$= T\omega$$

now
$$\omega = \frac{\pi}{30} \times 1008 \text{ rad/s}$$

$$\text{torque } T = \frac{\text{power}}{\omega}$$
$$= \frac{5280 \times 7 \times 30}{22 \times 1008} \text{ Nm}$$
$$= 50 \text{ Nm}$$

(b) As before, the power output is 5280 W

$$N_F = 560 \times \frac{20}{50}$$
$$= 224 \text{ rev/min}$$

$$\omega = \frac{\pi}{30} \times 224 \text{ rad/s}$$

$$\text{torque } T = \frac{\text{power}}{\omega}$$

$$= \frac{5280 \times 7 \times 30}{22 \times 224} \text{ Nm}$$

$$= 225 \text{ Nm}$$

Problems (MT2)

1. A particular rope pulley tackle has 4 pulleys in the upper and lower sheaves. The tackle is capable of lifting a load of 1.12 kN. If an effort of 160 N is required to lift this load, determine:

    (a) the velocity ratio,

    (b) the mechanical advantage, and

    (c) the efficiency.

    Ans: (a) 8. (b) 7. (c) 87.5%.

2. A toolmaker's jack (a small screw jack) has a single-start screw with a pitch of 2.5 mm. The effort is applied at a radius of 70 mm. Determine the velocity ratio of the jack and then calculate the mechanical advantage and efficiency when raising a load of 27 N with an effort of 0.75 N.
    Take $\pi = \frac{22}{7}$.
    Ans: V.R. = 176, M.A. = 36, efficiency = 20.45%.

3. The knee, cross-slide, and table of a milling machine together have a mass of 655 kg. A component of mass 15 kg, including its fixtures, is clamped to the table. The operating handle for raising the table has an effective radius of 196 mm. The table is raised by a single-start screw of 5 mm pitch.

    (a) Calculate the velocity ratio.

    (b) If it is known that the efficiency is 22%, calculate the effort required at the handle in order to raise the table.

    Take $\pi = \frac{22}{7}$, and assume that $g = 10 \text{ m/s}^2$.
    Ans: (a) 246.4. (b) 123.6 N.

4. The saddle of a lathe has a mass of 160 kg and the coefficient of friction between the saddle and its slides is 0.1. The velocity ratio of the traversing mechanism is 5. During a particular turning operation

the tangential cutting force exerts a downward force of 880 N on the saddle and traversing has to operate horizontally against an axial cutting force of 440 N in addition to friction. Determine:

(a) the frictional force resisting traversing, and

(b) the effort required at the traversing handle if the efficiency of the gear is known to be 75% for the given conditions.

Assume that $g = 10$ m/s^2.
Ans: (a) 248 N. (b) 183.5 N.

5. A chain block and tackle is used to lift a machine which exerts a load force of 2.52 kN. The larger and smaller pulleys of the block and tackle have 15 and 14 chain recesses respectively. Determine:

(a) the velocity ratio,

(b) the mechanical advantage if the efficiency at the given load is 42%, and

(c) the effort required.

Ans: (a) 30. (b) 12.6. (c) 200 N.

6. A worm and wheel hoisting device has a double-start worm which is operated by a belt-driven pulley 140 mm in diameter. The worm wheel has 50 teeth and the load drum diameter is 105 mm.

(a) Calculate the velocity ratio.

(b) If a load of 2.2 kN is to be lifted, determine the effective pull in the driving belt if the efficiency is 33%.

(c) Neglecting any losses in the belt drive, determine the power needed to drive the worm at a speed of 180 rev/min under the above conditions.

Take $\pi = \frac{22}{7}$.
Ans: (a) $33\frac{1}{3}$. (b) 200 N. (c) 264 W.

7. A differential wheel and axle has an effort wheel 200 mm in diameter. The stepped axle has diameters of 150 mm and 100 mm. If the efficiency is 80% when raising a load of 224 N and the effort rope has a diameter of 4.1 mm, determine the stress set up in the effort rope. Neglect the diameter of the effort and load ropes when calculating the velocity ratio.
Ans: 2.652 MN/m^2 (effort = 35 N).

258   MECHANICAL ENGINEERING SCIENCE

8. A screw jack has a single-start square thread of 4 mm pitch, and the effort is applied at a radius of 112 mm. It was found that an effort of 18.5 N was required to lift a mass of 45 kg and that an effort of 34.7 N was required to lift a mass of 90 kg. Taking g to be 10 m/s^2, determine:

   (a) the law of the machine in the form $P = aW + b$, and

   (b) the limiting efficiency.

   Take $\pi = \frac{22}{7}$.

   Ans: (a) $P = 0.036W + 2.3$. (b) 15.79%.

9. A flypress has a three-start square thread of 25-mm pitch and the effort is applied at a radius of 609 mm. The effect of gravity on the balls and the screw unit can be assumed to constitute an additional ramming force of 880 N. If the efficiency is 55%, determine the total ram force and the pressure exerted by the forming tool over an area of 440 mm^2, given that the effort applied is 200 N.

   Ans: 6.494 kN, 14.76 MN/m^2.

10. The effort P N required to lift various masses M kg on a geared winch are given in the following table:

P N	18	32	46	62	79	90
M kg	10	20	30	40	50	60

    (a) Assuming that $g = 10$ m/s^2, plot the graph of effort against load and hence determine the law of the machine in the form $P = aW + b$, and state the significance of the constants a and b.

    (b) If the velocity ratio is 8.8 determine the limiting efficiency of the winch.

    Ans: (a) $P = 0.15W + 2$. (b) 75.76%.

11. During an experiment on a lifting tackle, the following values of the effort E N to lift a load of W N were recorded:

E N	45	49	58.5	68	76.5
W N	225	270	360	450	540

    Plot these values, E vertically to a scale of 40 mm = 10 N, and W horizontally to a scale of 40 mm = 100 N. Draw the best straight line for the plotting.

    (a) If E and W are connected by a law of the type $E = aW + b$, determine suitable values for the constants a and b.

SIMPLE MACHINES

(b) If the tackle has a velocity ratio of 32, find the effort and efficiency when lifting a load of 900 N.

C.G.L.I. (modified).
Ans: (a) $a = 0.1$, $b = 22.5$. (b) $E = 112.5$ N, 25%.

12. The law giving the relation between the effort P N and load W N for a differential chain block and tackle is $P = 0.16W + 10$. If the limiting efficiency is 62.5% determine the number of recesses on the large and small pulleys if the difference between these numbers of recesses is 3.
Ans: $N = 15$, $n = 12$.

13. A hydraulic press has a ram diameter of 160 mm and an effort piston diameter of 40 mm. The limiting mechanical advantage of the press is 14 and the effort required to operate the ram with no load is 8 N. Determine:

    (a) the law of the machine, and

    (b) the effort, mechanical advantage, and efficiency when the load is 5.6 kN.
Ans: (a) $P = \dfrac{W}{14} + 8$. (b) $P = 408$ N, M.A. = 13.73, efficiency = 85.8%.

14. Determine the rotational speed and direction of rotation of the follower in the crossed belt drive shown in Fig. 9.21.

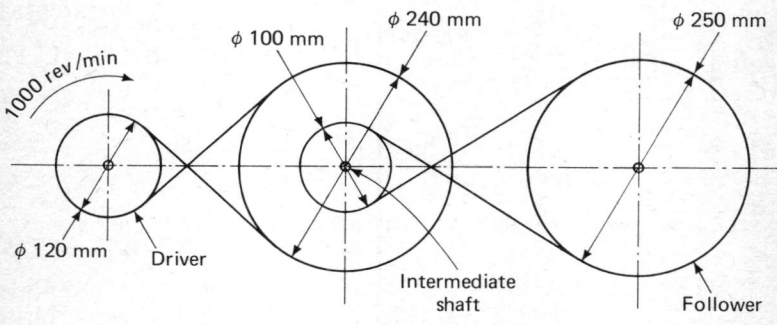

Fig. 9.21

Ans: 200 rev/min (clockwise).

260 MECHANICAL ENGINEERING SCIENCE

15. A worm and worm-wheel drive is operated by an electric motor. The pulley on the motor shaft is connected by belt to a pulley keyed to the worm shaft as shown in Fig. 9.22. The diameter of the pulley on the motor shaft is 75 mm and the diameter of the pulley on the worm shaft is 120 mm. The number of teeth on the worm wheel is 30 and it is driven by a single-start worm. The motor provides 2.2 kW of power at a motor shaft speed of 1440 rev/min. If the overall efficiency is 30%, determine:

(a) the input torque and the effective pull of the belt drive,

(b) the rotational speed of the worm wheel, and

(c) the output torque at the worm wheel.

Take $\pi = \frac{22}{7}$.

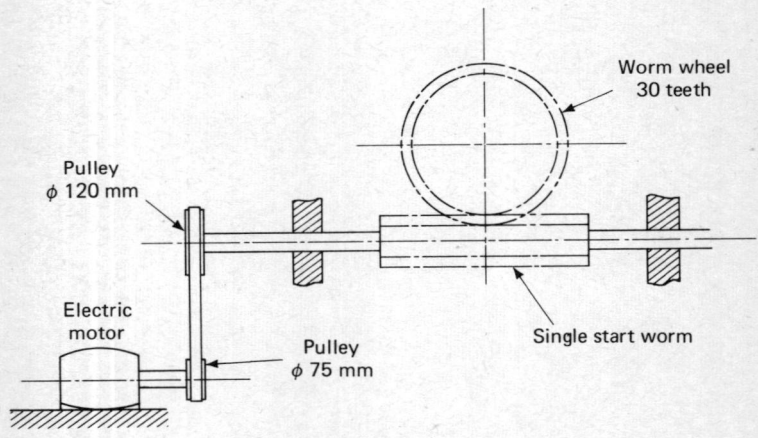

Fig. 9.22

Ans: (a) 14.6 Nm, 389.3 N. (b) 30 rev/min. (c) 210 Nm.

16. For the belt-driven gear train shown in Fig. 9.23, determine the rotational speed and direction of rotation of the gear A. The numbers of teeth on the gears are as follows: A, 60; B, 30; C, 50; and D, 25.

SIMPLE MACHINES 261

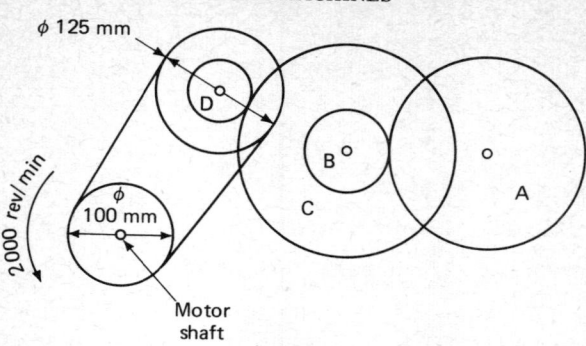

Fig. 9.23

Ans: 400 rev/min (anticlockwise).

17. In the cone pulley and gear drive shown in Fig. 9.24 the two cone pulleys are identical, having step diameters of 150 mm, 100 mm, and 50 mm.
    (a) If the maximum rotational speed of the shaft E is to be 1625 rev/min, determine the number of teeth on the gear D and then calculate the other two possible rotational speeds that can be obtained at the shaft E.
    (b) If the input torque at the motor shaft is 20 Nm and the overall efficiency at all three speeds is 70%, calculate the range of three torques available at the shaft E.
    Take $\pi = \frac{22}{7}$.

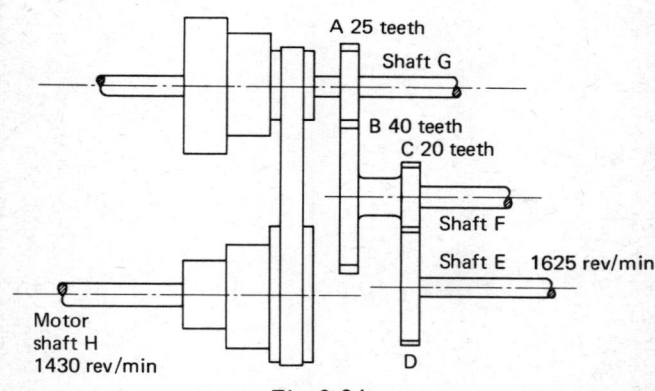

Fig. 9.24

Ans: (a) 33, 541.7 rev/min, 180.6 rev/min. (b) 12.32 Nm, 36.96 Nm, 110.9 Nm.

18. A lathe has a leadscrew pitch of 6 mm and a set of gear wheels ranging from 20 teeth to 120 teeth, in steps of 5. Calculate suitable trains of gears to cut the following screw-threads:

   (a) single-start, 2.5-mm pitch;

   (b) two-start, 4-mm pitch;

   (c) single-start, 12.5-mm pitch;

   (d) three-start, 22-mm pitch.

   Ans: $\dfrac{\text{drivers}}{\text{followers}} = $ (a) $\dfrac{25}{60}$; (b) $\dfrac{40}{30}$; (c) $\dfrac{25 \times 50}{30 \times 20}$; (d) $\dfrac{60 \times 110}{20 \times 30}$

   or any other suitable trains giving the same ratios and using the wheels available.

19. Figure 9.25 shows the elements of a simple hand-operated arbor press. The rack has a pitch of 6 mm and the pinion has 33 teeth, the efficiency of the gearing being 80%. An effort of 54 N is applied tangentially at a radius of 350 mm. Determine:

   (a) the pitch-circle diameter of the pinion, and

   (b) the ram force.

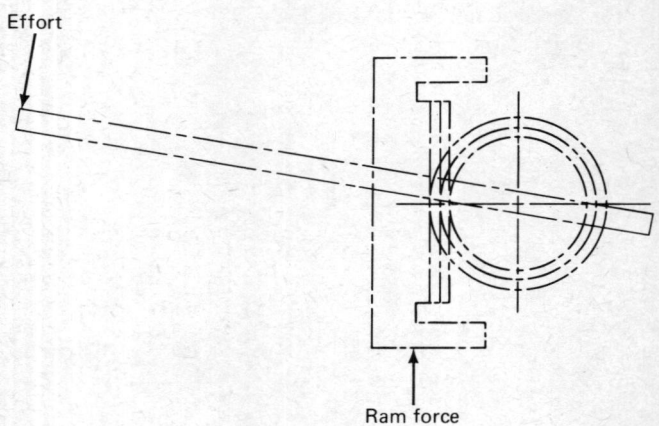

Fig. 9.25

Take $\pi = \frac{22}{7}$.
C.G.L.I. (modified).
Ans: (a) 63 mm. (b) 480 N.

20. In the gear train shown in Fig. 9.26 each gear has a module of 1.5 mm. The numbers of teeth on the gears are as follows: A, 64; B, 40; C, 80; D, 32.

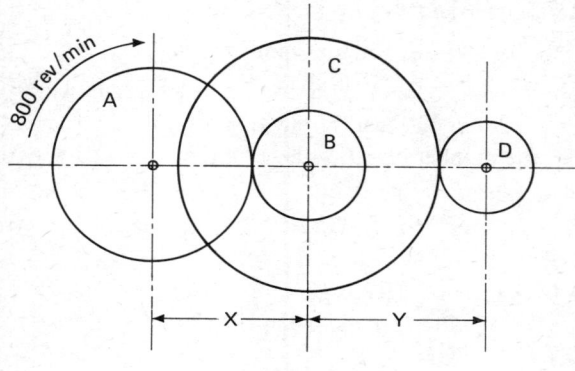

Fig. 9.26

(a) Calculate the centre distances X and Y between the three shafts.
(b) Calculate the rotational speed of D if A rotates at 800 rev/min.
(c) If the input torque at the shaft carrying gear A is 400 Nm, determine the torque at the shaft carrying gear D, taking the efficiency of the gearing to be 90%.

Ans: (a) X = 78 mm, Y = 84 mm. (b) 3200 rev/min. (c) 90 Nm.

21.

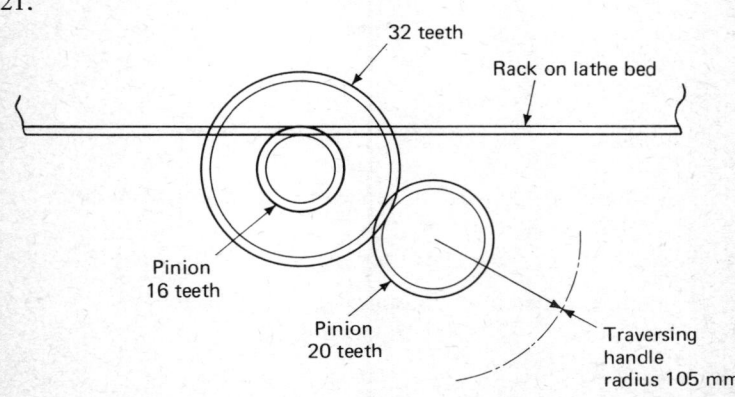

Fig. 9.27

Figure 9.27 shows the outline of part of the gearing arrangement for a lathe saddle traversing system. The pitch of the rack is 6.6 mm.

(a) Calculate the module of the pinion in mesh with the rack.

(b) Determine the overall velocity ratio of the system.

(c) If the feed rate is 100 mm/min calculate:

(i) the time taken for the tool to be traversed along a length of 132 mm during a turning operation, and

(ii) the number of turns made by the traversing handle.

Take $\pi = \frac{22}{7}$.

Ans: (a) 2.1 mm. (b) 10. (c) (i) 1.32 min, (ii) 2 turns.

22. (a) A 'Weston' or 'differential' pulley block is chain operated and has 20 flats on the large pulley and 19 flats on the small pulley. Calculate the velocity ratio.

(b) It is found that this block will lift a load of 900 N with an effort of 90 N and a load of 1.8 kN with an effort of 135 N. If the load W and effort E are connected by a law of the type $E = aW + b$, determine the values of a and b.

(c) What is the efficiency of this particular pulley block when raising its maximum permissible load of 2.25 kN?

C.G.L.I. (modified).

Ans: (a) 40. (b) $a = 0.05$, $b = 45$. (c) 35.71%.

23. (a) A milling machine vice has a velocity ratio of 300. When an effort of 67.5 N is applied the efficiency is 40%. Calculate the resulting load applied to the moving jaw.

(b) The vice clamps a rectangular bar so that there are two friction surfaces. The milling operation uses a side- and face-cutter of diameter 180 mm, cutting parallel to the jaw. What is the maximum torque that can be applied to the cutter before the work slips in the vice?

Assume a coefficient of friction of 0.2 at each friction surface.

(c) Calculate the power consumed when the cutter operates due to a torque of 147 Nm at 100 rev/min.

Take $\pi = \frac{22}{7}$.

C.G.L.I. (modified).

Ans: (a) 8.1 kN. (b) 291.6 Nm. (c) 1.54 kW.

SIMPLE MACHINES

24. A lifting machine has a velocity ratio of 20. Under test the loads and associated efforts produced the following data:

Load W N	36	108	288	648	1008
Effort E N	13.5	22.5	45	90	135
Load W N	1368				
Effort E N	180				

Determine the efficiency at each load and then plot a graph of efficiency against load, using scales of: efficiency (vertically) 10 mm = 2%, and load (horizontally) 10 mm = 90 N. It should appear from the graph that the efficiency will never rise above a certain value. State this value on your graph and add to this a reason why the load will not 'run back' if the effort is removed.
C.G.L.I. (modified).
Ans: 40%. Will not run back because the efficiency is less than 50%.

25. (a) Determine the velocity (movement) ratio of the hand-operated geared winch shown diagrammatically in Fig. 9.28.
    (b) The maximum load that should be lifted is 15.12 kN and it is found that at this loading the effort is 252 N. Calculate the mechanical advantage (force ratio) and the efficiency at this maximum loading.
    C.G.L.I. (modified).

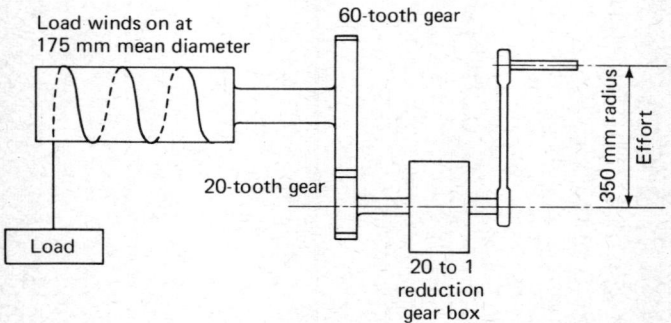

Fig. 9.28

Ans: (a) 240. (b) M.A. = 60, efficiency = 25%.

26. A double-purchase winch has an effort handle radius of 200 mm. A pinion with 32 teeth is keyed to the effort shaft and drives a gear with 40 teeth keyed to an intermediate shaft. A pinion with 20 teeth is also keyed to the intermediate shaft and this drives a gear with 64 teeth keyed to the load drum shaft. The load drum diameter is 100 mm. If an efficiency of 70% is expected when raising a load of 400 N calculate:

(a) the overall velocity ratio,

(b) the mechanical advantage, and

(c) the effort required.

Ans: (a) 16. (b) 11.2. (c) 35.7 N.

10. Conversion of energy

10.1 Heat produced by friction and machining

It was stated in chapter 3, paragraph 3.1, that heat is a form of energy transfer. Heat energy may be converted to mechanical energy, for example, the combustion of petrol in a motor car engine releases heat energy. The presence of this heat energy then causes a rapid rise of pressure which forces the piston in the car engine cylinder to move and do some mechanical work. On the other hand, the performance of mechanical work, as in a machining operation such as turning, milling, or grinding gives rise to an increase of heat energy, thus making it necessary to use a coolant when the temperature rise becomes excessive. We may say, in fact, that heat energy and mechanical work are mutually convertible, and this is a statement of a law known as the first law of thermodynamics. Heat is also generated when work is done in overcoming friction. Remember that energy is a store of work and cannot be created or destroyed. Energy can exist in a number of different forms and whenever there is a change from one form to another some work is done, the amount of work done being equal to the change of energy. The following list can act as a reminder of the SI units of energy and power:

$$1 \text{ joule (J)} = 1 \text{ newton metre (Nm)}$$

$$1 \text{ kilojoule (kJ)} = 1000 \text{ J}$$

$$1 \text{ watt (W)} = 1 \text{ joule/second (J/s)}$$

$$1 \text{ kilowatt (kW)} = 1000 \text{ J/s}$$

The unit of one kilowatt hour (kWh) is also frequently used and this is equal to 3600 kJ.

Example 1 (MT2)

The power absorbed in overcoming friction at an engine bearing is 64 W. The lubricating oil has a specific heat of 2 kJ/kg K and one litre (l) of the oil has a mass of 0.85 kg. Calculate the rate at which lubricant must be supplied to the bearing in litres per hour (l/h) in order to limit the temperature rise to 8°C. Assume that 80% of the heat generated is absorbed by the lubricating oil.

$$\text{The rate of heat generation} = 64 \text{ W}$$
$$= 64 \text{ J/s}$$
$$= 64 \times 3600 \text{ J/h}$$
$$= 64 \times 3.6 \text{ kJ/h}$$

80% of this heat is absorbed by the oil

$$= 0.8 \times 64 \times 3.6 \text{ kJ/h}$$

Now the rate of heat absorption can also be expressed as mct (chapter 4, paragraph 4.4) where

m = mass of oil in kg/h
c = specific heat of the oil
t = temperature rise

$\therefore \qquad 0.8 \times 64 \times 3.6 = m \times 2 \times 8$

$$m = \frac{0.8 \times 64 \times 3.6}{2 \times 8} \text{ kg/h}$$

one litre of the oil has a mass of 0.85 kg

$$\text{rate of flow} = \frac{0.8 \times 64 \times 3.6}{2 \times 8 \times 0.85} \text{ l/h}$$
$$= 13.55 \text{ l/h}$$

Example 2 (MT1)

In a band-sawing operation the cutting speed is 748 m/min and the cutting force is 50 N. Coolant is applied to the work at the rate of 0.85 l/min. The specific heat of the coolant is 2.2 kJ/kg K and one litre of the coolant has a mass of 0.8 kg. Assuming that 80% of the heat generated is carried away by the coolant determine its temperature rise.

CONVERSION OF ENERGY

The rate of heat generation $= 50 \times 748$ Nm/min
$= 0.5 \times 74.8$ kJ/min

The amount absorbed by the coolant
$= 0.8 \times 0.5 \times 74.8$ kJ/min

This is also equal to mct where

m = rate of flow of coolant in kg/min
c = specific heat of coolant in kJ/kg K
t = temperature rise in °C

but the rate of flow is given in litres per minute (l/min), thus

$$0.85 \text{ l/min} = 0.85 \times 0.8 \text{ kg/min}$$
$$0.8 \times 0.5 \times 74.8 = 0.85 \times 0.8 \times 2.2 \times t$$
$$t = \frac{0.8 \times 0.5 \times 74.8}{0.85 \times 0.8 \times 2.2} \text{ °C}$$
$$= 20°C$$

Example 3 (MT2)

A bar of steel is being turned on a lathe to 56 mm diameter. The rotational speed of the work is 400 rev/min and the cutting force is 900 N. Calculate the rate of flow of coolant (in litres per minute) required to keep the temperature rise at 5°C. The coolant carries away 84% of the heat generated and has a specific heat of 2 kJ/kg K. One litre of coolant has a mass of 0.88 kg.

Take $\pi = \frac{22}{7}$

The cutting velocity $= \pi DN$ mm/min (paragraph 8.4)
$$= \frac{22 \times 56 \times 400}{7} \text{ mm/min}$$
$$= 70\,400 \text{ mm/min}$$
$$= 70.4 \text{ m/min}$$

work done per minute = heat generated per minute
$$= \text{force} \times \text{velocity}$$
$$= 900 \times 70.4 \text{ J/min}$$
$$= 63.36 \text{ kJ/min}$$

The coolant carries away 84% of this heat energy

$$= 0.84 \times 63.36 \text{ kJ/min}$$
$$= mct$$

where
- m = rate of flow (kg/min)
- c = specific heat
- $= 2$ kJ/kg K
- t = temperature rise
- $= 5°C$

$\therefore \qquad 0.84 \times 63.36 = 2 \times 5 \times m$

$\therefore \qquad m = 0.84 \times 6.336$ kg/min

one litre $= 0.88$ kg

$$m = \frac{0.84 \times 6.336}{0.88} \text{ l/min}$$
$$= 6.048 \text{ l/min}$$

10.2 Conversion of electrical power to mechanical and heat energy

The conversion of electrical power to mechanical work is commonplace in the workshop. An electric motor is connected to the electricity supply and the motor shaft drives belt-driven pulleys and gearing to the machine spindle. We have already seen in chapter 2, that when an electric current exists in a conductor, the conductor is surrounded by a magnetic field, thus producing magnetic forces in the vicinity of the conductor. When an electric current is passed through the coils of an electric motor the magnetic forces induced produce the rotary motion required for the motor shaft, thus, in this way electrical energy is converted to mechanical energy.

Example 4 (MT1)

During a particular grinding operation the electric motor takes a current of 2.2 A at 400 V, and the force exerted at the periphery of the grinding

CONVERSION OF ENERGY

wheel is 30 N. If the efficiency of the electric motor is 90% and the efficiency of the machine itself is 80% calculate the peripheral cutting speed in millimetres per second (mm/s) during the grinding operation.

From chapter 2, paragraph 2.6, electrical power (watts) is equal to current (amperes) × potential difference (volts), therefore, the input power to the electric motor

$$= 2.2 \times 400 \text{ W}$$
$$= 880 \text{ W}$$

but the efficiency of the electric motor is 90%, therefore, the output power from the electric motor

$$= 0.9 \times 880 \text{ W}$$
$$= 792 \text{ W}$$

The machine has an efficiency of working at 80%, therefore, the power available at the grinding wheel

$$= 0.8 \times 792 \text{ W}$$

Also power is equal to force (N) × cutting velocity (m/s)

$\therefore \qquad 0.8 \times 792 = 30 \times \text{cutting velocity}$

$\therefore \qquad \text{cutting velocity} = \dfrac{0.8 \times 792}{30} \text{ m/s}$

$$= 21.12 \text{ m/s}$$
$$= 21\,120 \text{ mm/s}$$

Example 5 (MT1)

A pump for delivering coolant to the cutting zone on a grinding machine has an efficiency of 80% and is driven by an electric motor with an efficiency of 95%. The motor takes a maximum current of 0.2 A at 400 V when working at maximum power. If the coolant has to be raised through a vertical height of 1.3 metres calculate the maximum possible delivery rate of the coolant in litres per minute if one litre of the coolant has a mass of 0.92 kg.
Assume that $g = 10$ m/s.

$$\text{Input to motor} = 0.2 \times 400 \text{ W}$$
$$= 80 \text{ W}$$

the motor efficiency is 95%, therefore the motor output

$$= 0.95 \times 80 \text{ W}$$
$$= 76 \text{ W}$$

the pump efficiency is 80%, therefore the pump output

$$= 0.8 \times 76 \text{ W}$$
$$= 60.8 \text{ W}$$
$$= 60.8 \text{ J/s}$$
$$= 60.8 \times 60 \text{ J/min}$$

let the delivery rate $= m$ kG/min

$$= 10 \, m \text{ N/min}$$

therefore, the power absorbed in pumping the coolant up through a vertical height of 1.3m

$$= 10 \times 1.3m \text{ Nm/min}$$
$$= 13m \text{ J/min}$$
$$13m = 60.8 \times 60 \text{ J/min}$$
$$m = \frac{60.8 \times 60}{13} \text{ kg/min}$$
$$= 280.6 \text{ kg/min}$$
$$= \frac{280.6}{0.92} \text{ l/min}$$
$$= 305 \text{ l/min}$$

Example 6 (MT2)

In a particular milling operation the mean cutting force exerted was 2 kN. The operation was carried out using a cutter of 175 mm in diameter and an arbor rotational speed of 60 rev/min. If, under these conditions, the machine and electric motor efficiencies were 75% and 92% respectively, calculate the current taken by the motor at 420 V.

Take $\pi = \frac{22}{7}$.

The power developed at the milling cutter in watts (W) is equal to the cutting force (N) × cutting velocity (m/s).

Now cutting velocity $= \dfrac{\pi DN}{60}$ mm/s

$= \dfrac{22 \times 175 \times 60}{7 \times 60}$ mm/s

$= 550$ mm/s

$= 0.55$ m/s

output power $= 0.55 \times 2 \times 10^3$ W

$= 1100$ W

the machine efficiency is 75%, therefore, the input power from the motor

$= \dfrac{1100}{0.75}$ W

the motor efficiency is 92%, therefore, the input power to the motor

$= \dfrac{1100}{0.75 \times 0.92}$ W

$= 1596$ W

power = potential difference × current

$1596 = 420 \times$ current

current taken $= \dfrac{1596}{420}$ A

$= 3.8$ A

Another effect of electricity mentioned in chapter 2, paragraph 2.1, was the heating effect. The heating effect can be made more pronounced by using conductors with a small cross-sectional area, and also by increasing the electric current in the conductor. As far as the workshop is concerned, the chief examples of the conversion of electrical power to heat energy occur in the use of electric furnaces, soldering irons, and electric arc-welding plants.

Example 7 (MT1)

An electric furnace is used for the purpose of raising the temperature of batches of components from 25°C to 825°C. Each batch has a mass of 9 kg and the specific heat of the component material is 0.5 kJ/kg K. If the furnace takes a current of 10 A at 250 V and the furnace efficiency is 80%, determine:

(a) the time taken to heat each batch through the required temperature rise, and

(b) the cost of heating 100 batches at the rate of 0.8 new pence per unit.

Note: One unit of electrical energy for costing purposes is 1 kWh.

(a) The heat energy required for each batch (Q)

$$= mct$$

where
$$m = 9 \text{ kg}$$
$$c = 0.5 \text{ kJ/kg K}$$

and
$$t = 825 - 25°C$$
$$= 800°C$$

∴
$$Q = 9 \times 0.5 \times 800 \text{ kJ}$$
$$= 3600 \text{ kJ}$$

The furnace takes 10 A at 250 V

∴ furnace power rating $= 10 \times 250$ W
$$= 2.5 \text{ kW}$$

At an efficiency of 80% the useful output
$$= 0.8 \times 2.5 \text{ kW}$$
$$= 2 \text{ kW}$$
$$= 2 \text{ kJ/s}$$

$$\text{time taken} = \frac{\text{heat energy required}}{\text{rate of heat energy supply}}$$

$$= \frac{3600}{2} \text{ seconds}$$

$$= 30 \text{ min}$$

(b) The time required for 100 batches
$$= 3000 \text{ min}$$
$$= 50 \text{ h}$$

power rating $= 2$ kW

CONVERSION OF ENERGY

therefore, the number of units of energy used

$$= 2 \times 50 \text{ kWh}$$
$$= 100 \text{ kWh}$$

therefore, the cost at 0.8 new pence per unit

$$= 0.8 \times 100$$
$$= 80 \text{ new pence}$$

now there are 5 new pence in one shilling, therefore,

$$\text{cost} = \frac{80}{5} \text{ shillings}$$
$$= 16 \text{ shillings}$$

Example 8 (MT1)

In a particular process components have to be immersed in a bath of boiling water. The water is heated by an element with a resistance of 200 Ω and the bath contains 120 l of water. Assuming an overall efficiency of 80%, calculate the current taken by the element in heating the water from a room temperature of 20°C to the boiling point of 100°C in 40 minutes. One litre of water has a mass of one kilogramme. Assume that the mean specific heat of the water is 4.19 kJ/kg K.

Quantity of heat energy needed (Q)

$$= mct$$

where

$$m = 120 \text{ kg}$$
$$c = 4.19 \text{ kJ/kg K}$$

∴
$$t = 80°\text{C}$$
$$Q = 120 \times 80 \times 4.19 \text{ kJ}$$

The efficiency is 80%, therefore, the energy required from the element

$$= \frac{100}{80} \times 120 \times 80 \times 4.19 \text{ kJ}$$

This energy is required in 40 min

∴
$$\text{power required} = \frac{100 \times 120 \times 4.19}{40} \text{ kJ/min}$$
$$= 5 \times 4.19 \text{ kJ/s (kW)}$$
$$= 5 \times 4.19 \times 10^3 \text{ W}$$

Now electrical power P in terms of current I amperes and resistance R ohms is given by

$$P = I^2 R \text{ (chapter 2, paragraph 2.6)}$$

$\therefore \quad 5 \times 4.19 \times 10^3 = 200\, I^2$

$\therefore \quad I^2 = 25 \times 4.19$

$\therefore \quad I = 5\sqrt{(4.19)} \text{ A}$

$\quad\quad\quad = 10.24 \text{ A}$

10.3 Conversion of heat energy to mechanical work and electrical energy

In order to produce electrical energy in sufficient quantity for domestic and industrial needs energy interchanges are inevitable. The plant in a power station is used to bring about the necessary energy changes as shown diagrammatically in Fig. 10.1.

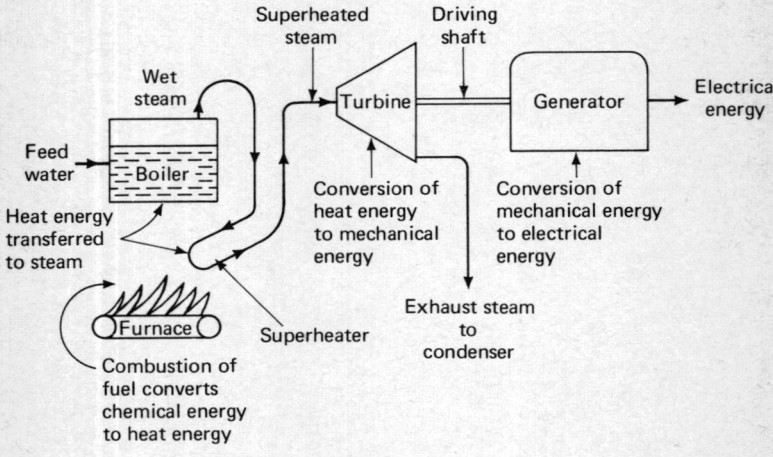

Fig. 10.1

Note that a generator works on a principle which is the reverse of that of an electric motor. In the case of a generator, the coils are made to rotate in a magnetic field by a turbine or engine. When the coils pass through the lines of magnetic force an electric current is induced in the

CONVERSION OF ENERGY

coils. A considerable amount of the energy possessed by the fuel will not be converted to electrical energy because some heat energy will pass out through the flue. Radiation, conduction, convection, and friction will also prevent some of the energy from being usefully applied. Also there will be some heat energy remaining in the steam when it has done the necessary work and is passed to the condenser.

Electrical energy can also be produced on a smaller scale by means of a diesel engine driving a generator.

Example 9 (MT1)

A steam turbine drives a generator and is supplied with steam at the rate of 10 kg/s. Each kilogramme of the steam has 1270 kJ of heat energy available to drive the turbine. The efficiencies of the turbine and the generator are 84% and 96% respectively. Calculate the generator output in MW.

$$\text{Energy per kg of steam} = 1270 \text{ kJ}$$

therefore, the energy supplied per second from the steam

$$= 10 \times 1270 \text{ kJ/s}$$
$$\text{power input} = 12\,700 \text{ kW}$$
$$= 12.7 \text{ MW}$$

the turbine efficiency is 84%, therefore, the power output from the turbine

$$= 0.84 \times 12.7 \text{ MW}$$

the generator efficiency is 96%, therefore, the power output from the generator

$$= 0.84 \times 0.96 \times 12.7 \text{ MW}$$
$$= 10.24 \text{ MW}$$

Example 10 (MT1)

An oil engine drives a generator, the output of which is 7.5 kW. The overall thermal efficiency is 25% and the fuel oil used has a calorific value of 46 MJ/kg. Calculate the fuel consumption in litres per hour given that one litre of the fuel oil has a mass of 0.84 kg.

$$\text{The useful output} = 7.5 \text{ kW}$$

but since the overall thermal efficiency is 25%, the input power

$$= \frac{100}{25} \times 7.5 \text{ kW}$$

$$= 30 \text{ kW}$$

This is supplied by the fuel oil itself,

therefore, $\quad\quad\quad 30 \text{ kW} = m \times$ calorific value

where $\quad\quad\quad\quad\quad\quad m =$ fuel consumption (kg/s)

now $\quad\quad\quad$ the calorific value $= 46 \text{ MJ/kg}$

$$= 46\,000 \text{ kJ/kg}$$

∴ $\quad\quad\quad\quad\quad\quad 30 = 46\,000 m$

∴ $\quad\quad\quad\quad\quad\quad m = \dfrac{30}{46\,000} \text{ kg/s}$

$$= \frac{30 \times 3600}{46\,000} \text{ kg/h}$$

One litre has a mass of 0.84 kg,

therefore, $\quad\quad\quad\quad m = \dfrac{30 \times 3600}{46\,000 \times 0.84} \text{ l/h}$

$$= 2.795 \text{ l/h}$$

Problems

Section A (MT1)

1. Lubricating oil is supplied to a machine bearing at the rate of 5 l/h and the temperature of the lubricant at the bearing settled to 28°C while the machine was in use. Assuming that 95% of the heat generated by friction at the bearing is carried away by the lubricant, and that the room temperature is 16°C, calculate the power absorbed in overcoming friction.
One litre of the lubricant has a mass of 0.9 kg and its specific heat is 2.1 kJ/kg K.
Ans: 33.16 W.

CONVERSION OF ENERGY

2. The coolant supply for a milling machine cutter has a specific heat of 2.2 kJ/kg K, and is supplied to the cutting zone at the rate of 1.5 l/min. The tangential cutting force is 1.11 kN and the cutting velocity is 333.3 mm/s. Determine:

   (a) the power due to cutting, and

   (b) the temperature rise of the coolant if it carries away 75% of the heat generated.

   One litre of the coolant has a mass of 0.925 kg.
   Ans: (a) 370 W. (b) 5.455°C.

3. In a particular drilling operation on a radial drilling machine the feed motor takes a current of 0.5 A at 400 V. The feed-rate set for the drill is 0.4 mm/rev, and its rotational speed is 375 rev/min. If the efficiencies for the electric motor and the feed gear transmission are 90% and 85% respectively, calculate the axial feed force.
   Ans: 1.02 kN.

4. An electric furnace operates at an efficiency of 75% and takes a current of 15 A at 240 V while melting an aluminium ingot with a mass of 4 kg. Taking the specific heat of aluminium to be 0.88 kJ/kg K, its melting point to be 660°C, and its latent heat of fusion as 387 kJ/kg, calculate:

   (a) the time taken to melt the ingot if its initial temperature is 20°C when being placed in the furnace, and

   (b) the cost of melting 25 ingots at 0.75 new pence per unit.

   Ans: (a) 23.46 min. (b) 5.28 shillings.

5. In a tempering operation cold chisels each of mass 125 g are immersed in an electrically heated salt bath where the temperature of the cold chisels is increased from 14°C to 254°C. The specific heat of the steel used for the chisels is 0.5 kJ/kg K, and the chisels are immersed in batches of 20. Assuming that the salt bath has a thermal efficiency of 60% and that 10 batches are dealt with in one hour, calculate the current taken by the element if its resistance is 14 Ω.
   Ans: 9.959 A.

280   MECHANICAL ENGINEERING SCIENCE

6. A copper hot-water tank has a mass of 10 kg and contains 100 l of water. The heating element takes 10 A at 250 V. If it takes 2½ h to increase the temperature of the water and the tank from 20°C to 60°C, calculate the thermal efficiency.
Take the specific heats of copper and water to be 0.4 kJ/kg K and 4.2 kJ/kg K respectively.
Ans: 75.4%.

7. A generator is driven by a steam turbine and has an output of 12 MW. The total heat energy (enthalpy) of each kilogramme of the steam is 3450 kJ on entering the turbine and 2400 kJ at the turbine exit. Taking efficiencies for the generator and turbine to be 95% and 80% respectively, determine the mass of steam supplied per hour to the turbine.
Ans: 54 130 kg/h.

8. An oil engine develops an output power of 51 kW and uses fuel with a calorific value of 42.5 MJ/kg. If the thermal efficiency of the engine is 30% calculate the fuel consumption in litres per hour. One litre of the fuel has a mass of 0.8 kg.
Ans: 18 l/hour.

Section B (MT2)

9. During an experiment for testing the suitability of certain lubricating oils, lubricant was applied to a journal bearing carrying a load of 40 N. The rotational speed of the shaft was 105 rev/min and the temperature of the lubricant settled at a constant value of 30.5°C. The shaft diameter was 25 mm. One litre of the lubricant has a mass of 0.88 kg and its specific heat is 2 kJ/kg K. Assuming that the lubricant carries away 80% of the heat energy produced by friction determine the probable approximate value for the coefficient of friction between the shaft and bearing material if the room temperature is 18°C and the lubricant is applied at the rate of 0.05 l/h.

Take $\pi = \frac{22}{7}$

Ans: 0.069 44.

CONVERSION OF ENERGY 281

10. A soluble oil mix used as a coolant in a machining operation has a specific gravity of 0.8 and a specific heat of 3.78 kJ/kg K. While it passes through the cutting zone at the rate of 18 l/min its temperature rises from 15°C to 20°C.

   (a) What quantity of heat, in kJ/min, does the coolant absorb?

   (b) If this amount of heat represents 80% of the heat generated at the tool point, what is the number of watts consumed in cutting?

   One litre of water has a mass of one kilogramme.
   C.G.L.I. (modified).
   Ans: (a) 272.2 kJ/min. (b) 5670 W.

11. The coolant used in a particular machining operation was a mineral oil having a mass of 0.72 kg/l and a specific heat of 1.68 kJ/kg K. The coolant was supplied to the cutting zone at the rate of 45.5 l/min, and during the passage through the cutting zone, the temperature of the oil increased by 5°C.

   (a) Calculate the heat given to the oil in kJ/min.

   (b) If this heat represented 80% of the power used in cutting, calculate the power consumed (in kW) in the cutting operation.

   (c) If the vertical distance from the sump to the delivery point was 1.65 m, calculate the power required (in watts) to lift the oil from the sump to the delivery point.

   Assume that $g = 9.81$ m/s^2.
   C.G.L.I. (modified).
   Ans: (a) 275.2 kJ/min. (b) 5.733 kW. (c) 8.84 W.

12. In an end-milling operation the tangential cutting force was 420 N on a high-speed steel cutter of 20-mm diameter. The rotational speed of the cutter was 350 rev/min and the coolant was supplied at a rate sufficient to limit its temperature rise to 4°C. One litre of the coolant has a mass of 0.9 kg and its specific heat is 3.2 kJ/kg K. Determine:

   (a) the torque exerted on the cutter,

   (b) the power absorbed in cutting, and

   (c) the rate of coolant application in litres per hour, assuming that the coolant carried away 75% of the heat generated by cutting.

   Take $\pi = \frac{22}{7}$.

   Ans: (a) 4.2 Nm. (b) 154 W. (c) 36.1 l/h.

13. During an experiment to investigate the effect of cutting speed on tangential cutting force and power absorbed when turning a bar of steel on a lathe with a constant feed and depth of cut, the following observations were made:

Work diameter	77 mm
Tangential cutting force	900 N at 40 rev/min
Tangential cutting force	765 N at 400 rev/min

Taking the power transmission efficiency from the motor to the tool point to be constant at 80%, and the motor efficiency also constant at 95%, determine the current taken by the motor at 440 V:

(a) at the lower speed, and

(b) at the higher speed.

Take $\pi = \frac{22}{7}$.

Ans: (a) 0.4342 A. (b) 3.692 A.

14. A small generator plant has an overall efficiency of 25%, the generator being driven by a diesel engine using a fuel with a calorific value of 40 MJ/kg. The generator driving shaft is driven at a rotational speed of 490 rev/min with a torque of 180 Nm. If fuel, with a specific gravity of 0.85, is used at the rate of 3.6 l/h, calculate:

(a) the thermal efficiency of the engine,

(b) the generator efficiency, and

(c) the generator output.

One litre of water has a mass of one kilogramme.
Take $\pi = \frac{22}{7}$.

Ans: (a) 27.17%. (b) 92%. (c) 8.5 kW.

15. A small electric motor takes 660 W from a 240-V supply and has an efficiency of 90%. Calculate:

(a) the current taken by the motor, and

(b) the torque available at the motor shaft at 1400 rev/min.

Take $\pi = \frac{22}{7}$.

Ans: (a) 2.75 A. (b) 4.05 Nm.

Index

air
    composition of, 4
    dry, 4
    moist, 4
alloy, 3, 4
ammeter, 13
ampere, 13
angle of lap, 203, 204
anode, 12
arbor press, 93, 94, 100
armature, 37, 38
assymetrical vee, 82, 83
atomic number, 2
atomic weight, 2, 3
atoms, 1-3, 7, 11, 12

battery, 12-14, 19
beams
    simply-supported, 95-99
bearings, 171
    ball, 171, 172
    journal, 210
    plain, 171
    roller, 171, 172
    wear on, 171
belt drive, 202-204, 238-240
    crossed, 204, 240, 241
belt speed, 239-241
belt tension, 203, 204
bimetal strip, 46, 47
Bow's notation, 82

calorific value, 68
calorimeter, 66
cathode, 12
cell, 13, 14, 19
centre of area, 109-119
centre of gravity, 106-109
centroid, 109-119
    of a parallelogram, 109, 110

centroid—*cont.*
    of a rectangle, 109, 110
    of a semicircle, 110
    of a triangle, 110
change of state, 1, 44
change wheels, 249
chemical
    action, 14
    change, 1, 44
    combination, 2
    equation, 6-8
    reaction, 3, 4
    symbols, 2, 3
circular pitch, 250-252
clutch
    simple, 164
    single-plate, 170
combustion, 1, 6, 267
    complete, 7, 8
    heat of, 5
    products of, 6-8
compound, 2-4
compressive strength, 146, 147
compressive tests, 143
concurrent, 81, 91
condenser, 276, 277
conduction, 63, 64, 277
conductors of electricity, 12-14,
    16, 36, 37, 270, 273
cone pulley, 242
contraction fit, 46
convection, 63, 64, 68, 277
corrosion, 1, 4-6, 12
coulomb, 13
couple, 105

demagnetizer, 39
differential chain block and tackle,
    225, 226
    velocity ratio, 225, 231

INDEX

differential wheel and axle, 224
   velocity ratio, 225
double purchase winch, 167, 246, 247
double shear, 135, 140, 141
dryness fraction, 60-62
ductile material, 142
ductile property, 143

efficiency, 193, 221, 222, 231-237, 248, 253
   electrical, 31
   electric motor, 271-273
   furnace, 69, 70, 274
   generator, 277
   limiting, 235-238
   mechanical, 193-196, 200-202, 271
   pump, 271, 272
   thermal, 68, 69, 277, 278
   turbine, 277
efficiency-load graph, 236
elasticity, 141, 147
elastic limit, 141, 143, 147
electric
   bell, 37, 38
   circuit, 13-15, 19
      parallel, 24
      series, 20
   current, 11, 13, 44, 270
      chemical effect, 12
      heating effect, 11, 273
      magnetic effect, 12, 270
   furnace, 273
   motor, 270, 271, 276
electric charge, 11, 13
   negative, 1
   positive, 1
electrode, 12
electrolyte, 12
electromagnet, 37, 38
electromotive force, 14, 20, 21, 29
electrons, 1, 11-16
electroplating, 12
elements, 2, 3
   combustible, 6
elongation percentage, 143-145
emulsion, 3

energy, 14, 15, 44
   electrical, 15, 16, 23, 30, 270, 276
   heat, 32, 44, 56, 267, 270, 275
   input, 193
   mechanical, 267, 270
   output, 193
   transfer, 44, 56
   unit of, 29, 267
enthalpy, 60
   of vaporization, 60
   specific, 60
equilibrant, 78, 82
equilibrium, 78, 94
expansion, 45, 46
   linear, 47
      coefficient of, 47-51
expansion fit, 46

factor of safety, 143, 146, 147
feed, 191
force, 78
   clamping, 82, 83
   compressive, 132, 133
   cutting, 102, 189, 190, 269
      axial, 81
      radial, 81
      tangential, 104, 194
   equilibrant, 78, 82
   feed, 191, 192
   frictional, 159, 160, 209
   horizontal component of, 88, 89, 161, 162, 180
   out-of-balance, 86
   propulsive, 79
   reaction, 95
   resultant, 78, 80, 204, 205
   shearing, 132, 135
   tangential, 105
   tensile, 132, 135
   vertical component of, 88, 89, 161, 162, 180
   wedging, 91
friction, 158, 159, 164, 171, 277
   coefficient of, 159-170, 181, 197, 210
   experiment, 162-164
   force of, 170
   laws of, 158, 159

friction—*cont.*
  static, 158, 159
  useful, 164
  wasteful, 171
  work done against, 179, 181, 182
frictional resistance, 158, 159, 164, 165, 171, 172
fulcrum, 92, 95, 96, 99, 100

gauge length, 143, 144, 148
gear trains
  compound, 245-247
  for screw cutting, 248, 249
  simple, 242-244, 249
generator, 14, 276, 277
gravitational acceleration, 78, 132
gravitational force, 97, 106, 107, 132, 179
gravitational pull, 78, 84, 106, 178
gravity
  work done against, 180

heat, 44, 267
  absorption, 268
  generated, 268
  interchange of, 64
  latent, 59-61
    of fusion, 59, 61, 67, 70
    of vaporization, 59-63
  losses of, 68
  quantity of, 57-61
  sensible, 56, 60-63, 70
  transfer of, 63-65
Hooke's law, 141
hydraulic jack, 228
  velocity ratio, 228, 233

idlers, 243, 244
insulators, 13

jib, 85, 86
joule, 14, 29, 30, 177
journal friction, 208, 209

kelvin, 57
kilowatt hour, 30-32, 267, 274

lamina, 109

leadscrew, 249
lever
  bell crank, 100
  cranked, 101, 103
  first order, 99
  second order, 100
  simple, 93, 99
  third order, 100
limit of proportionality, 141, 142, 148
load
  indeterminate, 143
  limit of proportionality, 144, 145
  maximum, 143, 144, 146
  moving, 143
  shearing, 135, 139
  wind, 143
  yield, 142, 144, 145
load-extension graph, 142, 148
lubricant, 171, 172, 210
lubricator, 210

machine, 220
  the law of, 234, 235, 237
  lifting, 234
  overhauling of, 236, 237
magnet, 34-36
  bar, 12, 35
  electro-, 12, 37, 38
  permanent, 34, 35
magnetic
  chuck, 12, 38, 270, 276
  circuit, 36, 37, 39
  devices, 38
  effect, 12
  field, 12, 36, 270, 276
  force, 34, 164, 166, 167, 270, 276
    lines of, 36
  materials, 34
  poles, 12, 34, 35
mass, 78, 106
mechanical advantage, 220-222, 230-234, 253
  limiting, 235, 236, 253
mid-ordinate rule, 184, 185
mixture, 3, 4
module, 250, 251

INDEX

molecules, 2, 3
molecular weight, 2, 3, 6, 7
moment of a force, 92
moments
  of area, 110-118
  of forces, 92-103, 168, 169
  of volume, 107-109
  out-of-balance, 94
  principle of, 94
  turning, 104, 199

neutrons, 1, 2, 11
newton, 78, 132, 177
newton metre, 92
north pole
  geographic, 34
  magnetic, 34, 35
nucleus, 1, 2, 11

ohm, 16
Ohm's law, 16-21, 25, 27, 30, 33
oxidation, 4, 5, 44
oxygen
  theoretical minimum for complete combustion, 6-8

parallelogram of forces, 80
  law, 80, 81
  method, 82
physical change, 1
pitch circle, 250
pitch diameter, 250-252
point of concurrency, 85
polarity, 35
potential difference, 15-30, 33
power, 29, 189, 199
  absorbed in cutting, 190-192
  absorbed in friction, 197, 198, 209, 210
  due to feed, 191, 192
  due to gear drive, 254
  due to torque, 199, 202, 204, 206, 208
  electrical, 29-34, 270, 273, 276
  input, 193-196, 271-273, 277, 278
  output, 193-196, 271-273, 277, 278
  rating, 189, 274

power—*cont.*
  transmission of, 193, 194, 200, 203
  unit of, 190, 267
pressure
  atmospheric, 45
  cutting, 195, 196
pressure vessel, 139
protons, 1, 2, 11
pulley drive, 202, 239
pulley speeds, 239-242
pulley tackle, 226, 227
  velocity ratio, 227, 234
pyrometer
  optical, 45
  thermocouple, 45

rack and pinion, 251
radian, 186
radiation, 63, 64, 68, 277
reduction, 4, 5
reduction of area percentage, 144, 145
resistance, 16, 17, 20, 31, 44, 275
  equivalent, 23-25, 28
  internal, 20, 21, 24-27
resistances
  in parallel, 23-29, 32, 33
  in series, 19-21, 32, 33
resistors, 19-29, 32-34
  variable, 19, 21, 22
resolution of forces, 88-92
resultant, 78-81
rotational frequency (speed), 186, 187, 240, 242, 244

screw jack, 222, 223, 230
  velocity ratio, 224, 230
screw thread, 223
  double-start, 223
  lead, 223, 224, 248
  pitch, 223, 248
  single-start, 223, 248, 249
  square, 223
    double-start, 230, 248
    four-start, 249
seger cones, 45
sensible heat, 56, 60-63, 70
shearing strength, 102, 137, 138

INDEX

single shear, 135
slip gauges, 158
solenoid, 37
solute, 3
solution, 3, 4
solvent, 3
south pole
   geographical, 34
   magnetic, 34, 35
space diagram, 82-87
specific heat, 57, 58, 211
   of copper (experiment), 66
   of superheated steam, 61
   of water, 57, 61
speed, 186
   average, 186
   cutting, 186-193
   machining, 186
   reduction ratio, 200, 243-245
   surface, 201
steam, 60, 62, 276, 277
   dry, 60
   superheated, 60, 61, 63, 276
   wet, 60-62, 276
steam turbine, 276, 277
stiffness, 102, 142
strain, 132
   compressive, 134
   direct, 132, 133
   intensity of, 132, 133, 135
   shearing, 134
   tensile, 133
stress, 132
   compressive, 134
   direct, 132, 133
   intensity of, 132, 133
   limit of proportionality, 143, 145
   maximum, 140
   nominal breaking, 143
   safe working, 143, 146, 147
   shearing, 134
   tensile, 133
   ultimate tensile, 143
   yeild, 142, 145
superheat, 63
switch
   push-button, 37, 38
   simple, 19

temperature, 44, 45, 47
   Celsius, 45, 47
   Kelvin, 45, 57
   melting point, 61
   saturation, 60
   tempering, 44
tensile strength, 143, 144, 146
tensile test, 135, 184
   to destruction, 142
thermal conductivity, 64
thermodynamics
   first law of, 267
thermometer, 45
   constant volume, 45
   mercury-in-glass, 45
   mercury-in-steel, 45
thermo-static control, 46,
tie, 85, 86
toggle mechanism, 89, 90
toolmaker's jack, 237
torque, 104, 105, 166, 167, 171, 199-201, 255
   driving, 203, 204, 206
   frictional, 208-210
torque-angle diagram, 205-207
triangle of forces,
   law, 81
   method, 82

vector, 78
   diagram, 82-84, 86, 87
   quantity, 186
velocity, 186
   angular, 186-188, 202, 203
   cutting, 194, 195, 269-273
   feed, 191, 192
   linear, 186
   of sliding, 158, 159, 162
   peripheral, 186, 188
velocity ratio, 220-222, 236, 237, 253
   gear drive, 243-247
   pulley drive, 239-242
viscosity, 172
volt, 14, 29
voltage, 14, 31

wall jib crane, 85
watt, 29, 30, 190, 191

wedge, 91, 92
work, 14, 29, 44
   diagrams, 183, 184
   input, 193
   mechanical, 267, 270
   output, 193, 196, 197
   useful, 192
work done, 177-179, 189, 199
   against friction, 179, 181, 182, 197, 209, 267
   against gravity, 180
   by a constant torque, 199, 205
   by a variable force, 183, 184
   by a variable torque, 206, 207

work done—*cont.*
   in cutting, 182
   in rotation, 186, 198
   unit of, 177
worm
   multi-start, 229, 230
   single-start, 229, 232
worm and wheel, 229
   velocity ratio, 230, 232
worm wheel, 229

yield point, 142
Young's modulus of elasticity, 142

Printed by William Clowes and Sons Limited
London, Colchester and Beccles